Bob Crow: Socialist, leader, fighter

MANCHESTER
1824

Manchester University Press

Bob Crow:
Socialist, leader, fighter

A political biography

GREGOR GALL

Manchester University Press

Published by Manchester University Press
Altrincham Street, Manchester M1 7JA

www.manchesteruniversitypress.co.uk

British Library Cataloguing-in-Publication Data
A catalogue record for this book is available from the British Library

Library of Congress Cataloging-in-Publication Data applied for

ISBN 978 1 5261 0029 0 hardback

First published 2017

Typeset in 10.5/12.5pt Sabon by
Servis Filmsetting Ltd, Stockport, Cheshire
Printed in Great Britain
by CPI Group (UK) Ltd, Croydon, CR0 4YY

To his comrades in arms, Mark Serwotka and Matt Wrack

Contents

Acknowledgements

My thanks are due to John Kelly for his advice in redrafting the manuscript, Caroline Wintersgill of Manchester University Press for her support, and Martin Donohue and Unjum Mirza for providing contact details of those who worked with Bob Crow before he became general secretary of the RMT.

Abbreviations

ACAS	Advisory, Conciliation and Arbitration Service
AEEU	Amalgamated Engineering and Electrical Union
AEU	Amalgamated Engineering Union
AGS	assistant general secretary
ASLEF	Associated Society of Locomotive Engineers and Firemen
ASTMS	Association of Scientific, Technical and Managerial Staffs
AWL	Alliance for Workers' Liberty
BFAWU	Bakers, Food and Allied Workers Union
BNP	British National Party
CFDU	Campaign for a Fighting and Democratic Union
CoE	Council of Executives
CWU	Communication Workers Union
FBU	Fire Brigades Union
GGC	General Grades Committee
ITF	International Transport Workers' Federation
LU	London Underground
LUL	London Underground Limited
NGA	National Graphical Association
NSSN	National Shop Stewards' Network
NUJ	National Union of Journalists
NUM	National Union of Mineworkers
NUR	National Union of Railwymen
NUS	National Union of Seamen
NUT	National Union of Teachers
PCS	Public and Commercial Services Union
POA	Prison Officers Association
PPP	Private–Public Partnership
RMT	National Union of Rail, Maritime and Transport Workers
SLP	Socialist Labour Party
SOGAT	Society of Graphical and Allied Trades
SSP	Scottish Socialist Party
STUC	Scottish Trades Union Congress
SWP	Socialist Workers Party

Abbreviations

TfL	Transport for London
TGWU	Transport and General Workers' Union
TOC	train operating company
TSSA	Transport Salaried Staffs' Association
TUC	Trades Union Congress
TUCG	Trade Union Co-ordinating Group
TUI	Trade Unions International of Transport Workers
TUSC	Trade Union and Socialist Coalition
UCU	University and College Union
URTU	United Road Transport Union
USDAW	Union of Shop, Distributive and Allied Workers

Introduction

Although he was the leader of the small, specialist National Union of Rail, Maritime and Transport Workers (RMT), Bob Crow was by far the most widely known British union leader of recent times. According to the *Financial Times*, he was 'the stand out figure of the UK's trade union movement; a household name with charisma and clout in an age when many union leaders have become colourless and marginalised'[1] and 'Britain's most famous trade union leader'.[2] The *Independent* opined: 'To many people, he was the only recognisable face in the modern trade union movement ... He was the nearest [it] had to a celebrity ... seem[ing] to loom larger than the organisation he represented.'[3] But it was not just a case of profile but also effectiveness, for before his death, the *Guardian* noted: 'By nearly any measure you care to choose, Crow is far and away the most successful leader in his field.'[4] All this was because Crow was a distinctive person with a colourful and confident public persona, as well as a set of combative, oppositional politics that matched this persona, leading the *Guardian* to comment that he was 'one of the last socialist household names left'[5] and the *Mirror* to believe that he was 'the greatest trade unionist of his generation'.[6] These characteristics went hand in hand with his being the leader of a union whose members – especially on London Underground (LU) or London Underground Limited (LUL) and the railways – have more potential bargaining power than most other workers. The combination of 1) the person, 2) the politics and 3) the potential power of RMT members made Crow the significant figure he became for the union movement and for politics more generally in Britain.

This biography will chart and explain his development from a youngster through to adulthood and then his steady rise through his

1 *Financial Times* 12 March 2014.
2 *Financial Times* 25 March 2011.
3 *Independent* 12 March 2014.
4 *Guardian* 13 December 2010.
5 *Guardian* 7 February 2014.
6 *Mirror* 12 March 2014.

union's ranks to its pinnacle as general secretary. The purpose is not to put Crow on a pedestal by writing a 'great man' history in which Crow delivered pay rises or Crow stopped employers from victimising members. Rather, it is to understand sociologically how and why he was able to make the contribution he did, on the basis of the inter-relationship between himself and the RMT members, where the triad of person, politics and (members') power is uppermost. Most biographies of left-wing union leaders explain what a particular individual did and, in a mechanical fashion, how the individual did it. But few are able to explain why the individual was able do what they did and why their actions resonated as they did. From this standpoint, the purpose here is to identify the wider lessons that emerge for workers and unions from studying Crow as a leader, fighter and socialist in terms of how to be effective. Effectiveness is essentially an equation concerning contending power, material interests and ideologies whereby trajectories of intention, process and outcome come into being. Simply put, worker or union (collective) power in pursuit of goals and objectives is ranged against employer and state power, where intention is guided by material interests, ideology and power considerations, with process concerning action and interaction with other agencies and comprising patterns of conflict and cooperation, while the outcome of the interaction is primarily the result of the balance of forces or power between contending parties. A positive outcome is one where benefits outweigh costs, covering a range of categories (economic, power, consciousness, organisational). Taking Crow and his leadership of the RMT, then, means examining how unions can rebuild their power – in the face of a concerted neoliberal offensive by capital and the state – so that they can prosecute members' material (principally economic) interests in the direction of socialist change.

To do this, leadership needs to be situated as a potential power resource for unions in their search for effectiveness. Here, the leadership demonstrated by Crow needs to be broken down into its constituent components (agenda setting, public speaking, negotiating, strategising, communicating, caucusing, alliance forming and so on) in order to better understand what he did, how he did it and why he was effective. On the Left, it is often assumed that if policies and strategy are correct, then advances will automatically flow. The case of Crow shows starkly that knowing how, when and where to apply these strategies is neither self-evident nor automatic. Rather, it is the leadership qualities expressed through a person and their persona that are critical to ensuring that the outcomes gained are both desirable and effective. But equal measure of recognition must also be given to acknowledging the basis upon which

2

Crow worked, namely, leading a relatively small, homogeneous and cohesive union with high levels of membership affinity to a particular identity, since the task of leading a bigger, much more diversified general union with less membership affinity represents a different, and perhaps more difficult, challenge. The potential power of the members Crow relied upon in negotiations with employers requires recognition just as much as his shrewd use of it, given that the RMT used 'yes' votes in strike ballots as much as – if not more than – strikes themselves to gain bargaining objectives. Other workers have strategic industrial power but it must be identified, constructed and then used skilfully to maximise leverage. The advantage many RMT members also have, especially in rail transport, is that, despite privatisation, public transport is still seen as a public (rather than a private) 'good', so that industrial action there has significant political effects, creating usable leverage.

Crow's wider significance must be understood within the context of the radical Left's depleted forces. He cut a bigger figure because there was relatively little in the way of competition for its leadership in the union movement. Moreover, he was a voice for the voiceless, showing that popular political disenfranchisement had become acute. He was able to take radical industrial and political positions because he led the RMT during a period when it delivered for its members (especially on wages). This luxury is not always afforded to left-wing union leaders. Consequently, when he spoke out against governments, whether Tory or Labour, on issues outside of his industrial brief, his criticism was seen by members as well founded, appropriate and legitimate – and not just because of their own discontent with the government. In this sense, the RMT under Crow practised a very political form of trade unionism.[7] Indeed, it often seemed that the RMT operated at times like a quasi-political party.

Posthumous tributes

From the outside the RMT, the tributes paid to Crow on his death in 2014 by the PCS general secretary, Mark Serwotka, the FBU general secretary Matt Wrack, and the former *Times* industrial editor, Christine Buckley, were as insightful and sympathetic as any:

> Bob Crow was the greatest trade union leader of his generation ... [he] was without doubt a towering force in our movement. He represented the very best of trade unionism. ... he was not just a skilled negotiator and strategist,

---

7 See Darlington (2014b).

he was a warm-hearted and funny man, and brilliant company. ... I hope his legacy is a wider recognition that we need more people like [him].[8]

Bob was an outstanding leader for the labour movement and the best known trade unionist of his generation. He was a fighter of unbending principle ... During a time when socialist ideas have been dumped by many, he proudly stuck to the idea that society could be organised in a different way.[9]

The union movement lost an inspirational and powerful figure when he died. For a journalist, he was a dream – a colourful, entertaining, tough speaking union leader who could command more column inches and more airtime than any of his peers. More importantly for the RMT's members, he was highly effective – a tough negotiator who secured good results, a man who fought for ideals but knew the importance of cutting a deal for the working people he represented.[10]

From inside the RMT, the tribute paid by Peter Pinkney, then RMT president, was just as glowing and significant:

Bob changed our union for the better. People forget just how much trouble we were in when he was elected general secretary. We were down to 48,000 members and falling. We were in real danger of being swallowed up by a bigger union. We had sold ... our education centre, and were very probably about to sell Maritime House. Bob came in and the first thing he did was sort out the finances. He found money that we had, but nobody seemed to know about. This gave us the breathing space to invest and increase our finances. He also set up the Organising Unit to help increase membership. This has a twofold effect: it increases income coming in, and helps build a bigger and stronger fighting workforce. However, the biggest impact that Bob had, in my opinion, was his vision and investment regarding education.[11]

Pinkney added: 'He held this union together by his commitment, knowledge and genuine compassion ... We have to go forward and progress his vision ... He gave us the tools and we should use them.'[12] Geoff Revell, a longstanding NUR/RMT activist who then worked for Crow on special projects from 2002 to 2014, recounted: 'He was in your life, not just in your branch ... [He] is dead but we inherit his legacy.'[13] Pinkney's suc-

8 *Huffington Post* 11 March 2014.

9 FBU press release, 11 March 2014.

10 Email correspondence, 19 November 2015. Buckley was industrial editor between 1999 and 2009, and has been editor of the NUJ's *The Journalist* magazine since 2009.

11 *RMT News* April–May 2014.

12 *RMT News* July–August 2014.

13 *Morning Star* 17 March 2014.

cessor, Sean Hoyle, said that Crow was 'the greatest general secretary our union has ever or is ever likely to have'[14] and 'the greatest general secretary the trade union movement has ever had'[15] (while current CWU general secretary, Dave Ward, believed that 'He was the greatest trade union leader in our generation').[16] Many years before his death, an RMT activist captured the difference Crow made:

> Bob's election was a breath of fresh air, because the whole cautious approach that the union had had, which had done us no good whatsoever, [was overturned] ... overnight we had a figurehead who – rather than trying to block activists on the ground – wanted to take on an employer, who would actively encourage it. He would look at reasons to go into dispute rather than reasons not to, which was totally opposite to what we had seen beforehand ... I think that in itself has encouraged people to join us, because they can see that there is somebody there who does want to do something for 'me'.[17]

There were many other tributes (see Appendix 2) but these sufficiently capture the breadth and depth of Crow's contribution to the RMT and the wider union movement. In doing so they go some way towards explaining why the phrase, 'loved by the workers, feared by the bosses', adorned many of the banners and placards commemorating him upon his untimely death.

Methodology

One fortunate aspect of writing a biography of Crow is that, as an extremely well-known union leader of a strategically powerful group of workers, what he did and said was copiously covered by the media. Indeed, it sometimes seemed that Crow himself was the 'story'. Many of his speeches and television interviews that went unreported in newspapers were available on media such as YouTube and the union's own channel, *RMTv*. The overall extent of coverage was very much helped by the triad of his persona, politics and (members' potential) power. He became a regular of long interviews and features in the *Guardian*, *Evening Standard*, *Daily Mail*, *Financial Times*, *Mirror*, *Times* and *Telegraph*. These allowed him to speak directly – he was often quoted verbatim – and on issues well beyond RMT members' immediate pay and conditions. Coverage ranged widely from the enthusiastic to the

14 *RMT News* January 2016.
15 *RMT News* July–August 2016.
16 *CWU Voice*, April–May 2014.
17 Cited in Darlington (2009b: 96).

ambivalent and, in some cases, the explicitly hostile. That he was also a key figure on the Left meant that what he did and said was covered widely by the left-wing press.[18] The RMT also published its own members' magazine, *RMT News*, for which Crow wrote a column as editor as well as some articles.[19] Crow was heavily featured in *RMT News* in terms of not only his attendance at events such as meetings, picket lines, demonstrations and lobbies, but also addressing branch meetings, awarding membership honours and providing comments on various subjects.[20] The RMT under Crow also issued several press releases per day on industrial and political matters and each would go under his name. The way the press releases were constructed allowed Crow's authentic voice to be heard.

Of course, it would have been much better to have interviewed Crow directly, putting to him specific questions or asking him to tell of his life in the manner of the biographic-narrative interpretive method.[21] However, the inability to do this was mitigated by gaining plentiful testimony from many who worked with him within and beyond the NUR/RMT (see Appendix 1). With regard to the former, many were people who worked with him before he became assistant general secretary (in 1994) or general secretary (in 2002) when media coverage of him was less widespread. Unfortunately, official RMT cooperation was not secured because the union acceded to a request from Crow's family not to cooperate with any biography that had not been commissioned by them. Consequently, access to a number of potential interviewees and internal documentation was not possible. However, not gaining RMT cooperation was not fatal because of the aforementioned wealth of material and testimony. Moreover, trying to secure RMT cooperation would have presented its own challenge, namely trying to navigate an independent course through the image that the union wanted to portray of Crow (and, therefore, of itself). Before his death, and magnified by his effect of his death, the RMT, through its officers and leading lay officials, was extremely loyal to Crow. As a tight-knit family, no perceived criticism from outsiders was brooked. This meant that it would

18 This primarily includes the *Morning Star*, *Socialist Worker*, *Solidarity* and *The Socialist*.

19 Although Crow was the general editor, RMT official Brian Denny was the managing editor responsible for the production of the magazine.

20 This included photographs as well.

21 This is where the fieldwork interview is not so much an interview (with questions, structured or otherwise) but the opportunity for the subject to tell of the flow of decisions in their lives and then explain the flow of decisions in the telling of their story.

have been difficult to get honest, open and frank assessments, especially ones that allowed for balanced critique as well as personal, individual reflections.

From 2005 to 2010, I worked with the RMT through its national organising coordinator, Alan Pottage, to write annual overviews in the *Morning Star* of the union's progress in developing its organisational strength and bargaining agenda. Four were re-published in *RMT News*.[22] This experience, together with being a frequent media commentator and writer for the *Morning Star*, *Scotsman* and *Guardian* on matters affecting the RMT, meant that I became an 'RMT watcher', which also involved hearing Crow's speeches at RMT, STUC and TUC events as well as at many other meetings where he spoke about campaigns to repeal the anti-union laws, create a new shop stewards' network and build a new socialist Left. On various occasions, I publicly defended Crow and the RMT.[23] And, in 2009, I dedicated an edited book called *The Future of Union Organising: Building for Tomorrow* to Crow, saying that he was 'probably one of the finest union leaders of his generation in Britain today'.

In writing any biography, conflating the individual with the collective social forces around the person must be avoided, for it wrongly situates the individual, in the process de-contextualising them. The end product is something like a 'great man' history. What Crow thought and did cannot be read directly from the actions of the RMT and its members. Crow and the RMT (and its activists and officers) were two separate, albeit closely aligned, agencies. Throughout this biography care has been taken to avoid conflating Crow and the RMT – falling prey to the fallacy that Crow 'was' the RMT and that the union had no existence separate from him, or the opposing idea that Crow was, in the end, just a cog in the RMT machine. So when working out Crow's impact, recognition must be made of the mediating and facilitating agencies involved, principally but not exclusively RMT members and activists. This task was not always easy because Crow did very much dominate the RMT's public persona and he had the lion's share of the media focus on the union.

22 See *RMT News* August 2005, September 2006, November 2007 and September 2008.

23 This included letters to *Scotland on Sunday* (17 August 2003, 18 March 2007, 2 July 2007).

Theoretical and conceptual approaches

Given that Crow's political belief system was 'communist/socialist',[24] critical Marxism is an appropriate analytical tool by which to study him because it can fully appreciate and understand the motivation behind his words and deeds. Using it shows Crow's ideas and actions will be subject to constructive criticism and evaluation. Within the parameters of a Marxist approach, the key components deployed are 1) dialectical materialism, whereby the formative influence of syntheses of agency and environment, individual and collective, and ideas and actions are accorded prominence as means of understanding social processes and outcomes (albeit with materialist concerns forming the foundation upon which the approach rests); and 2) a holistic form of political economy where politics and economics are held to be different but indivisible parts of society. This entails giving prominence to the influence of capitalism, the capitalist (neoliberal) state, and the struggle between capital and labour. Thus, Crow and the RMT represent a form of agency interacting with the environment in a process of mutual osmosis. Capital, market and state, as the stronger parties, set the overall terms of the relationship with Crow and the RMT, but Crow and the RMT were not completely subordinate, being able to influence the terms of that relationship.

This critical Marxist approach also facilitates an analytical framework to consider how Crow was shaped by the RMT *and* helped to shape the RMT. Being shaped by the RMT (and its predecessor) did not mean taking on all of its characteristics, for some features were rejected (while, of course, others were endorsed and taken up). The sense of being shaped by and shaping is not of a simple linear nature whereby Crow was shaped by the RMT until he became general secretary in 2002, and shaped the RMT thereafter. The dialectics of social processes, leading to social outcomes, are more complex than this. Yet it is the case that the agency of individual actors (when working with others as lieutenants) can have a greater impact upon the wider environment at some points than others. It is here that the influence of the synthetic interplay of the person, his politics and the potential power of members is at its sharpest. Out of this approach, three aspects are to the fore in examining Crow, namely, material interests (of his members and himself), ideology (his and members' political worldviews) and power resources (of his members and himself). These three aspects provide the conceptual categories by which a critical Marxist analysis is constructed and which productively anchors the person, politics and potential power of members.

24 *Guardian* 20 June 2009.

Critical Marxism also means not taking things at face value just because they came from a 'communist/socialist'. It means avoiding the 'spin' that Crow and the RMT put on the battles they fought, instead using independently arrived at criteria to judge what Crow said and did (such as was absent from a recent official RMT history).[25] Such independent criteria include those derived from classical Marxism (on defining the working class and the agency for socialism), social science (the health of the union movement, union democracy, strategic power), political science (political parties, political consciousness) and industrial relations (bargaining strategies and union building).

Following from this, a number of literatures are used to help study Crow and the triad of his personality, politics and members' power. Kelly conceptualised union militancy as having the following components: ambitious industrial and political goals (limiting compromise and concession), extensive membership mobilisation in pursuit of these (focusing upon self-reliance rather than a political party, a benign employer or the use of law), concentration upon collective bargaining (not third-party arbitration or consultation), and a worldview or ideology of labour–capital conflict. In practice, this means opposing social partnership, deploying frequent industrial action and taking radical, oppositional stances.[26] Thus, militancy involves more than just ambitious demands and stems from a wider perspective where the strategy to pursue demands is bound up with a radical way of seeing – and acting upon – the world. The contrast with moderation – defined as reasonable demands peppered with concessions, strong reliance upon employers, third parties and the law, infrequent threat or use of industrial action, and an ideology of mutual gains – clearly shows what militancy is about, and provides a checklist for assessing how comprehensive Crow's militancy was.

Kelly also provides a wider perspective on how unions mobilise members in workplaces and communities in order to generate collective power, arising from the development of grievances, material or otherwise.[27] Unions through their leaders can crucially help 'frame' issues in order to develop member consciousness and the confidence to collectively struggle for their interests. They do this by influencing the conception of their interests, attributing blame for grievances, and identifying windows of opportunity, the means to act and so on. But this mobilisation theory also contends that union leaders can not only

25 Berlin (2006).
26 Kelly (1996).
27 Kelly (1998).

help give legitimacy to workers' struggles by cognitively liberating workers through promoting a radical moral economy, but also embed and advance an organisational culture of conflict with capital. Again, this provides something of a template by which to judge Crow in terms of what he advocated and the impact of what he advocated.

On the sources of labour power, Batstone suggested a schema of 1) disruptive capacity, 2) scarcity of labour and 3) political influence, where each allows workers to impose sanctions upon employers.[28] The first comes from workers being located at points of production, distribution and exchange where their labour is crucial to allowing the process of work to take place; the second from workers being able to act collectively in the labour market by either taking advantage of the demand for labour or by restricting and regulating labour supply; and the third from workers establishing their own collective political agency. In noting that mobilisation is the act of pursuing goals using these three sources to collectively secure demands, Batstone acknowledged that 'economic' strikes are essentially a feature of the private sector (where the aim is to hurt the employer in the pocket) while 'political' strikes are essentially a feature of the public sector (where the aim is to undermine government legitimacy).

Traditionally, a number of different styles of leadership have been recognised such as autocratic, bureaucratic, delegative, democratic or participative, transactional and transformational. These are broad, overarching *idealised* styles to which individual leaders and the practice of leadership do not necessarily approximate *per se*, for some leaders will use different styles at different points in time or practise different elements at any one point in time. Within this, charisma, authenticity and pragmatism are not styles of leadership but components of some styles (such as transformational). Just as importantly, most of the different styles can be expected to be found in some measure when studying union leaders, since organisational constraints (such as rule books, democratic processes and organisational cultures) will exist. For leaders to lead requires followers to follow but the relationship is not a simple, linear one, as followers can range from passive to active recipients as well as being constructors and moderators of leadership (especially where followers are union members with a set of democratic rights). Therefore, there is a dynamic, osmotic relationship between leaders and followers comprising the person, position, process and outcome.

Political congruence exists when alignment occurs between the values, aspirations, expectations and desired outcomes of leaders, activists

28 Batstone (1988).

and members.[29] It is manifest in a common political project which is likely to bring about strategic renewal evidenced through membership growth and cultural and structural changes, comprising shared political frames of reference and collective identity, participation and socialisation (encouraged by innovative practice, networking and education) and mobilisation. Thus, the evidence of political congruence would comprise a political project which is 1) transformative in nature (of intentions, processes and outcomes) and 2) found agreeable by most members. In other words, a political project inside a union would have to set out what it was against, what is was for, and how to get there in terms of existing union practice, employers' interests and membership participation – and make considerable progress in realising these. Putting moves towards militancy together with increased membership and membership participation is one particular form of union renewal and revitalisation, especially when directed by the national union leadership and deployed as an 'organising strategy' to create more assertive and powerful workplace unionism.[30]

Returning to the equation of material interests, ideology and power, it is worth stressing there are two senses of power, namely, 'power for' and 'power over'. The former concerns workers' ability to generate resources of power (through collectivisation) and the latter the application (through mobilisation) of resources to a given situation to gain a certain outcome. Most importantly power should then be conceived as the *ability* of one party to force upon another an *outcome* that harms and contradicts their interests and ideology. This pertains not just to the relationship between capital, state and labour but also within the organisations of labour, namely, unions and political parties. There is a subjective element involved, for how power is perceived is important. The greater the extent to which power is perceived as being manifest, the stronger it is likely to be. And, as power comes to be perceived as legitimate, the more its exercise is seen as authoritative.

Given that Crow, as a socialist, leader and fighter, sought to change the RMT so that it became a larger, more militant and more powerful union as well as exerting influence on the wider union movement and the political Left, these frameworks and concepts are used to help assess the outcomes of his efforts as well as to analyse and understand the industrial and political perspectives held by him. Running throughout them is the triad of person, politics and power.

---

29 Croucher and Upchurch (2012) and Upchurch *et al.* (2012a, 2012b).
30 See Gall and Fiorito (2011) on the different manifestations and outcomes of 'union organising'.

Context

The RMT has many idiosyncratic characteristics and it had an important role in shaping Crow's ability to call upon particular resources in order to lead it in the way he did. It is worth getting some early perspective on these by noting the RMT's first three objectives. These are:

> (a) to secure the complete organisation of all workers employed by any board, company or authority in connection with rail, sea and other transport and ancillary undertakings and offshore energy; (b) to work for the supersession of the capitalist system by a socialistic order of society; [and] (c) the promotion of equality for all including through ... collective bargaining, publicity material and campaigning, representation, union organisation and structures, education and training, organising and recruitment, the provision of all other services and benefits and all other activities.[31]

So while its 16 objectives include the usual ones of improving members' terms and conditions of employment, they also stipulate industrial unionism and clear political objectives that go beyond the interests of RMT members and their families. This sets the scene for the RMT to be both an overtly industrial *and* political union in words and deeds. On both industrial and political fronts, the RMT under Crow became known as a 'fighting back' union. Indeed, under Crow, there was a sense in which the RMT went as far as any individual union could without becoming a political party as such – by which is meant offering its own candidates for elections to public office and under its own banner. More than most unions, the RMT under Crow never confined itself to merely speaking about and acting upon issues emanating directly from its members' experience of work. In setting up the Labour Representation Committee in 1899 (which became the Labour Party in 1906), unions decided to concentrate upon the industrial and economic spheres of the 'pounds and pence' of their members' wages and conditions, while funding Labour to concentrate on the political sphere where employment, among other issues, was regulated. Under the continued disillusionment with 'new' Labour from 1994 and then after leaving Labour in 2004, the RMT spoke and acted in the political field almost as its own party because of Labour's simultaneous rejection of social democracy and embrace of neoliberalism. In doing so, and for society as a whole, the RMT under Crow became the embodiment of radical Left oppositionalism, with Crow as its figurehead. He and the RMT, thus, spoke to the

---

31 RMT rule book (June 2012); see http://www.rmt.org.uk/news/publications/rmt-rulebook-2012/. See also Crow (2008: 21–22) on the NUR's demand for workers' control of the rail industry.

concerns of both their section of the working class and the organised working class more generally. Centrally underpinning all this was the demand, specific to the RMT, for rail renationalisation, which fused together the union's key industrial and political demands. It was this, primarily, that led to the RMT's involvement in helping to attempt to establish a new socialist party.

Related to these phenomena of political independence and self-reliance is the tightly cohesive internal RMT culture where identity with, and loyalty to, the union are to the fore. For example, being one of a small number of delegates to the AGM – called the RMT's 'supreme parliament' – is held to be an honour and privilege in a way that is not true of most other unions. More obviously RMT members were proud and protective of Crow as their general secretary, as indicated by the considerable turnout from across Britain to pay their last respects at his funeral. Many held either their own placards or those with the 'RIP Legend' slogan.[32] There is another aspect of the RMT which is note-worthy, namely that, while internal differences exist, especially over industrial politics and political worldviews, the RMT is more politically homogeneous than many other unions, where even its right wing is on the Left (that is, of an 'old' Labour type). Several other features are worth stressing at this stage. First, as with the Royal Mail, there is the special place of the railways in British society and in its people's psyche. This means that decent rail services are held to be critical to what it means to have a civilised society, making the RMT politically important and providing it with a particular kind of resource for bargaining with governments and political parties as well as employers (where govern-ments pressurise employers to settle disputes in order to restore services). Second, there are some practices concerning the joint regulation of work organisation that are not present elsewhere, whether in public or pri-vate sectors, which not only make the RMT a powerful force but also reflect its influence. For example, Transport for London (TfL) in 2011 employed 31 full-time and 371 part-time union reps,[33] with a majority of these being RMT reps. Twelve non-seafaring Council of Executives (CoE) members are paid full-time salaries by the RMT to carry out their jobs (while five shipping and offshore grades are paid for loss of earnings to attend meetings).[34] Third, in the time of Crow's leadership, the rail

32 They were joined by members from other unions, radical Left groups such as the Socialist Party and campaigning single-issue pressure groups such as CND.

33 *Evening Standard* 2 December 2011.

34 Prior to the creation of the RMT, the NUR's senior lay body was the National Executive which for simplicity's sake is not differentiated here from the RMT's CoE.

industry was buoyant, with expanding passenger numbers and relatively tight labour markets, generating a strong negotiating position.[35] Fourth, although the RMT was formed in 1990 from the merger of the National Union of Railwaymen (NUR) and the National Union of Seamen (NUS), the NUR side was by far the larger, and railway and Underground workers were not affected by the impact of the NUS's traumatic defeat by P&O Ferries (which led it to seek merger with the NUR).[36] Indeed, NUR members had not experienced a defeated strike in the 1980s that had damaged their union, as many other union members had. Fifth, the RMT has had stimulants to respond to in the form of aggressive employers and governments.[37] The train operating companies (TOCs), in particular, have some indemnity against losses caused through strikes, raising their resistance to such action and their willingness and ability to be aggressive. Sixth, the RMT is able to exercise both economic and political power through members' withdrawal of labour because 'economic' strikes against TOCs generate political pressure and 'political' strikes against London Underground generate economic pressure (by disrupting the economy). Seldom can other unions' strikes generate both. Lastly, strength of solidarity – as one part of a common identity – between many RMT members was regularly shown through members' willingness to strike (albeit after the exhaustion of internal grievance procedures) to defend fellow members who had been victimised, showing an active solidarity rather just passive sympathy,[38] which in turn suggested something significant – and critically, different – about the outcome of the combination of the nature of work, culture of workplace collectivism and industry-wide class consciousness on the railways and within the RMT compared to other industries and unions.

35 This contrasted with the situation from the 1960s to the 1980s, when NUR membership fell from 254,687 in 1965 to 180,429 in 1975 and 117,594 in 1987.

36 The strike by NUS members at P&O Ferries between 6 February 1988 and 9 June 1989 was against pay cuts, redundancies and increased working hours. It was one of the last great, defeated strikes of the 1980s.

37 See, for example, *Financial Times* 5 August 2003.

38 For example, between January 2013 and September 2015, the RMT successfully balloted members on 19 occasions to strike over the dismissal of individual members. Proportionately, this is far greater than other unions. The prevalence of victimisation (including the cases of Alan Pottage, Pat Sikorski and Steve Hedley) signifies the robustly contested nature of industrial relations on the railways and the Underground. Most other unions would pursue members' cases through employment tribunals after exhausting internal procedures.

Chapter structure

Chapter 1 deals with Crow's family background, childhood and early life up until the late 1980s. Chapter 2 covers the period of the late 1980s to early 2000s when Crow was elected to the RMT's national executive, the CoE, in 1992 and elected as its assistant general secretary (AGS) in 1994. Chapter 3 examines Crow's first term of office as general secretary, from 2002 to 2007. Chapter 4 covers his second term of office as general secretary. Chapter 5 deals with his last term of office and begins the work of assessing his impact and legacy, especially with regard to membership composition and growth. Because of the ongoing nature of the events that Crow was not only involved with but also helped to initiate and guide, it has not been possible to keep all content strictly to the time period of each chapter. Thus, the last four chapters do not follow a chronological order because it is not possible to fully assess Crow and his achievements chronologically. Thus, Chapter 6 examines his personal and family life while Chapters 7, 8 and 9 assess his importance, impact and legacy, drawing out lessons from his leadership, specifically concentrating on the interplay of 1) person and personality, 2) politics and 3) members' potential power.

1. Formative years

Examining Bob Crow's early years and family background provides insight into the process by which he became politicised and developed the strong and forceful personality he became known for and by which he pursued his political agenda. This is not to suggest that certain values or a certain personality were drilled into him at an early age but to show what social and political resources he was able to – and chose to – draw upon in order to develop his worldview as well as his sense of purpose in life and self-belief. His father's influence was critical in giving him an awareness of social justice as well as the determination to pursue this through individual and collective action. Crow chose to take on board these influences in a certain way. By contrast, his brother, Richard, chose to move in a different direction politically and professionally.[1] There were also significant turning points in Crow's life that explain why he became the person he did. The most obvious concerns his feeling of being picked on at work when he was 19 because this opened him up to a personal experience of a workplace union from which he never looked back.

Life in London

Robert (Bob) Crow was born in Shadwell in the East End of London on 13 June 1961, the son of George Crow and Lillian Hutton. His father was then a docker and Transport and General Workers' Union (TGWU)

---

1 Richard said: 'We've both got the same sense of social justice – we get that from our dad. But we come at it from different angles on the best way to achieve it. We see things differently and we always will' (*Daily Mail* 2 July 2011). He continued: 'If me and Bob get together, we'll talk about football, sport and life in general. We get on until it comes to politics and unions. As soon as we talk about that, we clash ... I do think he genuinely believes in what he says, but he's extreme ...' (*Daily Mail* 2 July 2011). Upon Bob's death, Richard paid tribute to his brother: 'He was honest, he looked after the people he was supposed to look after, and he was a great man as far as honesty and beliefs went ... When people have a high office in life they fall for the big trappings of the flash cars and the big hotels and big houses. But Bob wasn't like that; he was a genuine person of the people. He was one of those loveable little rogues, one of those guys that had bundles of friends' (*Daily Mail* 12 March 2014).

member. His grandfather was also a casual docker, but he was also a stonemason and a famous East End boxer nicknamed 'Punch Crow'.[2] His mother worked as a cleaner in the retail chain WH Smith to help the family make ends meet. She died from bowel cancer when Crow was eight years old[3] (although he attributed his battling character to her influence).[4] His parents had three other children – his older brother by three years, Richard, and two sisters (one of whom took her own life in her twenties). Richard recalled: 'After our mum died, Ann – who was 12 years older than me – looked after us for a couple of years. Then Dad married again and we all went to live with them on the edge of Epping Forest: me, Bob, my dad and Ann, my stepmum, her son and daughter. And they had a cousin too. There was eight of us all in a three-bedroom semi.'[5] In his last interview before he died, Crow told BBC Radio 4 that his family lived in poverty until they were moved out of the East End by London County Council to Hainault Forest in the Greater London/Essex area when he was four.[6] The house was a two-storey, three-bedroom prefab on a council estate. In the East End, the family had no cooker but just two electric rings, and four families shared a single bathroom.[7] The juxtaposition of wealth and poverty was close at hand, as Crow recalled that from their window they could see money being counted in the Royal Mint.[8]

Crow recalled his childhood with fondness:

I think the 1970s was a great time … people say they were bad times but I think they was fantastic times. Sunday afternoon, for example – everyone had their dinner at the same time, half-past two, everywhere you walked round east London all you could smell was roast beef and Yorkshire pudding, everyone's old man was down the pub having a drink Sunday lunchtime, every kid was on the wall outside the pub with a bottle of Coke and packet of crisps waiting for their old man to come out the pub. There was jobs everywhere, people would come out of one job and into another. We had the big match on Sunday afternoon, and everyone was happy.[9]

He also recalled growing up in a very union-orientated and political environment:

2 *Independent* 13 September 2007; 'RMT leader Bob Crow talks salary, strikes and Boris', http://www.bbc.com/news/uk-politics-26529361, 11 March 2014.

3 *Daily Mail* 11 March 2014.

4 *Financial Times* 10 September 2004.

5 *Daily Mail* 2 July 2011.

6 Radio 4, 10 March 2014.

7 Radio 4, 10 March 2014.

8 Radio 4, 10 March 2014; *Financial Times* 25 March 2011.

9 *Guardian* 13 December 2010.

When we used to come home at 6 o'clock at night, the news was always on and the old man had an opinion about everything. So we just naturally thought everyone was in a union. All the big industries were unionised. All my mates' dads' families were in unions. It was just a fact of life. Now, it must be very difficult for people – youngsters know nothing about unions.[10]

Crow went to Kingswood Upper School which then merged with Hainault Forest High School.[11] He recalled that it was 'fun' but there was little encouragement to excel or to strive for further education.[12] Consequently, he left school at 16 without any formal qualifications, preferring football to books.[13] It was an indication of what a remarkable individual he would become that this would not impede him becoming a skilled negotiator and union leader. Indeed, it was the 'school of hard knocks' and the 'university of life' along with Communist Party membership that provided him with his actual education – he told the *Financial Times* 'Anything I've learnt is about using my wits',[14] while the *Guardian* noted that he had 'a very keen brain and strong emotional intelligence'.[15] Paul Jackson, London Underground Engineering branch secretary, recalled that 'He was a street fighter and had the instincts and wit of a working class cockney.'[16] His desired career option was to become a professional footballer but he recognised that he did not have the ability: 'I realised I had to do something [else]'[17] and 'I never dreamt of driving a red bus or a red train when I was young. I really wanted to play professional football, but I had to give up on that when I was 14. I'd had a really hard time getting into the school team, so I realised that getting into a club was probably beyond me.'[18] But his love of football and cricket (and sport more generally) meant that he knew all the rules. 'Even when we were in primary school, he'd go down the local sport

10 *Independent* 13 September 2007.

11 *Guardian* 2 July 2004. His stepmother reported: 'He's been back there to see them in the past couple of years. He went there – they asked him if he wanted to go and see the children' (*Ilford Recorder* 6 September 2007).

12 *Financial Times* 10 September 2004.

13 *The Mirror* 15 April 2002.

14 *Financial Times* 10 September 2004.

15 *Guardian* 12 March 2014.

16 Email correspondence.

17 *Financial Times* 10 September 2004. Later in life, he said if he had not become a union leader, he would have liked to have been a meteorologist as he developed a keen interest in the weather (*Observer* 17 February 2002) – although that would have meant having a degree and science qualifications from school. A few years later he gave a different reply – asked by the *Independent* (29 June 2009) 'What would you be doing if you weren't a trade unionist?' he responded, 'No idea. It's in my blood. Certainly wouldn't be a nightclub crooner though.'

18 *Independent* 17 February 2004.

shop and buy pocket books with all the official rules. And he'd learn them off by heart', recalled his brother, Richard.[19] If this was evidence of a young mind capable of detailed recall and the ability to apply rules to situations, then it served Crow well later in life as an activist and negotiator who needed to know union rule books and collective bargaining agreements and how best to apply and interpret them.

The idea of working for London Underground came not from company milk rounds but because 'I saw these guys on the track, stripped down to the waist and working in the sun, and thought, I wouldn't mind that.'[20] Crow took the initiative to write to London Underground and three months later he was offered a job as junior track man. But because he was not yet 18, he was not allowed to work on the track itself. First, he made tea: 'My gang leader said: "You learn the job by making the tea, and placing bets for us, and watering the plants in the chairman's office." So at 16 I sat in the chair of the chairman of London Transport!'[21] One day, the chairman gave Crow a bunch of flowers and said: 'Go and give these to Mum.' So he went home and presented his mother with the bouquet. Next day, the furious chairman sought him out and asked why he had left work. Crow realised his mistake when he was told 'Mum' was, in fact, the nickname of the elderly cleaner.[22] However, it was not this event that marked a turning point in Crow's life but one a few years later.

Political epiphany

Turning 18, Crow was now able to fell trees as a lumberjack on the overground sections of the Underground, based at Loughton, and to work on track renewal doing heavy repair work. He also joined the NUR on 6 May 1979[23] – just three days after Margaret Thatcher was elected prime minister. It was said he was as much attracted to joining by the social side of beer and darts as anything else.[24] Given that his work was often physically arduous and not pleasant (involving jobs such as rodding blocked drains),[25] Crow developed into a tough,

19 *Daily Mail* 2 July 2011.
20 *Financial Times* 10 September 2004.
21 *Financial Times* 10 September 2004.
22 As recounted by Peter Pinkney in *RMT News* April 2014.
23 *RMT News* April 2014.
24 *Observer* 17 February 2002.
25 *Financial Times* 25 March 2011. He told the interviewer the worst job he ever had was 'rodding drains' in the Underground as a 19-year-old: 'There was a stench, it was full of rats, all kinds of sexual contraceptives you could think of, we used the

strong character. One day he was sent to Harrow on the Hill, which he felt was as remote to him as being posted up to Scotland – or Outer Mongolia.[26] Feeling that the posting was malicious and, thus, victimisation, he recalled: 'My gang leader didn't like me. I'd stood up to him about something. I objected, and he said it was for upsetting the applecart.'[27] So Crow went to a union meeting to complain about his treatment: 'I was 19, and it was full of all these old people. I thought they were old, but probably the same age I am now [43].'[28] Not long afterwards, it was suggested to him he become a local representative and join the branch committee. But before he agreed to this, he sought to negotiate: 'This bloke asked me if I wanted to get involved, and I said, "If you change the branch meetings from a Friday night then I'll get involved. Cause all my mates are going to be out clubbing and meeting women while I'm stuck in here."'[29]

He joined the branch committee and this led to him being sent on an NUR scholarship to the Labour Party summer school in 1980.[30] According to the *Guardian* and the *Independent*, he fell in love with the union movement so much that he ended up seeing it as his vocation and hobby.[31] At the same time, he was elected as a local union rep and, thus, from 1982 to 1992, served as the representative for Sectional Council 8, working on behalf of thousands of Underground infrastructure maintenance and renewal workers, called Permanent Way staff. In 1987, he gained full-time facility time release as a Permanent Way representative on the sectional council of London Underground's union–management bargaining structure. In these positions, Crow benefited from a situation recalled by former branch officer Jeff Porter: 'As London Underground had suspended the machinery of negotiation in the mid-1980s, leaving it in a state of suspended animation, sectional council reps [were]

---

long rods to clear out debris and leaves from the drains along the lines.' However, he enjoyed the work, telling the *Independent* (13 September 2007) that it was: 'Fantastic. Yeah, I mean, it's hard, heavy work, but we were all young lads. I've still got the same friends that I had then. [It b]uilt up great camaraderie.'

26 In other interviews, he recalled it was Rickmansworth, an hour's journey by train, but it was to him still 'the other side of the world' (*Independent* 13 September 2007).

27 *Financial Times* 10 September 2004. Later on he recalled it as 'a stupid issue really, now I think about it. In the gang, everyone had different duties that changed. One week you'd have to make tea. Other people had to write letters. It was my turn to do something – I can't remember what it was – and I had a row with my ganger' (*Independent* 13 September 2007).

28 *Financial Times* 10 September 2004.

29 *Independent* 13 September 2007.

30 *Times* 9 May 2009.

31 *Guardian* 9 June 2009, 20 June 2009; *Independent* 13 September 2007.

nominated by the union rather than elected by the membership, thus ... favouring those with good contacts with the union leadership.'[32] Crow was also the chair of the sectional council from 1983 to 1985 and held the secretary's post from 1985 to 1992. In 1984, he was awarded the NUR's Youth Award by the general secretary, Jimmy Knapp.[33] He was also Holborn branch chair from 1984 to 1986, Stratford No. 1 branch secretary from 1987 to 1993 and LUL Signal, Electrical and Track branch secretary from 1993 to 1994. Between 1984 and 1994, Crow was also a regular delegate to NUR/RMT annual and special general meetings as well as TUC and Trade Union CND congresses.[34] In 1986, he was elected to the executive committee of the London Transport District Committee. He was also a tutor at the NUR's education centre (called Frant Place), which gives some indication of his early ability – and confidence – for spreading the gospel of trade unionism and organising and negotiating. However, former branch secretary Pam Singer recalled:

> [We] were both chosen to be lay tutors at the same time. We did our training together. He was terrible! He didn't know how to go beyond lecturing and doing all the talking. Needless to say, he was not chosen to do much tutoring. The education coordinator was very relieved when Bob was elected to the Executive, because then he was not eligible to do any tutoring![35]

In 1990, Crow took part in an occupation of the South African Embassy after he managed to get into the building after demonstrating outside it against apartheid.[36] This event was an early indication not just of his belief in internationalism and solidarity across borders, but also his commitment to personally putting the 'theory' into practice.

Crow's first time on strike was the day after he returned from honeymoon in 1982.[37] Pam Singer recounted of this time:

32 Email correspondence.
33 This involved being given a book which he later gave to Mick Rix as 'a memento of our friendship' (email correspondence, 8 September 2014).
34 See Peter Pinkney detailing Crow's lay positions in his obituary in *RMT News* April 2014. See also *Independent* 19 April 2004.
35 Email correspondence.
36 Berlin (2006: 100).
37 *Guardian* 20 June 2009; *Observer* 17 February 2002; *Financial Times* 12 March 2014. However, the *Independent* (13 September 2007) reported '1980: Crow's first strike – a national day of action, called by the TUC. He was also involved in stoppages in 1982', following on from the *Observer* (17 February 2002): 'His first strike was a national day of action in 1980, called by the TUC. He was involved again in stoppages in 1982.'

I met Bob at my very first branch meeting in November 1982 when we were both members of Neasden 1 branch ... There was a very serious issue facing the Permanent Way workers: the replacement of wooden sleepers with concrete sleepers. A dispute was brewing. I walked in to my first meeting to see various Permanent Way gangs arguing fiercely about what to do. A very charismatic young rep stood up and addressed the meeting, holding everyone's attention. It was Bob, of course. He exuded confidence, spoke with passion and conviction. If I remember correctly, he inspired everyone to take strike action.[38]

Around the same time as becoming active in the NUR, Crow joined the Communist Party of Great Britain.[39] In his memoirs, Kevin Halpin, former AEU convenor of London Underground's Acton Works and Communist Party industrial organiser, recalled Crow's recruitment and subsequent training by party cadres on the railways in London,[40] with Jeff Porter recalling that Crow was a 'protégé of Halpin ... who was on the Stalinist wing of the party'.[41] He would remain a member until 1995, sitting on its national executive.[42] The Communist Party was a well-organised, if declining, force in the NUR as well as more widely at this time, so there was still an attraction in it. However, the rise of Bennism in the early 1980s and the move of Trotskyists such as the IMG (International Marxist Group) into Labour could have acted as a counterbalance to this. It seems that the influence of his father (see below), the likes of the former leading Communist Party member in the NUR, Jock Nicolson,[43] and his visit to the Labour Party summer school were more important in influencing Crow's decision to join, and a clear indication that he believed Labour was not a socialist party. As a result of Communist Party membership, he received an education: 'I used to go to

38 Email correspondence.
39 *Guardian* 20 June 2009. After the CPGB's dissolution in 1991, the main part of the former CPGB was constituted as the Communist Party of Britain (CPB, commonly referred to as the Communist Party, which was formed earlier in 1988) and is not to be confused with the existing Communist Party of Great Britain, formed in 1991 and whose full title includes 'Provisional Central Committee'. Among the other splinters from the original CPGB at the time of its dissolution were the Communist Party of Scotland and the Democratic Left (associated with *Marxism Today*). Crow also played a role in establishing the CPB from the remnants of the CPGB (*Central Fife Times* 7 September 2016).
40 Halpin (2012: 133). Although Crow remained sympathetic to the Communist Party and its initiatives, Halpin conveys the sense that Crow had left his natural political family and that he had little to do with Crow thereafter.
41 Email correspondence.
42 *Morning Star* 13 March 2014. Crow was never attracted to the Eurocommunist wing of the CPGB or the politics of *Marxism Today*.
43 Crow (2009: 5).

their lectures, I used to read the theory – they weren't just revolutionary phrase-mongers, they actually had a science',[44] and he recalled that his membership provided him with 'all my political understanding – it was a university education on its own'.[45] In this sense, it would allow him to operate instinctively. He also met Mick Rix (who became ASLEF general secretary, 1998–2003) through the Communist Party, forming a lifelong friendship with him: 'I've known Mick since 1984, when we went on a youth delegation to East Germany. Beer was 10p a pint and they gave us two pounds pocket money a day.'[46] On one of these Communist Party arranged trips for young trade unionists to the Eastern Bloc, Crow had an altercation with another future ASLEF general secretary: in Prague, he took offence at Shaun Brady's treatment of a female fellow delegate, punching him.[47]

Those working with Crow in the 1980s found him to be a tough, determined operator but sometimes a lone voice. According to Pam Singer:

> There was a large left-wing contingent and Bob was seen as being on the 'right' of the left ... he always wanted to concentrate on pay rises because he thought that pay was a unifying issue across London Underground ... many others wanted to concentrate on the bigger picture, i.e., re-organisation, eventual redundancies, job losses etc. This might be because his sector was, indeed, a lower paid sector than the operational side. Or it might have been the *Morning Star* 'line' ... He was politically isolated during the 1980s, as other *Morning Star* supporters had retired. [However], he was always prominent and stood his ground during difficult times [and] ... he always held the support of those in the infrastructure side because they knew that he was a tireless fighter. His appeal had to do with his bluntness, honesty and tireless conviction that he could make things better for his members ... Despite the raging debates that took place, there was never a major falling out with Bob. He did not give up, and retained a comradely view towards those who disagreed with him and often outvoted him on the Regional Council.[48]

Jeff Porter had similar recollections:

> Bob was very articulate but his most impressive attribute was his total honesty ... [his] power base was within the Permanent Way where he was very popular ... [he] never showed much flexibility in his broader politics and used to lose political arguments in the branch all the time, but generally

44 *Telegraph* 16 February 2002.
45 In Murray (2003: 103).
46 *Telegraph* 16 February 2002. See also *Evening Standard* 26 September 2002.
47 *Times* 18 November 2003. See also *Guardian* 17 April 2004, 2 July 2004; and *Independent* 25 May 2004.
48 Email correspondence.

with good grace. I do believe though that Bob was a pragmatist and knew when a deal must be struck, he didn't allow his political opinions to interfere with broader issues although he never lost sight of his principles ... Probably one of Bob's key attributes was his self-confidence and lack of self-doubt. This was reflected in his karaoke performance. Unfortunately, Bob was tone deaf and a terrible singer but up on the karaoke stage he would belt out a tune like a pro while the audience would grimace happily![49]

Former senior lay activist Martin Eady recalled Crow as both keen and eager to learn:

Bob stood out for his diligence in visiting Permanent Way gangs (spread out all over the Underground) especially on night shifts, and relentlessly pursuing the industrial issues and problems that members raised. Not all Sectional Council reps did this. As an LTDC delegate and ... [then] Executive Committee [member] he was noteworthy for constantly asking questions and learning all he could about the union both industrially and politically. Although personally confident, he did not stand out as a speaker or debater at this time. [In the 1980s], he spent a great deal of time with ... experienced members asking questions, always learning.[50]

Former branch secretary and RMT parliamentary officer Ann Henderson also recalled that at the NUR's 1988 AGM, Crow did not speak but instead was intent upon listening and learning.[51]

In this period, Crow's ascendance was also aided by 'many prominent activists from the infrastructure side ... retiring, and there were not many replacements'.[52] But there were other factors as well. There was a broad left-wing working unity on the London Transport Regional Council, and his role as a leading lay official of the London Transport Regional Committee 'got him known around the region'.[53] Given the drinking culture among RMT members and activists, these factors outweighed Crow 'never [being] much of a socialiser – he would always leave after meetings and rarely stayed for a drink afterwards. He kept his private life and the union very separate.'[54]

An activist from Crow's own branch recalled in 2007: 'I joined RMT some 20 years ago and was inspired by a young firebrand Crow who laid out the evils of the anti-union laws and the need to break them.'[55]

49 Email correspondence.
50 Email correspondence.
51 Email correspondence.
52 Pam Singer, email correspondence.
53 Jeff Porter, email correspondence.
54 Jeff Porter, email correspondence.
55 'Campaign for a fighting democratic union', *Off The Rails*, 6 November 2007, http://www.workersliberty.org/node/9511.

Another recollection was: 'I remember first hearing Crow speak at Cockfosters train depot in the mid-1980s, when I was working as an electrical fitter for London Underground. He stood out even then as a loud, charismatic character who had the ability to impress.'[56] And a future RMT AGS, Steve Hedley, recalled:

> I was sitting in a fairly humdrum meeting of the London Midland NUR district council in 1989 when a large gentleman with shoulder length curly hair made his way to the rostrum. I didn't recognise the man at all. I worked for British Rail at the time but a colleague whispered to me that's 'Bob Crow from London Underground'. The next ten minutes changed my life. Bob ... lambasted the anti-union laws, the union leadership, the bosses, the Tories, the cowardice of the (soon to become) 'New' Labour Party and, indeed, the whole capitalist system. The whole room was electrified. I had never heard such radical ideas put across in a way that I could understand and grasp instantly. The themes which Bob outlined so clearly in that speech became the tenets of our union.[57]

Therefore, it was not a surprise that Crow was elected to the CoE as the representative for London Underground in 1992[58] and in 1994, aged 33, he became the youngest ever AGS in the RMT's history.

Fatherly influence

Crow's father, George, was a docker and then a Dagenham car worker as well as trade unionist and communist, becoming a union convenor at Ford for the TGWU.[59] He advised his son to read the *Morning Star* and the *Financial Times* – and to believe the opposite of everything the latter said.[60] Crow junior fondly recalled his father's influence: 'The last thing my dad told me as I went to work on my first day was: Enjoy yourself, don't misbehave and the first person you sign up with is the manager and the second person is the union official ... I asked him which union to join and he said "The biggest one".'[61] As a result of his father's influence, 'socialism and trade unionism were drummed into me from an early age'.[62] Interviewed in 2006, Crow said of his father, who died in 1996:

56 Russell (2014).
57 Piece intended for the *Morning Star* 3 April 2014.
58 The *Guardian* (20 June 2009) noted that this was a position 'traditionally filled by a radical'.
59 *Daily Mail* 2 July 2011.
60 *Financial Times* 25 March 2011.
61 *Independent* 11 September 2002.
62 In Murray (2003: 103).

Looking back, I would have to say that my father, George, was my mentor ... We never really sat down every day and discussed what I should do. But at least 90% of what he said to me was good advice. He always imparted factual common sense. He was always good to bounce ideas off. What do you think of that, dad? What do you think of this? He was never general in his reply.

After I left school, I would talk more and more to him about work. He used to say to me, for example: 'A boss will never sack a good worker. Anyone can get a name for being lazy. But to get a name for being a good worker always goes down well.'

My father was very proud when I became assistant general secretary of the RMT. He instilled in me the core attributes of being a good union leader. All you can do is represent people, but do it to the best of your ability. Ask them what they want to do next and don't dictate what they should do next.

His inspiration for me was when he came home from work and put the six o'clock news on. He would always follow the news and that helped him to be a great speaker on current affairs. He could speak on worldwide politics through to football.

My father always said the Conservative government was no friend to working people. He knew that people need more than good pay and working conditions; they need a proper social structure that includes a decent national health service and state pensions system. His concerns went further than just the interests of union members.

Ultimately, my father taught me to be truthful. You have to be honest to people, even when people may not like what you have to say. On a number of occasions, I've had to go into a hostile meeting, in which it would be easier to tell people what they wanted to hear rather than the facts. But my father instilled an honesty in me that may upset people. As long as you stick to the truth, you'll be OK.

My job is to look after railway workers and seafarers. Sometimes their interests clash with what the travelling public wants. But looking after my members doesn't mean treading on others to get better conditions. It is about looking after the interests of people you represent, but also having the responsibility that is wider than the people you are looking after. And that's what my father has passed on to me.[63]

It is highly likely that his father also informed him of the East End struggles of the matchgirls and dockers in the 1880s, the 1936 Battle of Cable Street, and the fight against fascism in the 1970s in Brick Lane in order to make a more tangible connection between socialism and his locality. The influence of his father on him chimed with the times the young Crow was living through, for he later commented: 'Starting my

63 *Guardian* 18 February 2006. See also Murray (2003: 103).

career with these people in charge of unions, and working in a national-ised industry with people who had put in 30 or even 40 years of service, helped shape my views.'[64]

Crow also believed that his father's experience of the Second World War and the demand for a new world after defeating fascism had given him a sense of fearlessness and courage: 'The war changed people. My dad told me when they came back from the war they were going to have what they didn't have before. They weren't frightened no more. These people had just fought fascism and beat it. A miner from Wales had just built a national health service!'[65] Socially too, father and son were close, watching Millwall together. Richard recalled at home: 'It was always unions, unions, unions. It used to drive my mum, Lillian, mad. I think she had a dislike for it all. There'd be a strike going on the TV and he'd be going on about it and she'd be saying, "I wish you'd belt up."'[66] He also thought: 'I was more influenced by my mum and Bob was more influenced by my dad, probably because I had more time with my mum.'[67] His elder brother also remembered that the young Crow developed good advocacy and bargaining skills over pocket money for jobs, when Richard would be browbeaten by his father into giving Bob more than he thought his work warranted: '[W]hen we got home he'd complain to my Dad and demand the same pay as every-body else. So that's where it all started, isn't it? I'd say he hadn't done as much work as everyone else but my dad would say, "Oh give him another penny."'

Conclusion

By an early age, Crow had been shaped by a number of key influences, whether his father, working in a nationalised industry, being brought up in relative poverty or growing up when unions were significant actors. Together these became powerful forces for a young, energetic and challenging mind. This was all the more so when they provided the intellectual resources to help bring about a political epiphany, representing the application of ideas to a personal situation. From his father in particular, Crow gained a radical worldview as well as an ability to be courageous and forthright. Getting involved with a par-ticular union with its own particular culture and politics was another

---

64 *Scotland on Sunday* 10 August 2003.
65 *Guardian* 20 June 2009.
66 *Daily Mail* 2 July 2011.
67 *Daily Mail* 2 July 2011.

big influence. But the young Crow was not a mere empty vessel waiting to be filled up with noisy ideas. He exercised choice in these matters, preferring to go down certain routes, as the next chapter makes clear.

2. The 1990s

While Crow had many of the right starts in life for later becoming a union leader, these were necessary without being sufficient. Other components were also needed such as a strong and confident personality, and attacks by management to provide springboards for members to collectively respond to. If this particular mix of the necessary and sufficient had not been the case, then either Crow would not have emerged as he did or many other 'Crows' would have emerged, supplanting or rivalling him. The Company Plan on London Underground provided the most obvious instance, being the beginning of the process that manifestly brought all the aforementioned components together in a forceful outcome. Opposition to the Company Plan was preceded by a revival of combative, offensive strikes in the late 1980s and early 1990s over pay and working hours, as the economy grew and inflation rose.[1] At a national level, the engineering unions' successful 'drive for 35' strike campaign had begun in 1989. London was often the epicentre of these confrontations, with the steel erectors, for example, being a group of militant workers able to gain higher wages by striking at a time of demand for their labour. There was also the first national rail strike for many years in 1989, and action on London Underground as well. While the national strike did not achieve all the NUR wished, it gained most of what it wanted,[2] indicating that 'collective action and solidarity were not a thing of the past'.[3] Crow's own view was that these strikes showed that 'collective action and solidarity were difficult, but still possible'.[4] He went further, stating:

A major breakthrough came in 1989, when NUR members delivered an overwhelming majority in favour of strike action and the union mounted the first major national railway strike in a decade, beating off an injunction

---

1 For a history of unions on the London Underground from the 1990s onwards, see Eady (2016).
2 Berlin (2006: 81).
3 Berlin (2006: 82).
4 Crow (2012a: 154).

sought by BR [British Rail]. The significance of the 1989 strike went well beyond BR capitulating on the immediate issues. For the first time a major union had not only conducted a successful strike ballot under Tory laws and won its case in court but was even able to run another strike (on London Underground) in parallel over separate issues ...[5]

Most importantly, these strike mobilisations, as with the unofficial postal strike of 1988,[6] did not continue the cycle of defeat and retreat that had become the norm in the 1980s with the miners, steelworkers, dockers, seafarers and printers.[7] So this was a good time for Crow to have a second coming of age because it reaffirmed in the run-up to the Company Plan that resistance could be successful if well executed and well timed. It certainly meant that the psychological legacy of the afore-mentioned defeats was not as powerful as it had once been.

Battle gets underway

For many years, London Underground had escaped the attention of cost-cutting Tory governments as they fought battles with other workers and privatised the 'family silver'. But towards the end of the 1980s, this began to change when government funding to the Underground started to tighten, requiring management to look to make savings in how operations were run. This took the form of the Action Stations initiative in 1989 to make working practices more 'flexible', end seniority and tighten up discipline.[8] NUR members organised five unofficial strikes and then, after pressure on their national union, six official strikes against Action Stations in mid-1989,[9] after which the proposals were withdrawn, but at the cost of a poor pay deal that year.[10] An unofficial coordinating group led the push for the (unofficial) strikes, but then withered as its role was supplanted by the national union leadership. Its mass meetings declined in size as it ceded control to the national union leadership, concluding that grassroots workers needed to

5 Crow (2012a: 154).
6 Gall (2003).
7 The rejection of strike action by NUR members against the recommendation of their national leadership over driver-only trains in 1985 (after unofficial walkouts in response to sackings for refusing to work on driver-only trains) was not a defeat comparable to those of the other unions previously mentioned. In particular, the spread of driver-only operation thereafter was relatively slow (Gourvish 2002: 185–186). Instead, it was comparable to the ASLEF defeat over its 1982 strike over flexible rostering, from which the union quite easily recovered (Gall 2012b: 13).
8 See also Berlin (2006: 75–76).
9 See also Eady (2010).
10 *Socialist Worker* 12 August 1989.

work to get more left-wing officials elected to replace the existing ones (including Knapp).[11] This conclusion fitted with the Communist Party's perspective, rather than the 'rank-and-filism' of the Trotskyist Socialist Workers' Party, and was thus more appealing to the young Crow. While Crow had been a leading officer of the Holborn NUR branch, he had since moved to the Stratford No. 1 branch, and so was not formally part of the process by which the Finsbury Park, Holborn and Camden branches rejected the poor pay deal that was accepted by full-time officers of the NUR but then overturned by the CoE.[12]

Pushed back somewhat and with no easing of government pressure, London Underground moved ahead with an even bigger restructuring involving redundancies and new employment contracts, which heralded new flexible shift patterns, shorter holidays, an ending of the seniority system for promotion, the cutting of many premium payments, a much harsher disciplinary code, and new devolved collective bargaining structures.[13] Although the Tube Workers' Action Group was established in early 1992 in response to the announcement of the Company Plan of late 1991, the Left on the CoE was slow to mobilise against the Company Plan, allowing the pace to be set by Knapp. This resulted in delays in balloting, with negotiations taking precedence (despite management intransigence), and consequent delays in taking action. Crow, now a CoE member, essentially for the Underground, wrote: 'We have no doubt that it will be a question of when – and not if – industrial action takes place … I won't accept the argument that such a move would "rock the boat" in the run up to the general election.'[14] Action did take place but not for many months – indeed, not until nearly a year later. But initial RMT resistance petered out as members and activists among train drivers and signallers became somewhat demoralised, since ASLEF and TSSA members were not also striking. This spread to other RMT members, with the result that 'a tactical retreat was the only way out'.[15] Darlington described the imposition of the terms of the Company Plan (although sweetened by a 6% pay rise for 79% of staff and a pay

11 See *Socialist Worker* 19 August 1989.

12 See *Socialist Worker* 12 May 1990.

13 It was testament to the historical strength of rail unions on London Underground that management had allowed such things as 'leave workers' (who wait around to replace workers who are ill or absent on holiday), 'spare turns' (where train crews are rostered in case they are needed), and 'split turns' (where drivers work during the morning rush, take four hours off and return for four hours in the evening peak, but are paid for 12 hours).

14 In the *Morning Star* in early February 1992 and quoted in *Socialist Worker* 8 February 1992.

15 Pam Singer, email correspondence.

cut for the remainder)[16] as a 'serious defeat' that brought the RMT, in particular, into a state of 'disarray'.[17]

However, there was an irony to the Company Plan because the tranche of redundancies lowered the age of the workforce, meaning that those who remained were more prepared to stay and fight, and it opened up union positions for new activists to move into.[18] These 'young Turks' secured their first victory by overturning the dismissal of *Socialist Outlook* supporter Pat Sikorski, in the summer of 1993, through industrial action. From this successful fight back, Sikorski was elected to the CoE (see below). Moreover, the Left learned a valuable lesson during the dispute, according to Martin Eady:

> [We] learned the hard way that strong groups like train drivers and signallers will not 'on principle' take strike action to defend apparently weaker groups like cleaners and catering staff. They may talk of 'solidarity' but when push comes to shove they will only strike if they can see a clear advantage for themselves. We did a lot of manoeuvring to try and align and co-ordinate action of the different groups so that weaker groups could benefit from action by stronger groups. I had some success with this when I was on the National Executive and organised the 1989 series of strikes. But the solidarity 'principle' unfortunately proved wanting when put to the test. Of course, Bob was part of this learning process. In fact, we eventually learned that the so-called weaker groups have their own strengths if organised effectively. People don't like dirty trains and hungry drivers don't work well.[19]

So while the resistance to Action Stations and the Company Plan indicated significant variance in processes and outcomes, they both showed to Crow that resistance could be mounted and that some types of action were more effective than others. But more than that, whether by a broad left-wing strategy of capturing the leadership positions of the national union or by dictating to it through 'rank-and-filism', Crow understood that he needed to play a part in transforming the RMT. The perspective of broad Leftism took precedence not just because of the influence of the Communist Party but also because the Employment Acts of 1990 and 1992 greatly undermined workers' ability to take unofficial, un-balloted and un-notified industrial action by increasing the costs of doing so to them and their unions. Reflecting back on the Company Plan's introduc-

16 *Evening Standard* 19 November 1992.
17 Darlington (2001: 10–11).
18 See Darlington (2001: 11). Something of a similar process took place on the railways.
19 Email correspondence.

tion, Crow sought to use his wit to undermine it: '[It] definitely hasn't worked, despite how much management like to say it has. There has been a definite increase in the number of white-collar managers. They go on more courses than Lester Piggott – it's costing a fortune.'[20] He used this hook to get media attention to explain his case, which was cleverly couched in terms of passenger safety and public money:

> The Company Plan has created a 'superstructure' of managers. Every line now has its own staff – that means that departments such as personnel, finance or marketing, which used to be handled at headquarters, are now duplicated. Yet on the track, for instance, there are not enough staff to deal with repairs. For every 100 hundred faults, only 10 are repaired each week – everything is patchwork. And in the long run repairs like that cost money because they have to be done again. The system now is for contractors to work on the track and the signal and electrical departments. They are replacing our own staff. Yet there is the ludicrous situation where staff are having to train these contractors, at the Neasden training centre, to do the work. But while track repairs are patched, our managers enjoy some of the best offices in central London. It must be prestigious for them to have a plush headquarters address in Westminster, but is it necessary?[21]

A new Left emerges

A Broad Left had existed in the NUR since 1988 and grassroots bodies such as the Manchester Rail Action Committee also came into being. And while the Left had some success (such as winning the 1991 RMT AGM vote by 50 to 36 against Knapp's line of supporting the position of Labour leader, Neil Kinnock, of maintaining the Tory anti-union laws),[22] it was not a particularly significant force outside AGMs. Crow was involved as a branch secretary in the establishment of the Broad Left, which had around 100 members (including several national executive council members), but he was not one of its office bearers, although he was a contact point for London Transport.[23] Knapp sought to clamp down on the circulars of the Broad Left.[24] The formation of a more influential hard Left took several forms. Set up in 1991, the Campaign for a Fighting and Democratic Union (CFDU) sought to revitalise and overhaul the union's internal democratic structures and challenge

20 *Evening Standard* 29 November 1993.
21 *Evening Standard* 29 November 1993.
22 *Socialist Worker* 6 July 1991.
23 Minutes of meeting of NUR Broad Left, 23 July, 26 November 1988.
24 See, for example, the NUR circular entitled 'Unofficial Circulars', 9 February 1990.

Knapp's moderate industrial and political leadership, specifically for not mounting sufficiently robust opposition to impending privatisation.[25] At its height in the mid-1990s, the CFDU brought together up to 300 left-wing union officials and activists, with the backing of some 40 union branches, some regional councils and CoE members.[26] It was proscribed by Knapp but relaunched itself in 1997 in a new guise called the Campaign for Public Ownership and Public Transport. While it did not exist on the Underground, 'from the early 1990s, there was the emergence of a similar, although less formally constituted, network of left-wing union activists to prominence. This involved a well-organised chain of influence stretching from union reps into the union branches, London Regional Council and Council of Executives.'[27] They numbered around 20–30 individuals and included Sikorski, who became known as 'the General' because of his ability to marshal his members as fighting troops.[28] Then with the setting up of the Socialist Labour Party (SLP) by Arthur Scargill after Labour scrapped its Clause IV commitment to public ownership in 1995, around twenty of the leading left-wingers, including Sikorski, John Leach and Crow, joined this new party as an organised embodiment of their industrial and political agendas.

Crow emerged strongly from these groupings and was at the head of its collective leadership as a CoE member from 1992 and then as AGS with responsibility for the Underground from 1994. Among his elders in this process in London were the likes of Geoff Revell, Alan Norman and Larry Cotton. From mid-1991 to early 1999, this overall Left leadership campaigned and mobilised for 25 strike ballots involving nine strikes (comprising 17 days of strikes) on the London Underground.[29] This provided a firm basis for the next mobilisation against the privatisation of the Underground. But Crow did not appear willing to move much outside this London-centric remit at this stage. For example, he was not known for his resistance to Knapp's calling off of the Manchester Piccadilly guards' strike after an injunction was granted against it in 1992.[30] Indeed, the RMT's unwillingness to defy the Tory anti-union

25 See Berlin (2006: 143–144).

26 See Darlington (2009a: 17).

27 Darlington (2009a: 17).

28 See, for example, *Evening Standard* 10 January 2002; *Daily Mail* 21 January 2002; and *Sun* 14 January 2002.

29 Darlington (2001: 5).

30 See *Socialist Worker* 26 September 1992. The same was true of the calling off of an Underground strike over pay after the granting of an injunction in 1994 (see *Socialist Worker* 15 October 1994).

laws would continue under Crow as it had under Knapp. Martin Eady recalled:

> I had a massive row with Bob at the LTDC in 1992 when he was the [CoE] member, over the privatisation of train cleaning ... TUPE (Transfer of Undertakings Protection of Earnings) was not invoked, mainly because no cleaners were prepared to carry on working for half their wages. No industrial action was called because under Tory laws it would have been declared political and, therefore, illegal. Much effort was wasted arguing the 'principle' laws should be challenged by having illegal strikes, which diverted our efforts away from the issue of fighting privatisation and its effects. There was great resentment at the union's (and Bob's) failure to organise any effective resistance, especially with the privatisation of building services. Eventually, after much debate and argument, we realised that the issue to fight on was not privatisation itself but its effects on pay, conditions, safety and pensions. These are clearly industrial not political demands so do not fall foul of the Tory laws. There was no point trying to fight the 'principles' of privatisation or illegal strikes.[31]

Similarly, advocating the practice of making common cause with other workers in the form of coordinated strike action was stunted. An opportunity came when the miners faced pit closures in 1992. Later, another opportunity presented itself with the postal workers' national strikes in 1996.

Although there was criticism from some on the far Left of his willingness to make concessions on opposition to the Company Plan, Crow cemented his leadership of the radical Left in the RMT and his reputation as a key union militant. Both enabled him to become a key player in the RMT at a national level as a result of his base on the London Underground. Of the CoE member for the Underground, the *Evening Standard* observed: 'While Jimmy Knapp ... is nominally the leader of the union, he has effectively been turned into a figurehead through the advance of Mr Crow and his colleagues.'[32] Crow did not wait to let others act even though he had not long been elected to the CoE and was just 31 years old. His powers of reasoning and speaking and ability to think on his feet became apparent in the Company Plan dispute. For example, he was able to paint the management as unreasonable, saying: 'Our key argument is that independent arbitration through the Wages Board has not been exhausted. We will call off the action today if management will say they are prepared to go to the Wages Board.'[33] He also

31 Email correspondence.
32 *Evening Standard* 19 November 1992.
33 *Evening Standard* 19 November 1992.

spoke to his members and defended his own position, saying 'The money's no good if you are sitting on a bullet being shot across the Grand Canyon' and 'I may be painted as the bogeyman, but in 1983 you would have thought Arthur Scargill had two horns and a tail, and now he is more popular [after outrage at pit closures in 1992] than John Major.'[34]

Elected assistant general secretary

Jimmy Knapp faced two challengers for re-election as general secretary in mid-1994, one from the Right (Norman Guy) and one from the Left (Jimmy Connolly). That he beat Guy by only just over 1,000 votes was seen by the radical Left as evidence of growing disenchantment with a supposedly left-wing general secretary. For example, the radical Left believed that Knapp had played down the significance of the political impact of striking (as with the RMT's 1993 British Rail strike for job security under impending privatisation when miners were fighting pit closures and both unions were part of the Triple Alliance); he would not sanction industrial action against privatisation *per se* because he regarded it as political and, thus, unlawful; and he orchestrated the choice not to implement six ballot mandates over the previous two years, of which four were on the London Underground (including two on the Company Plan).[35] Knapp argued that the turnouts were insufficiently high and falling. The radical Left pointed out that member cynicism – which diminished voter turnout – grew the more the ballot mandates were not implemented. Although Connolly's showing was relatively poor, the radical Left was able to gain a majority of 13 to 8 on the CoE. Sikorski was one of the new members.

This was the background to Crow, in early October 1994, beating Tony McGregor, the moderate incumbent, for the post of AGS by a margin of 2 to 1.[36] Showing that he was beginning to adopt a wider role, Crow benefited from having played a part in the signal workers' strike that summer, which gave him a national profile among RMT members outside London, while the incumbent was less advantaged since he came from the former NUS side of the union. According to Jeff Porter, Crow's

background as a track worker and on the engineering side [also] made it easier for him once he was on the CoE to engage with workers on other parts of the railway because of the shared experiences. London Underground members were not always regarded with great favour by

34 *Sunday Times* 22 November 1992.
35 See *Socialist Worker* 6 March 1993, 19 June 1993 and 17 July 1993.
36 Press Association 5 October 1994.

railway workers in other parts of the country. It is a mark of [him] ... that he was able to emerge from the comfortable world of London Transport 1980s' trade unionism and carve out a national role.[37]

Nonetheless, as Crow was known to many as a 'hard-line' and paid-up Communist Party member,[38] this was no small achievement and was a vindication of his views (at least in terms of their application to RMT matters). Crow's election as a 'young, belligerent [operator] – an outspoken critic of the union's leadership – was seen as a boost for the left and for industrial militancy'.[39] The *Evening Standard* noted that in the preceding years he had successfully led the opposition to further job cuts on the Underground and to inadequate pay offers.[40] According to an unofficial TUC document, Crow became 'associated with around 30 strikes in his 10 years in office [from 1992–2002]'.[41] Along with Sikorski, Crow emerged as leader of the hard Left.[42] However, Crow not only had the edge on Sikorski as the younger, more energetic and colourful character, but he had also attained higher office earlier on, so that it was not long before Crow became 'the undisputed leader of the RMT's hard-Left faction'.[43] Two other elements were critical here. The first factor in favour of Crow's continued ascendancy in the RMT was that his election as AGS at this time came about because, following his first three-year period on the CoE, he would not be able stand again for a further three years, meaning he would have to return to his trackside job (even if in practice he was on full facility time). The second factor was that Crow had shown that he was able to work productively with activists from different political backgrounds, including Trotskyists such as Sikorski and Greg Tucker. Indeed, although a Communist Party member, Crow did not participate exclusively in its formal closed caucuses since he worked with the wider Left in its more open and fluid informal gatherings, so that 'Bob was part of th[is process] despite having joined the CP, not because he joined them'.[44]

37 Email correspondence.
38 *Daily Mail* 6 October 1994.
39 Janine Booth, *Solidarity* 19 March 2014.
40 *Evening Standard* 22 August 1994.
41 *Evening Standard* 10 January 2002.
42 See *Daily Mail* 18, 26 July 1994; *Evening Standard* 1 October 1993; *Independent* 4 August 1994; and *Times* 19 July 1994. But later, others like Leach and Gordon emerged as well (see, for example, *Evening Standard* 16 May 2001).
43 *Evening Standard* 11 May 2001. Sikorski's star waned as he was seen as rather austere – see, for example, his handling of the Scotrail dispute in 2010 (*Sunday Herald* 8 October 2010).
44 Martin Eady, email correspondence.

The element of pragmatism that Crow developed, despite his perceived public stance of militancy, was also to be found in these early days. For example, he told the *Evening Standard* in a dispute over a case of disciplinary action: 'We are trying to keep the lid on this and hope management will take stock of the amount of feeling on this issue';[45] and he informed the Press Association during a dispute over pay with European Passenger Services (part of the Eurostar service), in which RMT members had rejected their pay offer by 70%: 'It is too early to start talking of an industrial action ballot but this is an option if we fail to make progress.'[46] The pragmatism also developed in another area, namely his relationship with Knapp, for loyalty and respect were tempered with criticism and opposition. For example, Crow opposed Knapp's attempt to end the practice of CoE members from the rail side being paid by the union to do this job full time.[47] Reducing them to part-time positions would have strengthened Knapp's control and undermined lay influence. Crow's opposition here was important in stopping Knapp getting his way at the AGM. There was also the instance of his criticism of Knapp's less than total opposition to privatisation, and of compelling Knapp to lead the signal workers into their long and drawn-out battle with Railtrack over pay in 1994.[48] Yet it was often reported that Crow tried to court and impress Knapp as a seasoned and successful negotiator,[49] with Crow, unlike the rest of the radical Left embodied by the CFDU, far less publicly critical of Knapp.[50] Crow's complex relationship with Knapp was to continue over the issue of standing for general secretary, as we will see.

Like many on the radical Left, Crow was prone to hyperbole. For example, talking as RMT AGS with responsibility for London Underground, he said: 'We've probably had more strike ballots than the trade union movement put together.'[51] This was patently not true, for in this period the average annual number of ballots across the trade union movement was well in excess of 200 a year.[52] But this tendency was very much part of

45 *Evening Standard* 12 January 1996.
46 Press Association, 11 January 1996.
47 This was on the basis of a supposed financial crisis for the union. Certainly, the union had challenges to deal with, but it turned out that these were being exaggerated to build the case for abolishing full-time CoE positions.
48 *Observer* 17 February 2002.
49 *Observer* 17 February 2002; *Sunday Times* 28 March 2010.
50 *Observer* 17 February 2002.
51 Cited in Darlington (2001: 17).
52 From 1994 to 2001, when Crow was AGS, there were just over 200 strikes on average per year and the number of ballots for strikes per year was always substantially in excess of the actual number of strikes. For example, between 2002 and

Crow's public persona and would become more obvious with time. Within the RMT, the tendency to exaggerate allowed him to present situations in stark terms. For example, in comparing the striking down of an industrial action ballot by an injunction to industrial vandalism and corporate kleptocracy, he asked 'did the 1,200 Jarvis workers get a vote when it went into administration ... did members at Scotrail get a chance to be balloted over the company's plans to introduce Driver-Only Operations?'; and he stated that the absence of elections to company boardrooms was 'a classic case of one law for the boss class and another for the working class'.[53] This style did not diminish him – instead, it allowed him to get his message across and to become an increasingly effective player in the union and on the Left. It fitted, as Crow recounted, with responding to an increasingly hostile and aggressive employer on London Underground:

> The last five years are littered with agreements reached one year which management seek to re-interpret the next year. London Underground sees agreements as a means of getting themselves off the hook in the short term. They think they can break these agreements whenever they like. How can trade unionists negotiate in a climate like this?[54]

His negotiating deftness allowed him to offer to suspend a strike ballot if management went to arbitration and withdrew an imposed pay rise. In 1996 he stated, with regard to London Underground, that 'negotiations had to be about compromise'.[55] The result of these negotiations after a joint RMT–ASLEF strike saw the trading of pay for hours, with the likes of *Socialist Worker* acerbically suggesting that the only practical difference between the politics of the Socialist Labour and Labour parties was in the size of pay cut.[56] And in 1998, again on the Underground, Crow offered to accept a 1% below inflation deal in return for a shorter working week, saying: 'When you go into negotiations and put all your cards on the table you can't complain when the other side nicks one or two.'[57] Crucially, this public persona allowed him to carry members with him when negotiating such deals.

As a result of how he conducted himself in public, the *Sunday Times* and *Evening Standard* could not help but identify Crow as a 'polished

---

2011, there were 8,123 ballots for striking but only 1,308 strikes. Comparable figures are not available for the period 1994 to 2001. Figures from 'Annual Article, 2011', 15 August 2012, Office of National Statistics.
53 *RMT News* April and November 2010, respectively.
54 *Socialist Worker* 30 August 1997.
55 *Socialist Worker* 10 August 1996.
56 *Socialist Worker* 7 September 1996.
57 *Socialist Worker* 17 August 1998.

media performer' and a 'polished union front man'.[58] Behind closed doors in union–management negotiations, he was also capable of giving 'articulate, reasoned arguments to back up the RMT's case, without resorting to the kind of table-thumping, loud-hailer diplomacy which used to dominate union negotiations'.[59] Time and again, Crow was able to draw comparisons to other issues to support his own arguments, making them seem eminently reasonable. In the case of calling for an investigation into a mystery radiation illness, he said: 'It would be easy to deride concerns expressed by members, but a few months ago we all thought British beef was absolutely safe.'[60]

Privatisation

The privatisation and fragmentation of British Rail in 1996 represented a defeat for the RMT on both industrial and political fronts, though it was not of the same magnitude as those defeats that had affected other unions. Most importantly, the rail industry was neither closed down nor de-unionised. In a similar way to the Company Plan, the removal of the 1956 Machinery of Negotiations had a mixed outcome. Its abolition ended the layered structure of collective bargaining, so that the lay union positions charged with undertaking bargaining at these levels became redundant. The loss of bargaining rights and the consequent disorganisation was a setback for the RMT, but with the redundancies of older workers and novel bargaining structures under privatisation, a new group of activists was able to emerge and fill the vacuum. The lack of a significant defeat for the RMT on the railways was important not just for the union but also for Crow, because he increasingly stepped out of his London Underground constituency, becoming a major player in the RMT nationally. Moreover, as privatisation did not reduce public subsidy to the railways but did facilitate profiteering and put further pressure on rail workers' terms and conditions, this provided a potent situation for the RMT to agitate within.

Socialist Labour

After the SLP's founding, Crow ended his Communist Party membership, joining the SLP in 1997 and becoming a member of its Executive.[61]

58 *Sunday Times* 25 August 1996; *Evening Standard* 22 August 1996.
59 *Evening Standard* 22 August 1996.
60 Press Association, 18 June 1996.
61 *Observer* 17 February 2002.

He had long admired Scargill, calling him 'The best trade union leader we've ever seen',[62] and believing that the miners' defeat in 1984–85 had not been the result of any deficiencies in Scargill's leadership.[63] The other aspect to leaving the Communist Party and joining the SLP was that Crow disagreed with the former's call to vote Labour and actively support its candidates in all but the tiny handful of constituencies where the Communist Party stood.[64] To Crow, this meant supporting many right-wing candidates. Along with more than half the CoE members,[65] he joined because he believed the SLP was a more viable vehicle to bring about the return of public ownership and the onset of socialism. For a short time, this seemed to be the case. Critically for Crow, the SLP – unlike the Communist Party – did not believe in trying to steer Labour to the Left or that gaining its election to office was desirable (as per the Communist Party's longstanding political approach embodied in the 'British road to socialism' perspective).[66] Among fellow SLP members were the CoE members Alan Pottage and Bobby Law.[67] Crow did not endear himself to his former Communist Party comrades, who regarded the SLP as an unwelcome further division and diversion on the Left. But this did not stop Crow from working with them, their *Morning Star* newspaper and others (especially on more general political matters) over the longer term. Yet in the initial years of the SLP, tensions did arise with his former comrades over the initiative to organise a union-based campaign for the repeal of the Tory anti-union laws, which 'new' Labour had made clear it would keep in place. Initially, this was the 'Reclaim our Rights' campaign, for which Crow, along with fellow SLP member John Hendy QC, authored a short pamphlet called *Reclaim Our Rights: repeal the anti-union laws*. This campaign mutated, on the initiative of the SLP and others, into the bigger United Campaign to Repeal the Anti-Union Laws.[68] Its founding conference on 28 March 1998 was

---

62 *Independent* 13 September 2007.

63 Crow was a strong supporter of the miners during their year-long strike and joined a Miners' Support Group in London. One part of this activity meant travelling up to Yorkshire and the Midlands to support the NUM on demonstrations (*Observer* 17 February 2002).

64 *Independent* 19 April 2004; *Guardian* 2 July 2004. He told the *Telegraph* (4 September 2003): 'The only thing I disagree with the Communist Party on now is that they unequivocally support Labour.'

65 *Guardian* 17 February 1996.

66 *The British Road to Socialism*, Communist Party, 1989, https://www.marx ists.org/history/international/comintern/sections/britain/brs/1989/.

67 *Herald* 2 February 1996; *Evening Standard* 22 October 1998.

68 Joining with Reclaim our Rights was the Free Trade Unions Campaign (established by the Alliance for Workers' Liberty and the Communication Workers'

attended by 700 union activists, officials and officers. Crow was elected unopposed as its chair, with Hendy as secretary. The tension with the Communist Party was essentially over whether the campaign duplicated what the Communist Party had started in the early 1970s with its Liaison Committee for the Defence of Trade Unions (LCDTU) when campaigning against the Industrial Relations Act 1971.

The SLP's early promise quickly foundered as a result of the way Scargill and his allies dominated the party. Initially, Crow did not seem overly concerned about Scargill using a block vote of affiliated members from the NUM to win votes at conferences, telling the December 1997 SLP conference when moving the party's industrial report (and in a characteristically blunt fashion) that 'The only reason these people are whining is because they haven't got 3,000 votes in their back pocket.'[69] However, by 1998 Crow had decided to leave the SLP – as many others had already done – because of the way in which the party began to degenerate internally and not because of its brand of socialist politics *per se*.[70] According to those leaving, Scargill became increasingly authoritarian and disciplinarian in the way he ran the party, insisting that the SLP stand against as many Labour candidates as possible, regardless of whether these candidates were socialists or not. For Crow, this was sectarian and the last straw.[71] After leaving, Crow never again joined another political party.[72] In this regard, he often said: 'You can be a communist and not be a member of the Communist Party just like you [can] go to the British Virgin Islands and not be a virgin.'[73] But he did support and participate in many initiatives that sought to unite the Left and to lay the ground for what some hoped would be the beginnings of a new mass party of socialism. Indeed, he believed that socialists should unite into a single new party.[74] In Scotland, the Scottish Socialist Alliance became the Scottish Socialist Party (SSP) in 1998 and an alliance of left-wing groups in England launched the Socialist Alliance in 1999. Crow

Union). The Campaign for Trade Union Freedom was established in 2013 following a merger of the CP-founded Liaison Committee for the Defence of Trade Unions and the United Campaign to Repeal the Anti-Trade Union Laws.

69 Spencer and Khamis (1998).

70 See *Guardian* 31 July 2002. The tendency for many to leave led the SLP to be dubbed 'Scargill's Leaving Party'.

71 *Guardian* 2 July 2004.

72 Although registered as a political party for the purposes of contesting public elections, TUSC is not a political party in the sense of having an independent existence outside of election periods.

73 *Independent* 19 April 2004; *Times* 12 September 2009; *Financial Times* 25 March 2011.

74 *Observer* 17 February 2002.

supported both. In the case of Scotland, he said on a number of occasions that he would probably join the SSP if he lived in Scotland.[75] The SSP aside and referring to the RMT's fundraiser for the Cuba Solidarity Campaign, he quipped: 'The only parties I'm really interested in now are garden parties.'[76] His non-membership of a party was enforced by events outside his control. Following the SWP's domination and then action to transform the Socialist Alliance into the Respect Party (led by the SWP and George Galloway), the Socialist Alliance fractured and atrophied after 2001. For Crow, this was another frustrating experience of what seemed like the Left spending more time attacking itself than training its fire on capitalism. It was another instance of the saying about the Left, namely, 'there is nothing quite so divisive as a call to unity'. Nonetheless, this type of experience never shook Crow's belief in the need for socialism nor the requirement for the Left to unite in order to prosecute the battle for socialism.[77]

Re-elected assistant general secretary

Although Crow had easily won the AGS position in 1994, this did not mean that he would sail through his re-election in November 1999. His challenger was Mick Cash, then a 35-year-old signal technician and deputy Labour leader of Watford Council. Cash's platform was that the extreme Left had 'too much influence' in the RMT, so that 'We have had more strike ballots than we have had annual pay awards'; he said that London Underground RMT activists

> remind me of a drunk on Saturday night. They will fight anyone, anywhere, any time for any reason. As far as I am concerned that is not leadership. The union needs to be more pragmatic in how it deals with today's world. It is not simple black and white issues any more. Using strikes all the time is not the answer.[78]

This was a clear challenge to Crow, where Cash represented the forces of 'old Labour' grouped around Knapp. Coming from the larger overground rail section of the membership, Cash only just lost to Crow by 6,795 to 7,137 votes. For many on the Left, the lack of enthusiasm for

75 *Independent* 19 April 2004. Another occasion when he said this was when he was presented with honorary membership at an SSP trade union conference in Glasgow on 20 September 2003 by the SSP national trade union organiser, Ritchie Venton.
76 *Independent* 19 April 2004
77 See, for example, *Guardian* 9 September 2013.
78 *Evening Standard* 22 September 1999.

Crow reflected disappointment in his inability to live up to his promises of delivering action at some key moments.[79] Not winning would not necessarily have ended Crow's career and influence, but it would have very much weakened them. Critically, he would not have been in a commanding position to stand for general secretary in 2002 as the unassailable leader of the Left.

From 1999 to 2001, Crow led the battle to stop the downgrading of the guards' safety role, under the slogan of preventing them from being reduced to 'ticket collectors and Kit-Kat sellers'.[80] Safety was written into all guards' responsibilities until 1999 when it was reassigned to Railway Safety Ltd, a Railtrack division.[81] The RMT argued that too much responsibility was now placed on drivers, for if a driver was injured or killed then no other staff members on the train would be able to deal adequately with accidents and incidents. The RMT also knew that retaining guards' safety-critical role was crucial to maintaining its industrial leverage. Over a period of time, the RMT was able to gain satisfactory compromises from TOCs so as to be able to call off its disputes on this issue. Even in the case of c2c, the most hard-nosed TOC and the only one not to have settled thus far, Crow showed flexibility, but it was thrown back. The RMT offered to call off a strike in return for a moratorium on introducing the practice, with Crow saying: 'It seems that they are not interested in solving this dispute.'[82] This was after many meetings over previous months[83] and an overtime ban which was initially called off to aid talks.[84]

To stand or not to stand?

Knapp was due for re-election in early 1999. Notwithstanding some caution and reticence, Crow had been one of his foremost and high-profile critics. Thus, it seemed logical to stand against him in order to change the RMT's direction. Moreover, Crow was in a strong position to do so, given that he had effectively become deputy general secretary.[85] But he did not stand. The *Herald*'s industrial correspondent, Roy Rodgers, speculated that his motives revolved around Knapp's relative popularity, so he was biding his time and not risking alienating mem-

79 See, for example, *Socialist Worker* 20 November 1999.
80 *Mirror* 15 October 1999. See also *Edinburgh Evening News* 22 June 2001.
81 *Times* 15 February 2003.
82 *Morning Star* 18 October 2001.
83 See, for example, *Morning Star* 17 July 2001.
84 *Evening Standard* 13 August 2001.
85 *Times* 7 May 1998.

bers.[86] This was the view of others like the *Evening Standard*.[87] It added: 'Mr Crow decided not to stand against him because of his genuine liking for [Knapp].'[88] On the Left, a similar conclusion was drawn. The Tube worker activist Janine Booth wrote: 'Cometh the hour, cometh Bob Crow? No. Although we needed a more militant, left-wing leadership there and then, Crow preferred to wait until Knapp's retirement, when he could be more confident of winning.'[89] Crow's later political allies, the Socialist Party (formerly Militant), agreed: 'The more obvious candidate for the left, however, would have been Bob Crow, an SLP member and the assistant general secretary, but he seems to be waiting for Knapp's retirement rather than taking him on head on.'[90]

In the event, it was Greg Tucker, a former Lambeth Labour councillor, CoE member and South West Trains driver, who took on Knapp, winning 4,535 votes to Knapp's 8,776. One factor not noted was that Crow calculated that his being able to influence the union politically and industrially in his existing AGS position would not be greatly augmented by being general secretary at this point. This was a further indication of pragmatism. Put another way, Crow understood that the timing of what one did could be as important as what one actually did in terms of the message imparted and the effect achieved. History was on Crow's side, for Knapp became seriously ill with cancer from 2000, being off work for a year,[91] and Vernon Hince – the acting general secretary – was due to take retirement within a few years. This meant that a power vacuum opened up, with Crow and his allies beginning to fill it. In other battles at the same time against the union's right wing, Sikorski stood against Hince for the senior AGS position, winning 4,521 votes to the incumbent's 5,421, and Mick Atherton stood unsuccessfully against John Cogger for the presidency (after the end of Crow supporter Phil

---

86 *Herald* 2 October 1998, 15 February 1999 and 26 June 1999. See also *Times* 14 September 1998.

87 *Evening Standard* 6 July 1998.

88 *Evening Standard* 13 August 2001. Phil McGarry confirmed that Crow had loyalty towards Knapp (interview). In this regard, Crow later promoted the Jimmy Knapp Cancer Fund, established in 2001, in *RMT News* (December 2006), where Knapp was described as 'respected and admired for his energy, passion and leadership'.

89 *Tunnel Vision*, AWL pamphlet, available as 'The fight against Tube privatisation reviewed', http://www.workersliberty.org/story/2004/07/02/fight-against-tube-privatisation-reviewed-part-1.

90 Mullins (1999).

91 The *Evening Standard* (16 May 2001) commented that Knapp's 'day-to-day effectiveness has been affected by major abdominal surgery – and more recently by a torn Achilles tendon when he fell while alighting from a train'.

Boston's tenure).[92] Another explanation for Crow's unwillingness to stand against Knapp was provided by a former activist:

> Knapp was Bob Crow's mentor and clearly a great influence, both in terms of left-wing politics and trade-union tactics. I remember huge meetings at Friends' Meeting House on Euston Road with Knapp as the main speaker. We used to laugh at Bob Crow's role as Knapp's 'warm-up man', where he played the role of management basher/stand-up comedian to great effect. Once the crowd had been softened up, Knapp would come in to tell us, 'They're trying to destroy our union, boys!' He would then proceed to lay out his tactic of one-day strikes. It was accepted that jobs would be lost, but the union must survive. Those of us who argued against this in favour of a better defence of jobs had little success. Bob and Jimmy were a powerful double act.[93]

This chimed with Crow's affection for Knapp. Its veracity is strengthened by recalling Knapp's suspicion of unelected RMT officers opposing his leadership. Although Knapp was the Broad Left candidate in succeeding right-winger Sid Weighell as general secretary, much of the existing officer cadre remained in place afterwards, with Knapp often feeling isolated and marginalised. Consequently, Crow's criticism of Knapp may have been blunted by seeing first-hand the treatment meted out to him, with the result that what the national union did was not always in Knapp's hands. Crow learned a lesson here about replacing the senior officers upon being elected general secretary himself.

London Underground

The 2001 London Underground dispute over cutting jobs and its implications for passenger safety (which involved a number of strikes and injunctions) highlighted much about Crow, the RMT and the complex interaction between them. Failure to support the strikes was to be expected from the Labour government, but it went further and condemned them, adding to the RMT's fervent dislike of 'new' Labour. But the RMT also came under pressure to stand down its strikes from the TUC, which 'pointedly delivered [its letter saying so] to Vernon Hince, the RMT's deputy general secretary, and not to Mr Crow, the

---

92 Sikorski was disciplined by the RMT AGM, at Knapp's behest, for allegedly circulating unofficial election material (*Socialist Worker* 10 July 1999). By contrast, neither Phil Bialyk nor Mick Cash were disciplined for soliciting external intervention in RMT affairs in the 2002 general secretary election.
93 Russell (2014).

assistant general secretary who ha[d] been leading the Tube talks'.[94] The Underground dispute initially involved much bluster, with Crow threatening that 'we will not just be taking action on one day, we will be taking action every day'.[95] This moderated somewhat into 'If the dispute is not settled ... it will not be just a one-day strike. There were will be more to come after that.'[96] But as a seasoned, tough negotiator, he knew when to pause for breath: 'We have now suspended industrial action on two occasions to allow for further negotiations ... We are hopeful that we can resolve our differences.'[97] But he would not bow to management when it required an immediate response. So when the RMT negotiating team needed time to discuss their response among themselves, Crow led what was depicted as a walkout from the ACAS-led talks.[98]

Behind the scenes, there were divisions within the RMT, as the CoE member for London Underground, John Leach, supported by Alex Gordon and another, opposed calling off the strikes, while Crow

> got the union's General Grades Committee (GGC) to vote again and again until it made the decision he wanted it to make ... RMT's London Underground members had good reason to reject the offer that Bob Crow wanted us to accept. At a meeting the following week at the Royal National Hotel, rep after rep made the case against it ... In all, 24 of the 25 reps who spoke were opposed to the offer. Crow later admitted that he had his 'balls chewed' at the meeting. The union's Executive accepted the reps' views, rejected LUL's offer, and kept the union in dispute.[99]

94 *Evening Standard* 2 May 2001.
95 *Evening Standard* 9 January 2001.
96 *Evening Standard* 9 March 2001.
97 *Evening Standard* 11 May 2001.
98 *Evening Standard* 16 May 2001. The accusation came from Anne Burfutt, London Underground human resources director. When she left her post a few months later, Crow presented her with a large fluffy dinosaur (*Evening Standard* 6 August 2001). In another sign of his not having a one-dimensional character, *The Business* (31 March 2002) revealed that Crow and Beverley Spears, the human resources director of South West Trains, had a longstanding friendship. She recounted: 'I met Bob in about 1983 when I was employee relations manager for engineering and he was the local union rep. In the 20 years I've known Bob, I've never heard him raise his voice. There have been people throughout my career who have become mentally or even physically abusive with me. He's always sorted them out without using violence, by frogmarching them over to apologise to me.' Crow said that when his wife had a bad car accident 'she [Spears] actually sent round one of her managers to see if we were all right'.
99 *Tunnel Vision*, AWL pamphlet, available as 'The fight against Tube privatisation reviewed' http://www.workersliberty.org/story/2004/07/02/fight-against-tube-privatisation-reviewed-part-1. The GGC is the section of the CoE that deals with industrial matters on the roads and railways.

Crow remained unscathed by this. The passion he displayed in defending members' interests sometimes came out in peculiar ways. In one negotiating session:

> he rolled up a copy of that morning's *Metro* newspaper and hurled it at the [London Underground] chief executive, shouting: 'What's all this, then?' 'This' was a report in the *Metro* on the results of a phone poll organised by LU on whether the travelling public were in favour of a Tube strike or not – with 4,224 callers against and just 358 in favour. But it further revealed that LU had made a claim of vote rigging – having traced 217 of the 358 calls in favour of industrial action to one telephone extension in Elephant and Castle, identified as an LU staff canteen. Mr Smith, 52, picked up the paper and tossed it back, telling Mr Crow that was no way to behave. A furious Mr Crow stormed out of the room and it took some time to persuade him back into the talks.[100]

Crow came under personal attack early on in the dispute, with the *Evening Standard* alleging that he was:

> a throwback to the 1970s – a stone-faced Stalinist who believes that public service unions exist solely to satisfy his own political ambitions, and ensure that the public provides services for his members. He is wholly indifferent to the fate of the passengers who suffer every day at his hands.[101]

Another *Evening Standard* article led Hince to jump to Crow's defence:

> I attended the recent marathon discussions at Acas, and I can tell you that Bob's negotiating skills and persistence were vital in ensuring that Tube management put forward proposals that would allow for a suspension of the industrial action on 3 May.[102]

Other militants coming to the fore at this time were Bobby Law, London Regional Council Secretary and then London Regional Organiser; future CoE member Olly New; and future presidents John Leach and Alex Gordon. As former Tube workers with responsibility for the Tube, Law and Leach were part of the RMT negotiating team. At first it may appear somewhat unusual that Crow was painted as a moderate. Referring to other disputes, *The Times* observed: 'Crow faces accusations of selling out his union because the recent strikes over waistcoats, name badges and other issues were ended instead of continued in a political protest

100 *Evening Standard* 16 May 2001.
101 *Evening Standard* 3 May 2001. It also added later that Crow was 'a figure so antiquated he could have stepped out of Peter Sellers' 1950s classic, *I'm All Right Jack*' (30 May 2001). This led Mark Seddon, then *Tribune* editor, to comment: 'In Bob Crow ... the *Evening Standard* has discovered a new Fred Kite' (*Observer* 13 January 2002).
102 *Evening Standard* 11 May 2001.

against privatisation',[103] while *Socialist Worker* approvingly quoted an RMT member saying of the Underground dispute:

> Many of us expect it from Monks and even from Jimmy Knapp ... But Bob Crow has played a good role up to now. He encouraged us not to cross picket lines when ASLEF union members were striking officially and our action had been declared illegal in the High Court. There is no way he should have gone along with calling off the strike.[104]

After the end of the dispute, *Socialist Worker* opined:

> about 30 percent of reps were for throwing [the settlement] out and going ahead with the strikes planned during election week. It is easy to see why. The union's campaign has won a better deal over jobs and safety than any other group of workers threatened with privatisation. But at the same time an opportunity to stop privatisation has been squandered.[105]

As already noted, one of those arguing for a harder line throughout most of the dispute was Leach (with Gordon in a supporting role).[106] Noting that neither Crow nor other union officers had a vote on the CoE, the *Evening Standard* concluded: 'the far Left is led by John Leach' and 'Crow, in turn, is regarded as unduly moderate by some members of the RMT executive committee'.[107] For Crow, there may have been considerations regarding how a continued strike would play with members outside London ahead of the 2002 general secretary election.[108] Yet it seems more likely that Crow thought a good deal had been done (in the form of a no compulsory redundancy agreement), being the best available in the circumstances and reflecting most members' views. Indeed, looking back on the dispute in an interview with Crow, the *Financial Times* reported that:

> His greatest negotiating triumph, he says, came in 2001 when he won long-term job security for London Underground workers as the service was part-privatised. It was a deal criticised by some in the press as a 'job for life' agreement. According to Crow, after weeks of grinding talks, management just gave in, saying: 'Please, just give them whatever they f***ing want.'[109]

Nonetheless, many RMT London Underground activists believed that the way their union had handled the dispute had squandered an

---

103 *Times* 6 June 2001.
104 *Socialist Worker* 12 May 2001.
105 *Socialist Worker* 9 June 2001.
106 *Evening Standard* 16 May 2001.
107 *Evening Standard* 16 May 2001.
108 *Evening Standard* 16 May, 13 August 2001.
109 *Financial Times* 25 March 2011.

opportunity to do more than just delay part-privatisation (represented by Private–Public Partnerships, PPPs).[110] This issue was not solely about Crow's leadership, for there were also divisions about how to campaign politically against PPP. Within the RMT London Region, the Campaign against Tube Privatisation (CATP) was launched in late 1998 as an alliance of workers and passengers. It had Crow's support but he was far less supportive when it put up its own candidates in the 2000 Greater London Assembly elections. One of the leading advocates for doing so was Sikorski. Standing against the other Left parties opposing privatisation, it gained just 17,041 votes (1%) in the London-wide list section. Other Left parties gained 48,252 votes (2.9%), suggesting that a united slate of the kind Crow traditionally supported might have had success in surpassing the 5% threshold needed for a seat.

Later in 2001, another dispute erupted with London Underground, this time over pay.[111] It again showed that the description of the RMT (and ASLEF) provided by Blair's favourite union leader, Sir Ken Jackson of the AEEU, of 'strike first, negotiate later' was wide of the mark.[112] Crow showed that he was prepared to engage in detailed and lengthy arguments[113] where he believed: 'The cause of this dispute lies squarely on the shoulders of LU, who have shown arrogant disregard for the views of the independent arbiter.'[114] In another Underground dispute in 2001 over facilities, he made it evident that 'This dispute should never have come about in the first place. We came to a clear agreement with LUL last year and the blame lies fairly and squarely at their door. It's quite prehistoric that women train operators are having to go into pubs to use toilet facilities because those provided by LUL are so inadequate.'[115]

Conclusion

As a result of opposition to the Company Plan, Crow first came to national prominence. The *Evening Standard* observed that he was 'committed, hard Left, articulate and intelligent ... [having] won the admi-

---

110 See also, for example, *Tunnel Vision*, AWL pamphlet, available as 'The fight against Tube privatisation reviewed', http://www.workersliberty.org/story/2004/07/02/fight-against-tube-privatisation-reviewed-part-1.

111 Crow also helped negotiate a 35-hour working week at GNER in 2001.

112 *Evening Standard* 11 October 2001

113 See his response to the attacks on him and the RMT by the *Evening Standard* (3 October 2001).

114 *Morning Star* 1 September 2001.

115 *Morning Star* 27 September 2001.

ration of colleagues for his ability as a negotiator and [being] quickly chosen as one of the few London Transport delegates to the union's annual conference'.[116] In its words, he had 'quickly built up a reputation as one of a new breed of activist-orators in public transport' and 'quickly established himself as a key figure' after joining the CoE.[117] The *Sunday Times*, in an article entitled 'The pin-striped militant who will bring the capital to a standstill', believed that he was 'leading a last stand by London Underground workers against management plans to change working practices that date back to the 1920s'.[118] These characterisations etched out the hallmarks of what he was to become, namely, a clever and dedicated socialist fighter and leader with a big personality and colourful character.

Despite the NUR/RMT regaining some of its collective confidence and attaining some victories in the late 1980s and early 1990s,[119] the unfolding of the 1990s showed that there were definite limits to the extent of its renewal. For example, Crow wrote:

> In 1993 ASLEF and RMT at first took strike action together to defend the agreement the unions had with BR that there would be no compulsory redundancies, but by the time of the second day of strike action the RMT was fighting alone. The union voted narrowly to enter further talks, but the momentum was gone and the outcome was a major setback for the fight against privatisation. For RMT there was another major sting in the tail, when BR vindictively ended the payroll 'check-off' system of deducting union subscriptions directly from wages, and the union's membership plunged as a result from 105,000 in 1992 to 59,000 in 1995 [and it was] unable to halt privatisation and fragmentation of the industry ...[120]

This was a difficult environment in which to work but one that did not deter Crow – rather, it seemed to strengthen his resolve to rebuild the RMT into a respected and effective fighting force. He was fortunate to have mainly worked within London Underground, because the RMT had been less beaten back there than elsewhere. Crow became the *de facto* leader of the radical Left in the union, eclipsing those in this milieu who were older or from outside London.

The London Underground disputes in 2001 and the many that preceded them on the railways plainly showed that Crow was not all about strikes and not strike-happy, as the *Daily Mail* and *Evening Standard*,

116 *Evening Standard* 19 November 1992.
117 *Evening Standard* 19 November 1992, 16 May 2001, respectively.
118 *Sunday Times* 22 November 1992.
119 Berlin (2006) and Crow (2012a).
120 Crow (2012a: 154).

on the one hand, and Tory and 'new' Labour politicians, on the other, painted him. The *Sun* declared that Crow was 'Public Enemy No. 1 for Britain's commuters'.[121] But before any striking took place under Crow's leadership, there was a fairly standard process to be gone through, including declaring a dispute, waging a media war, giving notice of a ballot for industrial action, giving notice of industrial action and offering to be available for talks. For any action to be contemplated there was also the not inconsiderable matter of sanction by the CoE or the General Grades Committee. Strikes were not the only form of action used, since there were also overtime bans and work-to-rules. In all, Crow led from the front in making sure that – whether through threats of action or action itself – an increasing amount of pressure was put on employers to settle on terms acceptable to RMT members. Clearly, when it got to the point when he thought no more could be gained, he saw no virtue in striking for striking's sake. This was even to the point of being criticised for this by his far Left comrades.

Throughout the processes, Crow showed he was capable of providing militant and successful industrial leadership (especially in London). In the former regard, the *Evening Standard* reported in 2002: 'Londoners are used to strikes and go-slows on the Underground. In the past 12 years, only 1992, 1997 and 2000 have been strike-free.'[122] Yet for all Crow's talents for effective leadership and for all its industrial muscle, on its own – or with its fellow rail unions, ASLEF, TSSA and what would become Unite – the RMT did not gain the renationalisation of Railtrack after its collapse in 2001, and nor could it, in Crow's words, 'stop the equivalent of a subterranean Railtrack fiasco'[123] with the introduction of PPP on the Underground in the same year. Much to Crow's chagrin, it did not become a 'poll tax on wheels' as he wished.[124] The same was true of the complete closure of Red Star parcels in May 2001 with the loss of 260 jobs. Such instances highlighted not only that sizeable amounts of industrial and political power had to be wielded in order to achieve desired goals, but also that the RMT needed to have the support of an influential union movement led by militants and supported by a significant socialist movement. The next chapter looks at how Crow as RMT general secretary tried to resolve these problems so that the RMT could become more effective in defending and advancing its members' inter-

---

121 *Sun* 14 January 2002. This was then used by many others such as the *Guardian* 18 February 2002.
122 *Evening Standard* 2 October 2002.
123 *Evening Standard* 10 July 2001.
124 *Morning Star* 6 February 2002.

ests. In doing so, Crow would need to call upon all the skills, training and experience he had built up. Indeed, the *Evening Standard* reckoned that he had 'gained a reputation for tough negotiation and upholding the power of the humble worker ... [with a] more polished front and smoother style [than any rivals]'.[125] What clearly emerges up to this point is that Crow had marked himself out as a young and confident radical leader. This was no small achievement given the domination of the NUR by older, more experienced activists and officers.

125 *Evening Standard* 11 May 2001.

3. Becoming RMT general secretary

It is not often that a deputy to a sitting general secretary becomes almost as well known and as influential as the general secretary. But due to his record of struggle, big personality, radical Left politics, responsibility for dealing with London Underground and powerbase in London, this was the case with Crow. This situation was heightened by Knapp's illness. Together these factors provided a strong basis upon which to become general secretary. Notwithstanding his refusal to stand earlier against Knapp, Crow had an accelerated path to becoming a national union leader. It is worth noting that this happened in 2002 and not in 2004 (when Knapp's term of office was to have ended) because were it not for Knapp's death from cancer, Crow would have had to sit and wait for his retirement. Yet compared to Knapp's tenure from 1983 to 2001, the RMT under Crow would develop apace in regaining lost profile and power. This would be no easy achievement but it was one that Crow was committed to achieving personally and politically.

Getting elected

Crow's election manifesto included such statements as: 'The union looks to the Government to protect our members on the big issues such as employment legislation and the reversal of the catastrophic policy of privatisation in … transport … If the Government will not fulfil our members' hopes then we will have no alternative but to do battle with the Government too';[1] 'Whoever's in government, your interests come first';[2] and 'The railway cannot operate properly on a fragmented basis with more than 3,000 companies alone registered with Railtrack. Renationalisation of the whole industry is my aim.'[3] Two others contested the election, the education officer, Ray Spry-Shute, and the South West regional organiser, Phil Bialyk. Although Spry-Shute

1 *Independent* 14 February 2002.
2 *Evening Standard* 30 January 2002.
3 *Independent* 14 February 2002.

had a background on the Left, was close to Knapp and was known to many members through his union role, it was Bialyk who offered the main opposition to Crow, having industrial bargaining experience. He was decidedly 'old' Labour and pragmatic like Knapp and, thus, was positioned as the main right-wing candidate. He was backed by 'new' Labour because there was no other serious alternative to Crow, Bialyk being the nearest thing to a moderate that there was. Bialyk's campaign was organised by Cash.[4] Crow's chances of being elected were enhanced not just by his being the most senior officer standing and by the RMT's increasingly left-wing inclinations but also by Spry-Shute and Bialyk splitting the anti-Crow vote.

While Crow organised a speaking tour (which was cut short as the result of an assault on him), the TUC was seen to intervene through one of its officials, Mike Power (although it subsequently reprimanded him for doing so).[5] The concern was not just that Crow would win but that so too would the Left, with replacements for Hince and Crow's AGS positions. The briefing note from Power to Cash – which Cash requested from Power – said:

> Crow has never shown any inclination to associate positively with the Labour government ... He has personally advocated ending the RMT's link with Labour ... He has been associated with around 30 strikes in his 10 years in office ... Subtle negotiation, leadership and diplomacy have never been part of his working methods. He favours a return to the Seventies and believes that strike action raises the class consciousness of the rank-and-file. This approach makes him a popular choice for the extremists.[6]

The briefing predicted that a Crow victory 'could result in the biggest changes within the union for a generation and be long-lasting and deep' with the winner being in post 'for up to 20 years'.[7] Political forces to Crow's right were not the only ones hostile or sceptical of his candidacy, for the *Daily Telegraph* quoted one far Left activist as saying: 'He will

4 *Socialist Worker* 19 January 2002.

5 *Morning Star* 11 January 2012. Mike Power also served as Bialyk's 'spin doctor' (*Morning Star* 11 January 2012).

6 *Evening Standard* 10 January 2002. See also *Socialist Worker* 19 January 2002.

7 The *Socialist Review* (February 2002) reported: 'At a regional meeting for RMT delegates from across south west England and south Wales with Bob Crow and his Blairite-supported rival, Phil Bialyk, the branch secretary of Swansea RMT demanded to know if Bialyk had been involved in preparing the document smearing Bob Crow which had emanated from the TUC. Bialyk refused to reply. The Swansea rep then said he would be moving a motion demanding an official union investigation and that, if it found Bialyk was involved, he would be arguing for his expulsion or a five-year suspension. The meeting endorsed this call.'

probably be regarded as the lesser of two evils, because he at least sup-ports the principle that the executive should be accountable to the rank and file.'[8]

The election result saw Crow as the runaway winner, with 12,051 (65%) of votes cast, 7,500 votes ahead of Bialyk on 4,512, with Spry-Shute on 1,997.[9] He was younger than either his predecessor or his successor.[10] Crow won without the aid of a split anti-Crow vote and the margin of victory was the biggest in the union's history. His victory highlighted that for the RMT, a much more forceful personality, effective deployment of bargaining power and radical politics were better suited to the turbulent times of 'new' Labour, privatisation and neoliberalism. Greeting his victory, Crow said: 'The members elected me because they wanted a fighter ... All I want to do is to improve the terms and conditions of working people.'[11] 'I am the first general secretary for over 100 years who is not affiliated to the Labour Party. I am a socialist and proud of it. I have been elected by a massive majority and whether I am a socialist or not, my views are the members' views.'[12] The *Guardian* quoted a 'moderate RMT official' as saying: 'They feel they have got nothing out of New Labour and backed Bob because he said he would stand up for them.'[13] To the media's annoyance, Crow was not available for interviews after the result – instead, he was celebrating with support-ers.[14] Outside the pub where the victory celebrations took place, a sup-porter hung a banner which read: 'Well done Bob – the revolution starts here'.[15] Newspaper copy such as 'the toughest of the new trade unionists ... [a] Marxist Millwall supporter'[16] greeted his election. Although he said he was not bothered by this, he was angered by accusations of being a 'wrecker' from Blair[17] and others:[18]

8 *Telegraph* 5 January 2002.
9 Turnout was 32% (*Labour Research* March 2002).
10 Knapp was 43, Sam McCluskie (NUS) 54, and Cash 54, while Crow was 41.
11 *Telegraph* 16 February 2002.
12 *Times* 14 February 2002.
13 *Guardian* 14 February 2002. The official was likely to have been Mick Cash.
14 *Evening Standard* 14 February 2002. The *Observer* (17 February 2002) reported: 'He chose to spend the night of his victory downing pints in a St Pancras pub rather than trading soundbites in the television studios. His supporters were delighted. Television executives and sober RMT officials were exasperated.' Crow admitted that he was drunk for most of the day in question (*Daily Telegraph* 16 February 2002).
15 *Evening Standard* 14 February 2002.
16 *Observer* 17 February 2002.
17 Not long afterwards, Blair said: 'Some unions led by particular individuals, for example the RMT led by the guy who supports Arthur Scargill, don't agree with the Labour Party. Today's Labour Party governs for the whole country and it can't be

Water off a duck's back ... I'm a track worker – I've only ever constructed a railway, I've never wrecked one. Dyson shut down its factory completely without a ballot. They threw 700 people out so they could move the firm to the Far East and get the wages paid 75 per cent cheaper. They're the wreckers.[19]

That was an absolute disgrace. I've been working for the expansion of the railway since I was 16. I was also a track worker helping construct the industry. Now I'm fighting for better pay and conditions for my members and the investment needed to get a better service for passengers. I see the railway as a public utility, like gas, electricity and water – part of the family silver.[20]

Later, he argued that the real wreckers were those responsible for the decades of under-investment in rail under both Tory and Labour governments.[21]

From the union movement, there were a few digs at him. Sir Ken Jackson, now Amicus joint general secretary, told the *Independent*:

Sid Weighell famously rejected the idea that unions could squeeze more money for themselves out of the coffers by unlimited strike action: 'the philosophy of the pig trough – those with the biggest snout get the biggest share'. Let us hope that the resonance of his words of wisdom has not died with him. His ... favourite saying was that 'for the triumph of evil it is only necessary for good men to do nothing'. And he was right.[22]

However, some commuters welcomed Crow's election:

In common with other passengers, I have suffered endless price rises, delays, train cancellations and spurious inter-company blame-shifting over the past few years ... I am therefore overjoyed ... [Crow's election] may herald a new wave of actions to challenge the rail companies' (mis)management and the Government's gleeful desire to extend this foolhardy approach to the Tube ... And while, because I rely on the rail network, [RMT] strike action ... will prove inconvenient to me over the short term, it is precisely because I rely on the rail network and want it to be run safely, effectively, and with the interests of passengers foremost, and because I fear that if no one makes

dictated to by the unions or anyone else' (*Daily Record* 22 February 2002). The only praise Crow ever gave Blair was: 'At least he's honest – we haven't got a lot from him but he never told us we would. He's been pretty straight. He's got his opinion' (*Telegraph* 16 February 2002).

18 See, for example, his detailed response to attacks on him and the RMT in *The Business* 20 January 2002.

19 *Telegraph* 16 February 2002.

20 *Mirror* 15 April 2002.

21 *Mirror* 15 April 2002.

22 *Independent* 22 February 2002.

a stand the situation will only worsen, that I hope that the RMT under Bob Crow proves as belligerent as your correspondent predicts![23]

Reflecting back on his election in 2014, Crow said: 'I suppose I've got Margaret Thatcher to thank for my career. The truth is I'd never have been elected if it wasn't for her. Our rulebook used to say you couldn't stand as general secretary unless you were a member of the Labour Party. I wasn't. But Maggie did away with that rule.'[24]

Before being elected, Crow suffered a serious assault. In the early hours of New Year's Day 2002, after coming home from a party, he challenged two men who were trying to break down his front door. As he confronted one, the second hit him with a metal bar, gashing his face so that he needed five stitches and corrective eye surgery: 'They were banging the door down. I started yelling, "What do you want?" As I did one of them came round the side and hit me with the bar. Thankfully I am a burly bloke and the two tore off up the road.'[25] In another account, he said:

> There was a black bloke standing there. I said, 'What do you want?' He didn't answer. He walked backwards, still looking at me. Then I saw a flash. Turned out it was an iron bar – one in the face and one on the arm. I thought I was dreaming. All I could hear was water splashing on the floor. I thought, 'I can't believe it, the pipes have burst'. So I turned on the lights and it was blood. Then I collapsed. I woke up again at about 5.30, went upstairs and woke my wife.[26]

At this stage he did not claim this to be the work of his opponents.[27] Once the police had ruled out a botched burglary and were favouring a premeditated assault, Crow speculated that the attack was the work of rail employers. He commented:

> It was hired muscle. They tried to finish me off. It has got me very worried. No way would I consider the union rivals to be a part of this. I think it's something to do with certain employers. They are worried about further industrial action. They are worried they could lose money in the stock exchange. I think it was someone giving me a hiding the day the ballot papers went out.[28]

Later he said: 'There are hundreds of subcontractors who didn't want me negotiating with them. It's intimidation: "Don't cause any

23 Rachel Cohen, Sheffield (*Independent* 22 February 2002).
24 *Mirror* 9 February 2014.
25 *Evening Standard* 4 January 2002.
26 *Financial Times* 10 September 2004.
27 See *Evening Standard* 4 January 2002; *Morning Star* 4 January 2002.
28 *Independent on Sunday* 13 January 2002.

aggro.""[29] The *Observer* quoted an unnamed RMT member as saying: 'He had a nerve to do that [b]ut it worked with the members', with a 'campaign adversary' saying that this displayed Crow's shrewdness, mastery of 'low cunning' and ability to manipulate the media.[30] Christian Wolmar believed that 'the culprits were more likely to have come from the then quite active far-right in Dagenham, where he lived',[31] although this was made highly unlikely by the fact that one of the assailants was black. After the attack, his house was fitted with a panic button, but Crow said he still felt 'vulnerable [because] you can't have a panic button for just walking down the street or taking a bus'.[32]

Despite Crow's victory, the hard Left did not manage to capture the position of senior AGS. In a five-way fight, Cash (with 6,736 votes) defeated John MacDonald (with 4,889) on his platform of 'I want the union to negotiate first and only call for strike action when you need it and all else fails ... I am fed up with our union being portrayed as strike happy and extreme.'[33] The three other candidates were Stan Herschel, Ken Usher and Andy Warnock-Smith. Given that the Left put up two candidates and the Right three, there was little possibility of a split vote benefiting one or the other. However, the hard Left did secure the number three position of (junior) AGS when Sikorski was elected in August 2002. He held the position for two terms of office until 2012, when he was beaten for re-election by Steve Hedley.[34]

First steps and responses

Overall, the RMT was somewhat down on its luck when Crow was elected.[35] It had not fared well in the battle to stave off and defeat privatisation (notwithstanding the unintended useful consequence of labour shortages as TOCs made staff redundant), it was in something of a financial mess, its membership was low and falling, and the national union had been without coherent leadership. There was much to put right and much that Crow wanted to achieve over and above simply righting the ship. Within days of taking office, and after the failure to stop PPP

29 *Financial Times* 10 September 2004.
30 *Observer* 17 February 2002.
31 *Guardian* 12 March 2014.
32 *Morning Star* 14 January 2002.
33 *Evening Standard* 28 March 2002.
34 Hedley was a member of the Socialist Party for a short period until 2013.
35 Alan Pottage wrote: 'In 2002 our union was looking into the abyss, with deep financial problems, continuing loss of membership, we were demoralised and inert' (*Scottish Left Review* May–June 2014).

on the Tube in 2001 through industrial action, Crow instructed John Hendy QC to act for the RMT in taking legal action against the scheme on the basis that 'the Health and Safety Executive has failed to oversee the public-private partnership properly ... [and] LU has failed to consult the staff safety representatives properly'.[36] As recounted earlier, Knapp had tried to make full-time CoE members part-time on the grounds of a financial crisis. Although this was rejected, Knapp used the lack of the right to emergency resolutions at AGMs to push through a cuts package after the deadline for resolutions and appeals against CoE decisions had passed. Crow instructed an officer to investigate the finances and found that the crisis was not all it seemed to be. That was not to say that all was well, but with work undertaken the result was that 'under Bob's leadership we became solvent – we owe not a bean to anyone'.[37] Indeed, over the years to 2014 the RMT returned small annual surpluses (save for one year) and had a rising income (from membership subs and shares) and appreciating assets (property, shares).[38] It held no sizeable debt, but it did have high and rising pension liabilities. Out of income, the RMT paid the CoE and branch secretary salaries (so that they were not dependent upon employers) as well as opening a series of new regional offices such as Doncaster and Southampton.

With the resources that did exist, Crow instituted the creation of an intranet for the RMT offices to aid communication and exchange of information.[39] This was part of his strategy to professionalise the union. This was taken further in 2006 when a government grant was gained (via the Union Modernisation Fund) to improve internal communications with information technology. However, his major initiative was to establish an Organising and Recruitment Unit in 2002, with Alan Pottage appointed as its national organising coordinator along with five staff members. Reflecting on the combined outcome of these processes, Cumbers *et al.* wrote:

> restructuring involved the reduction of the role of local branches and the strengthening of particular regional centres (Bristol, Liverpool, Birmingham, York and Glasgow) by recruiting extra union organisers ... Local branches are now much less important for the day-to-day operation of union business, with regional offices now providing more support, information and advice for company-based local activists ... The strengthening of the regional scale of organisation has been designed to support the crucial role of local negotiators and organisers.

36 *Evening Standard* 18 February 2002.
37 Alan Pottage, *Scottish Left Review* May–June 2014.
38 See annual returns to the Certification Officer.
39 *Evening Standard* 13 February 2002. See also Cumbers *et al.* (2010).

Interestingly, the localisation or 'downscaling' of negotiation and bargaining processes seems to coincide with a certain delocalisation of representation in relation to the reduced importance of traditional local branches in the recruitment and organisation of union members. Union officials … argued … the rescaling of organisational structures … strengthened communication between local activists and union leaderships, creating more seamless and flexible structures that transcend older hierarchies …[40]

Despite repeated changes to managerial structures under British Rail, union organisation had remained centralised and bargaining structures dense, layered and hierarchical, with a spirit of 'constitutionalism' pervading them.[41] This emphasised the scale of the rupture, with the era of privatisation bringing about fragmentation and decentralisation. Under Crow, the RMT rose to the challenge of decentralised managerial and bargaining structures (as well as the growth in the number of agencies to bargain with) by changing the locus of influence within its own processes and structures, and by seeking to maintain as much uniformity of members' terms and conditions as possible by working from an updated version of the former BR rule book in order to assert an industry standard.[42] Without a strong lead from the national union under Crow, this successful reorganisation would not have happened. Part and parcel of explaining this was not just Crow's dominant force but also the lessons he learned under Knapp, namely, beginning the process of replacing unelected union officers by introducing elections for regional and national positions and influencing the outcome of those elections in order to increase union democracy and union effectiveness. Martin Eady recounted:

Under Weighell, the union administration had considerable power and Knapp did not adequately deal with this when he took over. In fact, the power of the administration over elected reps, both lay and full-time, and officers was not dealt with until Bob himself as general secretary cleared out the 'Augean Stables' at head office. This restored power to the elected reps both at head office and locally. It was part of a necessary and overdue sea-change in the nature of our union which Bob initiated as soon as he took over.

[T]he union had been highly centralised, led by officers and administrators,

40 Cumbers *et al.* (2010: 135–136).
41 Pendleton (1997); Pendleton (1991a); Ferner (1985); Pendleton (1991b).
42 This provides an interesting counter-weight to Fairbrother's (2000) union renewal thesis of the decentralisation of managerial structures and collective bargaining (at the behest of the employer) providing the occasion for the renewal of workplace unionism. In the case of the RMT, the national union played a vital role in equipping the local and regional organisation to renew itself.

inflexible and wedded to the Staff Councils Scheme (a form of Whitleyism that lasted until 1993). This structure meshed with a centralised, nationalised management and provided a stable, comfortable environment for union officers, the administration and all too many local reps. But with the end of the Scheme in 1993 and the breaking up of the railway and Underground into separate companies, mostly privatised, all this changed. One of Bob's greatest achievements was to recognise this and decentralise the union, making it more flexible and reducing the power of the central bureaucracy. ... The plethora of companies and structures was much too numerous and complex for head office to service or control. Bob encouraged local lay reps to become involved in negotiations which previously they had not been trusted to do. This led to a revolution in the union, changing it to a democratic member-led organisation and as a result a much more left wing one.[43]

The reduction in headquarters staff also helped transform the union's finances, so that Crow 'found that once various abuses had been dealt with we were actually in quite a healthy position'.[44] In order to have control over remaining and new staff so as to avoid the fate that befell Knapp (see below), Crow 'persuaded the CoE to agree to give him control of all staffing matters, which meant he could easily run the union machinery'.[45] This was an indication of the power of Crow's personality and his creation of political congruence.

Another significant development was the launch of the RMT credit union in 2004 in recognition of its many low-paid members, high credit card charges and the aspiration to expand the RMT's presence. Less than two and a half years after Crow's taking office, the *Telegraph* reported: 'Even his opponents admit that the union is well run, with an extensive property portfolio.'[46] Away from the tub-thumping public speeches, this indicated that Crow was an efficient administrator, able to delegate work and manage those carrying it out.[47] This task was made easier by the respect he garnered from union staff and his experience of branch secretaryship. Finally, in terms of administration, Crow put an

---

43 Email correspondence.

44 Martin Eady, email correspondence.

45 Oliver New, email correspondence. Examples were appointing Andy Gilchrist as national education officer, and Brian Denny, Derek Kotz and Geoff Martin as media officers. All came from a radical Left background, often the Communist Party.

46 *Telegraph* 11 October 2004.

47 Many years later in 2013 (see Chapter 8), Crow showed he still had these skills when he dealt with the correspondence arising from the branch structure review. Here, he annotated the correspondence and listed action points for execution.

end to the practice of the union's legal work being undertaken by one company as there were suspicions that it had been overcharged.

However, one thing Crow did not act upon was the investment of RMT funds not just in capitalist corporations but in some of the most unethical ones. *Scotland on Sunday* revealed that the RMT had invested more than £900,000 in stocks, shares and bonds of companies and banks behind several PPP deals as part of its £7.7m portfolio. The response from the RMT was that Crow 'might reconsider some of the investments if they were deemed inappropriate'.[48] This was fair comment as Crow was new in post at this time. But later investigations showed that patterns of shareholding had not changed much. In 2013, the RMT held shares worth £15.35m in some of the world's largest banks and transnational corporations (such as HSBC, Barclays, LloydsTSB and Anglo-American, BP, British American Tobacco, Compass, Shell and Vodafone), receiving substantial dividends.[49] The official RMT response was 'RMT has an investment team that makes sure our members funds are looked after and don't get eaten away by inflation. If any trade union from any country in the world asks us to disinvest in a company we do so.'[50] Given that company profits come from exploiting workers, as Crow well understood, the attitude adopted by him and the RMT was pragmatic. It ensured that the union had the resources to fund its growth through the Organising and Recruitment Unit, as well as officers' salaries and pensions and membership benefits.

On the industrial front immediately following Crow's election, talks concluded whereby London Underground awarded drivers 'a pay rise of nearly ten per cent within a year', with Crow commenting: 'This is my second celebration in two weeks ... members [are] over the moon.'[51] After the threat of two two-day strikes (after a 9 to 1 'yes' vote) starting the following week, Tube drivers were offered a 5.7% rise to add to the previous year's one. Crow described the union's concessions to get the deal as a 'few bits of productivity that we always said we were prepared to look at. We are absolutely delighted that we are not taking industrial action next week.'[52] In addition to this dispute, there were a number of others that started before his election and that were resolved soon after

48 *Scotland on Sunday* 24 November 2002.
49 *Telegraph* 13, 20 July 2013. These details emerged from RMT annual reports to the Certification Officer. This situation did not appear to have changed by the end of 2015 – see the RMT's annual return for 2015 to the Certification Officer and the *Times* (11 August 2016).
50 *Telegraph* 13, 20 July 2013.
51 *Evening Standard* 28 February 2002.
52 *Evening Standard* 28 February 2002.

at Scotrail, South West Trains (SWT), Arriva Trains Northern (ATN), Silverlink and Docklands Light Railway (DLR). As ever, the media speculated that their intensity had been deliberately ramped up in order to enhance Crow's militant profile during the election.[53] However, the facts did not support this. Of the DLR dispute, Crow said: 'It is good to get a sensible deal without industrial action';[54] on Silverlink he commented: 'It is not too late for [the company] to step back from the brink and improve its offer' after a strike date was announced;[55] and on ATN he said: 'We are always ready to talk to the company.'[56] In the case of SWT, the RMT called off further strikes after a membership revolt.[57] In the Arriva case, the dispute and strikes continued into early 2003.

In his first big fight with London Underground since becoming general secretary, over safety under PPP, Crow had to vigorously defend himself and the RMT from widespread criticism. The *Evening Standard* claimed that 'The union has fabricated a complaint about "inadequate consultation over safety", but that is code for muscle-flexing over privatisation. The union hopes that public anger will be directed not at its members but at Tony Blair. The strike is a crude political gesture.'[58] It stated that 'Crow ... believes that strike action raises the consciousness of the rank-and-file.'[59] Crow responded: 'We do not want to inconvenience members of the public, and our members do not want to lose money by striking. But, on safety there is no room for compromise.'[60] Earlier, he made clear that 'London Underground are treating our members' safety fears with contempt and they have left us with no alternative but to strike';[61] 'Our members have every right to protect their own and the public's safety. This overwhelming vote is an indictment of LU's refusal to enter into meaningful consultation with our safety representatives. When lives are at stake there can be no room for compromise.'[62]

Although the strikes were successful, the fight to control the effects of the PPP regime on safety was not, with both the Health and Safety Executive and the London Mayor, Ken Livingstone, acquiescing in PPP's

53 See, for example, *Scotland on Sunday* 13 January 2002; and *Times* 4 January 2002.
54 *Evening Standard* 11 April 2002.
55 *Morning Star* 11 April 2002.
56 *Daily Post* 31 July 2002.
57 *Evening Standard* 13 February 2002.
58 *Evening Standard* 18 July 2002.
59 *Evening Standard* 15 July 2002.
60 *Evening Standard* 17 July 2002. This was in the form of a letter condemning the content of an *Evening Standard* article on 15 July 2002.
61 *Express* 11 July 2002.
62 *Evening Standard* 10 July 2002.

implementation. This fight was followed by another on pay later in the same year because, according to Crow, London Underground

> refused to go ... to mediation, as set out in our collective agreement ... this process that settled last year's pay round. We have, again, asked Acas to try to persuade LUL to take this path. [Its] reluctance to go to mediation could possibly be because it has tabled the worst pay offer of any train-operating company this year, and that management's position of refusing to negotiate an end to inequalities in pensions, travel concessions and working hours is unreasonable and untenable.[63]

Earlier, London Underground had asked for a no-strike agreement as part of its *quid pro quo* for a 3.2% pay off – once this was rejected, the offer was reduced to 2.5% and then increased to 3.0%.[64] The dispute was resolved when Livingstone intervened to facilitate effective independent mediation, with the pay settlement backdated six months.[65] Earlier in the summer, Livingstone had appointed Crow to the TfL board overseeing transport in the capital.[66] However, the productive relationship with Livingstone did not last long after Livingstone encouraged Tube workers to cross RMT picket lines in 2004.[67] Livingstone continually asserted that the RMT was more militant with London Underground as a better public-sector employer than with private-sector, rapacious TOCs. Underlying the fissure was the RMT's continued opposition to part-privatisation, which Livingstone subsequently – albeit reluctantly – accepted after losing his legal challenge against it. But also present was the RMT's ability to put more pressure – especially of a political kind – upon a public employer handling around 4 million passenger journeys per day.

A man of action and for action

From day one as general secretary, Crow was more forthright than nearly all other union leaders in saying not just what was wrong but also what was needed to right the wrongs. His lack of faith in Labour's ability to act progressively meant that he continually emphasised the need for

63 *Evening Standard* 26 September 2002.
64 *Evening Standard* 7 August 2002.
65 *Morning Star* 10 October 2002. This was a long time coming, as back in January Crow, as RMT AGS, had commented: 'We are disappointed that after submitting our claim to mediation LU has failed to implement the mediator's recommendation to harmonise passenger and engineering train drivers' pay' (*Evening Standard* 23 January 2002).
66 *Times* 15 June 2002.
67 *Evening Standard* 24 June 2004.

direct, mass action. For example, at the 2002 STUC congress, he said: 'It is not good enough coming to the rostrum and passing resolutions. We should be doing what the Italian workers are doing and saying – stuff your anti-trade union laws … It is not good enough passing resolutions. Go on the streets and defend and uphold workers' rights in Britain, Scotland and the world.'[68] Later in that year, he stated: 'If British workers want better conditions, then it's no use waiting for the EU to sort it out – they must do it for themselves';[69] 'I will be calling next week that we go on the streets like the Italians and Spanish and say: "You can stuff your anti-trades union laws."'[70] He kept up his calls the year after when, at the 2003 TUC congress, he urged 'workers to take to the streets in protest at employment laws', specifically the lack of the right to take secondary action, after a bus company in Devon had used strike breakers where the RMT was unable legally to call out its members at the depots that the strike breakers came from. 'If it is good enough for the bosses to understand what solidarity is, then it should be good enough for us to bring in laws that create secondary action that is legitimate as well.'[71] Earlier that year, he compared the anti-war movement to the Romanian revolution, which ended with Ceausescu's execution. As Blair was not listening to the protests, Crow made the allusion: 'Look at what happened in Eastern Europe when people didn't listen.'[72] In the run-up to the 2005 TUC, he argued:

> But what people have got to recognise is that we are not going to win things just by passing resolutions. Resolutions are fine in making sure that the strategy and theory are right, but that has to be turned into practice. That means solid trade union organisation, with unions that are prepared to lead from the front and take workers with them. That's how the anti-union laws were defeated in the 1970s and that's how they will be in the future.[73]

While making such calls at TUC congresses, Crow's relationship with its affiliates was not always smooth. In 2002, he suffered the embarrassment of not being elected on to its General Council, marking the first time the main rail union had been denied a place on the council for over fifty years. He came thirteenth out of fifteen candidates for the eleven places for unions with under 100,000 members. According to the *Guardian*: 'A TUC source suggested Mr Crow had "put people's backs up" for attack-

68 *Scotsman* 16 April 2002.
69 *Morning Star* 27 June 2002.
70 *Morning Star* 7 September 2002. See also *Evening Standard* 9 September 2002.
71 *Times* 9 September 2003.
72 *Independent* 11 February 2003.
73 *Socialist Worker* 17 September 2005.

ing Tony Blair and threatening strikes',[74] while *Socialist Worker* believed: 'TUC officials sympathetic to New Labour manoeuvred to keep him off the TUC general council'.[75] But this rebuff did not last long and it was precisely for attacking Blair and threatening strikes that he was elected in 2003, serving for two years until 2005. *The Times* speculated that Mick Rix's removal from the General Council had precipitated Crow's election, since Rix had failed to be re-elected as ASLEF general secretary, which meant that there was one less radical on the ruling body.[76] The TUC affiliates' on-off relationship with Crow would continue over the years. In 2005, *The Times* reported that Crow had 'suffered the indignity of losing his seat on the TUC's General Council. Worse, he was defeated not by another union firebrand but by Tim Poil, of the Nationwide Building Society's staff union.'[77] Crow was re-elected to serve on the General Council for 2006–07 but then lost his seat again. He was not re-elected until 2010, serving until his death in 2014. Of his time on the General Council, Mark Serwotka commented that Crow was 'always there to back up those critical voices from the left where he would not hold back but did so with humour which was disarming'.[78] However, according to Serwotka, one of Crow's big frustrations with the Left on the General Council was that it was never sufficiently tightly organised. So while the general secretaries of the 'awkward squad' unions met informally, this tended to be on an *ad hoc* basis, and never reached the stage of jointly agreeing strategy and tactics for prosecuting common grievances.[79] It was not until the creation of the Trade Union Co-ordinating Group (TUCG) in 2008 that this situation was remedied a little.

The beginning of the divorce from Labour

Although the RMT donated £37,000 to Labour in 2001 and supported 13 local constituency parties, Crow told the *Financial Times* that it could not support a Labour government that had 'deserted its working class roots and supporters and jumped into bed with its big business friends. Unless the disastrous policies are changed we will no longer support them politically or financially.'[80] But he did not call for outright

---

74 *Guardian* 11 September 2002.
75 *Socialist Worker* 19 October 2002.
76 *Times* 10 September 2003.
77 *Times* 14 September 2005.
78 Interview.
79 *Socialist Review* (September 2004) commented that 'Bob Crow no longer attends left caucuses'.
80 Quoted in *Labour Research* (February 2002).

disaffiliation, even though he said as an individual that Labour was 'not socialist enough for me'.[81] Along with Rix, he argued that Labour should be reclaimed and if it moved to the Left it would become more popular.[82] Crow himself said that the 'battle is on for the very soul of the Labour Party. Of course, we could do ['new' Labour] a favour by picking up our ball and going elsewhere. Or we can dig in our heels and reclaim the Labour Party as the party of labour.'[83] Early into his term of office, Crow signalled there would be a cut in funding to Labour, with the RMT channelling its resources towards those Labour MPs who supported rail renationalisation.[84] The rationale was, he said, 'We want our MPs to put up a bit more of a fight than some of them are doing. I want to see a Labour Party that's out there fighting as hard for workers as the Conservative Party is fighting for big business. I don't think working people are properly represented in Parliament now.'[85] Commenting on Chancellor Gordon Brown's speech to the 2003 TUC congress, he said: 'It was the same meat but with different gravy. He said nothing about workers' rights. Former Labour leader John Smith promised that workers would have employment rights from day one and Mr Brown had an opportunity to make an announcement about that today but he didn't. It seems that we can expect more privatisation of public services.'[86] This was the same line that he had pursued earlier at the 2003 RMT AGM: 'What's the difference between John Major with a blue rosette privatising you and Tony Blair with a red rosette privatising you?'[87] At this AGM he also stated with regard to alternative forms of political representation, 'sooner or later you've got to put your toe in the water'.[88]

The sense of anger and outrage – if not quite betrayal[89] – felt by Crow over what 'new' Labour represented and did was heightened by the Iraq war.[90] It led to an early example of his quick wit. Asked about the pros-

81 *Telegraph* 16 February 2002.

82 *Guardian* 1 May 2002.

83 *Morning Star* 1 May 2002. This indicates that Kevin Maguire's comment that 'In the past, Mr Crow has called for the RMT to sever its links with the Labour party' was inaccurate (*Guardian* 14 February 2002).

84 *Guardian* 1 March 2002.

85 *Telegraph* 16 February 2002.

86 *Guardian* 10 September 2003.

87 *The Socialist* 12 July 2003.

88 *The Socialist* 5 July 2003.

89 Having previously been a member of the Communist and Socialist Labour parties, Crow himself could not have felt betrayed because he did not believe Labour was either a socialist or a progressive party. But he believed RMT members had the right to feel aggrieved – see *Morning Star* 29 June 2003.

90 See BBC Forum interview, 9 September 2002, http://news.bbc.co.uk/2/hi/talking_point/forum/2234265.stm.

pects of war, he said: 'Yes, it seems to me that what's taking place, by the Bush Government and by Blair, is that whatever happens there's going to be a war. It's a bit like Henry Ford – you can have any colour[ed] car you want as long as it's black. Whatever happens, there's going to be a war.'[91] Along with other union general secretaries, Crow signed an open letter to the *Guardian* warning against an attack on Iraq in July 2002, and in the prelude to war in the spring of 2003 he called for 'a war on poverty and not on Iraq', branding Blair a 'war criminal' for contemplating war with Iraq. Later in the year, he said: 'Over-egged, sexed up or exaggerated – whatever words you use, it's quite straightforward: Blair took us to war for oil and he lied about weapons of mass destruction.'[92] Crow was a well-known figure holding Stop the War's national banner as it mobilised hundreds of thousands before and after the invasion of Iraq. In the run-up to the 15 February 2003 demonstrations in London and Glasgow, Crow 'sent out official circulars to all branches insisting upon maximising branch mobilisations combined with personal phone calls/texts to reps and activists and writing for rank-and-file publications'.[93] The Iraq war, Labour's record on privatisation and its handling of the firefighters' pay dispute became the fault lines for what was the beginning of the end for the RMT and Labour under Crow's leadership.

In November 2002, FBU members began protracted strike action in pursuit of a pay rise.[94] Quite apart from supporting fellow public sector workers battling for decent pay, the action caused concern for the RMT in terms of its members' safety and that of the travelling public (on the Underground in particular), as the army and its Green Goddess fire engines had neither the skill nor equipment to deal with major incidents. Early on, Crow raised the issue with London Underground but without any satisfactory response (such as the right to stop work due to safety concerns without being disciplined), and so the RMT threatened to ballot its members on industrial action.[95] This was suspended on legal advice[96] but some 300 RMT members refused to work during the first FBU strike and were sent home on full pay.[97] Those who refused to work

91 BBC Forum interview, 9 September 2002, http://news.bbc.co.uk/2/hi/talking_point/forum/2234265.stm.

92 *Guardian* 11 September 2003.

93 Unjum Mirza, email correspondence.

94 See Seifert and Sibley (2005).

95 *Evening Standard* 10 September 2002.

96 *Morning Star* 29 November 2002.

97 Crow had taken the lead by calling together RMT London Underground reps to get them to organise the campaign of non-compliance.

during the second strike were sent home without pay.[98] The *Guardian* criticised Crow for 'stopping the tube under cover of sophistry'[99] and the *Mirror* blasted his 'political opportunism … threatening rail strikes if there is no fire service [is] a self-serving sham'.[100] But they were wrong since, as with his approach on other matters as general secretary, he put his members' interests first. That he personally supported the FBU's strikes and wanted to see solidarity action taken to support them only came into play after this.[101]

Safety first

The first major RMT battle to be fought outside the capital under Crow's leadership was against downgrading the role of train guards, which affected some 5,000 RMT members. The TOCs effectively chose to re-open an issue that had previously been settled by not honouring the agreement – which was that they would abide by the independent assessment of the role of guards that had found that there needed to be specific provision for such duties.[102] Crow was able to encapsulate the essence of the issues into the accusation that the TOCs wanted to make guards into little more than glorified 'Kit Kat sellers' by transferring their duties in the case of accidents to train drivers.[103] Drivers then became overloaded with responsibilities, leading to errors.[104] He charged employers with having a 'hidden agenda' to abolish guards altogether in order to boost profits, and cited eight 'more progressive' operators (such as Great North Eastern, First Great Western and First Great Eastern) which had signed agreements over guard responsibilities, saying 'We are not asking the other [nine] train operating companies to do anything different.'[105] Over time more employers conceded, but the battle to get the remainder to agree was particularly hard, as the Strategic Rail Authority had

98 As on other occasions, Crow's predictions were wide of the mark – he predicted that 'all-out strikes could spread to the national rail network and London Underground if managers disciplined staff who stopped work because of safety fears during the firefighters' action' (*Independent* 16 November 2002).

99 *Guardian* 18 November 2002.

100 *Mirror* 22 October 2002.

101 *Scotland on Sunday* (1 December 2002) reported that Crow 'said his union would give financial support to the FBU to prevent firefighters being "starved back to work"'.

102 *Guardian* 7 March 2003.

103 Because the issue had been returned to at the employers' instigation, the term 'ticket collectors and Kit-Kat sellers' was sharpened up into just 'Kit-Kat sellers'.

104 *Guardian* 29 March 2003.

105 *Guardian* 29 March 2003.

indemnified them against any losses caused by RMT strikes (which Crow described as 'despicable' on the part of the government).[106] In his last act of his first term of office concerning TOCs, along with his ASLEF and TSSA counterparts, Crow agreed to stand down a strike threat in order to 'take part in a commission to investigate a £600m pensions deficit'.[107]

While a keen supporter of pursuing a health and safety agenda, Crow had to be persuaded of a particular case's merits as Unjum Mirza recounted:

> In 2004, a number of management 'sources' leaked out information to me about the significance of John Prescott's office's proposed changes to fire legislation, particularly the 'Section 12' Regulations ... that were introduced following the King's Cross fire in 1987 that killed 31 people. Among many things, the Regulations stipulated minimum staffing numbers on sub-surface stations. I remember approaching Bob and Bobby Law with quite a stack of paperwork, saying something like: 'We need to talk about this. It's important.' When they saw the amount of paperwork I was holding they both said: 'Fuck off!' I returned with a simpler bullet pointed report and Bob got all the paperwork transferred over to the union's safety team and did a report to the Parliamentary group. It was an extremely successful political campaign that won the retention of the 'Section 12' Regulations.

Making the break

Even before Crow was elected general secretary, and under his influence, the RMT had begun to scrutinise whether it was getting political value for money from its sponsored MPs and Labour affiliation. In 1998, its AGM voted narrowly against disaffiliation (by 27 votes to 21)[108] but it began reducing the funding it gave Labour and the number of members it affiliated.[109] Neither seemed to be delivering much of worth. Indeed, the opposite seemed to be true, with the RMT believing that Labour's actions were often antithetical to its interests and those of its members. Although its 2001 AGM voted to withdraw funding from those sponsored MPs who did not back rail renationalisation, the policy was (again) not implemented until Crow became general secretary. In prosecuting this growing scrutiny of where the RMT's money went

---

106 *Times* 26 March 2003.
107 *Independent* 7 June 2006.
108 *Socialist Worker* 4 July 1998.
109 Berlin (2006: 135). In 1998 and 1999, AGMs voted to withdraw support from Labour MPs who did not support union policies, but this was not implemented. The RMT also supported Ken Livingstone's campaign to become London Mayor when he was not the official Labour candidate.

and what it delivered, Crow said: 'We've supported the Labour Party but we're going to investigate what MPs are fighting for us – and some aren't. If they want to be sponsored, they've got to be seen rolling their sleeves up and fighting for us';[110] 'We deserve at least one meeting and a cup of tea [with them]. If they want our money, they have to roll their sleeves up and fight as hard as I do for the renationalisation of rail.'[111]

It was a brave move by the RMT, articulated and ultimately led by Crow, to allow individual branches in Scotland to affiliate to the Scottish Socialist Party (SSP), given likely expulsion from Labour and spending time in what many considered the political wilderness of being outside Labour's tent.[112] But twisting a well-known proverb, Crow asked why the RMT should continue to feed the hand that bit it. Moreover, it was not a case of being outside Labour, given that being inside delivered so little, but of seeking to establish other means of political representation. Crow did not rush into this situation, for even at the 2002 AGM he argued against disaffiliation.[113] Indeed, he responded to Labour minister Peter Hain MP in the *New Statesman*, saying: 'Peter Hain calls me a splitter and a saboteur ('Don't let Tories and Trots crow'). Had he been at the RMT annual general meeting, he would have heard me argue passionately not to pull out of the party that we helped set up in the first place because we needed a political voice for working people.'[114] This message was repeated by Crow in the *Morning Star*[115] and the *Guardian*[116] as well as at the 2002 conference of the Socialist Campaign Group within Labour, where he urged 'people to get involved in reclaiming the Labour Party for working people',[117] adding that unless this was successful, 'we are going to see [Labour] become totally unrecognisable from the Tory Party'.[118] Indeed, at the TUC in September 2002, 'despite his [own]

110 *Scotsman* 29 January 2002.

111 *Guardian* 26 June 2002.

112 One of these warning voices was likely to have been Cash. The *Guardian* (2 July 2003) reported that: 'One senior RMT official opposed to a breach with Labour said the union was "heading for the political wilderness"'.

113 Berlin (2006: 150).

114 *New Statesman* 15 July 2002. Hain's article was published on 8 July, in which he charged Crow with being a wrecker: 'A hundred years after the railway workers helped to establish the Labour Party, their hard-left leader, Bob Crow, wants to sabotage it. But any split with Labour would benefit the Tories, not his members.'

115 *Morning Star* 9 July 2002.

116 *Guardian* 25 June 2002.

117 *Morning Star* 22 July 2002. Crow was also still talking to Labour at this point, holding 'clear-the-air talks' with its then general secretary (*Guardian* 19 July 2002).

118 *Mail on Sunday* 21 July 2002.

views he did not believe that the RMT should disaffiliate from the party'.[119]

Prior to this, at the 2002 RMT AGM, Crow gave notice that at the following year's AGM disaffiliation would be debated, and he sent every RMT-sponsored MP a questionnaire, asking a series of questions about their position on privatisation. Delegates at the 2002 conference voted to cut the funding given to Labour by reducing its affiliation from 56,000 to 10,000 members, meaning that its donation fell from £112,000 a year to £20,000 a year.[120] The SSP, then led by Tommy Sheridan, had gained a further five MSPs in the 2003 Scottish Parliament elections, becoming a serious political force for the Left in Scotland and providing a model for how others could organise elsewhere in Britain. It was this and the amicable relationship between Crow and Sheridan that facilitated the RMT's decision at its 2003 AGM to allow branches to affiliate to political parties on the Left other than Labour.[121] Seven branches and the Scottish Regional Council subsequently affiliated to the SSP[122] (in Wales some branches supported Forward Wales, led by the former Labour MP and then Welsh Assembly member, John Marek). But even as this stage, Crow and the RMT did not advocate an 'either or' situation, for they wanted to remain affiliated to Labour *and* to be able to support other parties and candidates.[123] These were primarily the SSP, Plaid Cymru, the Greens, Ken Livingstone and George Galloway.[124] At this stage, it was an open question as to whether the RMT saw its political future as lying outside Labour or whether it was merely and temporarily using the SSP as a ginger group to push Labour to the left. The sense of Labour moving from being social democratic (or democratic socialist), sometimes referred to as 'old' Labour, to a version of neoliberalism (called 'social liberalism') often referred to as 'new' Labour was palpable. It was summed up in the common pronouncement: 'I have not left Labour – Labour has left

119 *Herald* 9 September 2002.

120 *Guardian* 26 June 2002.

121 *Socialist Review* (June 2003) reported: 'At the RMT conference this year, over a dozen branches plus the union's NEC have submitted motions which enable branches and regions to give money to groups like the Scottish Socialist Party, Socialist Alliance, Plaid Cymru or the Greens. Bob Crow has organised a survey and found that 50 of the 52 delegates have been mandated to back the proposals.' A year earlier, the 2002 AGM mandated the CoE to prepare such a rule change for voting upon as well as cutting direct sponsorship of MPs and the number of affiliated members (Berlin 2006: 153, 150).

122 See Gall (2012a: 146). There was some minor opposition to support for the SSP (*Herald* 12 December 2003).

123 *Guardian* 30 June 2003; *Independent* 8 January 2004.

124 *Guardian* 2 July 2003.

me.' In the RMT, Crow articulated this as 'If RMT's continued affiliation to the Labour Party has become controversial, it is the result of the hijacking of the party by a small group of people bent on destroying its working-class roots and pursuing policies opposed by the majority of our members.'[125] The 2003 RMT conference voted by 37 to 13 to halve its annual affiliation fees from £25,000 to £12,500,[126] with Crow saying: 'I think if the Labour party continues the way it is going I cannot honestly see that come five years' time, we will still be in it at all.'[127]

Relations with the Greens in England (led by Caroline Lucas)[128] became more cordial, given its policies on rail and road transport.[129] While the fact that the SSP advocated free public transport and rail renationalisation allowed the RMT to have a suitable political voice in Scotland,[130] it did not resolve the issue in England. The aforementioned dualism partly explains why – along with a sense of defiance and injustice including threatening legal action against expulsion[131] – Crow ensured that the RMT kept sending its cheques for affiliated members to Labour (and it kept sending them back uncashed).[132] Crow argued that the union had not been told which rule it had broken, had been denied the right of natural justice to put its case and had no right of appeal.[133] This led to another cutting quip – he told the Special General Meeting of 6 February 2004 which reaffirmed its 2003 AGM decision (by 42 to 8) that 'even Harold Shipman was given a hearing'.[134] The next day, at the Convention of the

125 *Independent* 8 January 2004.

126 *Independent* 2 July 2003.

127 *Guardian* 2 July 2003.

128 As the first Green MP, she later tweeted upon Crow's death that he 'embodied a bravery, passion & commitment that's rarely seen today'.

129 Crow told delegates at the Green Party's 2002 annual conference: 'If other parties want to denounce us for standing up for the people, then we are going to have to look for a political voice somewhere else'. He stressed the similarities between RMT and Green policies on issues including workers' rights, environmental protection and Iraq (*South Wales Evening Post* 19 September 2002). He voted for Green Party candidates for the London assembly and European Parliament on 10 June 2004 (*Guardian* 2 July 2004).

130 This also included Tommy Sheridan's bill to renationalise the railways in Scotland in May 2006 (see Gall 2012a: 137). However, it was quickly ruled out of order for dealing with reserved (to Westminster) business.

131 *Times* 6 February 2004.

132 *Guardian* 2 July 2004. This carried on subsequently. The sum was £3,000 per quarter. Labour responded by banning Crow from attending its 2003 annual conference. He responded by saying that he would attend as a journalist because he was 'a bona fide member of the National Union of Journalists and editor of the newspaper of the RMT' (*Times* 28 July 2003).

133 *Guardian* 4 February 2004; see also *Independent* 16 March 2004.

134 *Solidarity* 19 February 2004.

Trade Union Left in London, with characteristic bluntness and forceful-ness, he said of 'new' Labour: 'I'd rather see an independent campaigner stick up for the workers' interests than someone with a red rosette stab-bing workers in the back.'[135] He also showed his ability to turn his oppo-nents' arguments against them, telling the Convention:

> They kept telling us we had to abide by rule 2A, which says that everyone must abide by the programme and manifesto of the party ... But I asked, 'Are top-up fees in that manifesto? If it is in the manifesto, are you going to expel the MPs who voted against it? And if it's not in the manifesto, are you going to expel Brown and Blair for bringing top-up fees in?'[136]

Taking concrete steps to resolve practical issues explains why Crow was prepared to win agreement for the RMT to affiliate (along with ASLEF, BFAWU, CWU, FBU and NUM) to the Labour Representation Committee (LRC) which was founded in 2004 by John McDonnell MP and was named after the original LRC of 1900. It worked to spread the socialist message and restore socialist principles within Labour (although its affiliates were not necessarily Labour members).[137] Affiliating to the LRC again indicated that Crow and the RMT could work – and needed to work – with some elements of Labour MPs as part of a multi-pronged political strategy. But the LRC, like the NSSN and TUCG (see below), was insufficient to significantly augment RMT influence or socialist resistance.

For those who believed that not being affiliated to Labour meant being cast into the political wilderness, the RMT took the opportunity to reorganise its parliamentary presence. It had done this originally in 2002 after Crow was elected general secretary, and took further steps in 2004. On a value-for-money basis, the RMT decided only to work with MPs who agreed with, and worked to prosecute, RMT policies and interests, specifically rail renationalisation and state support for the merchant navy. This process saw the ending of the relationship with former member, then deputy prime minister, John Prescott, and spon-sored MP Robin Cook (along with eleven others including former RMT official and deputy chief whip Keith Hill)[138] and the beginnings of a new

---

135 'The awkward squad and the rank-and-file', *Labournet* 7 February 2004, http://www.labournet.net/ukunion/0402/satul01.html.

136 *Socialist Worker* 14 February 2004.

137 Respect, founded in 2004 and led by George Galloway, did not receive backing from the RMT (see also Berlin 2006: 164) although Crow was reported to have supported it initially (*Sunday Times* 23 November 2003), having said that Galloway was 'a massive loss' to Labour following his expulsion: 'He has been a principled working class fighter all his life, an excellent MP and trade unionist who made a principled stand against the war' (*Telegraph* 24 October 2003).

138 This also included the Crewe and Nantwich MP, Gwyneth Dunwoody

relationship with new Labour MPs, most of which were members of the Socialist Campaign Group.[139] The RMT had to vigorously defend its right to act and spend its money how it saw fit, with Crow writing to the *New Statesman*, saying:

> At no time has the RMT sought to impose a loyalty oath on its parliamentary group, or to dictate how MPs vote. To suggest that cutting our funding [to Labour] was a 'deliberate insult' to anyone is insulting to the delegates who voted unanimously to reduce our affiliation base. Of our 60,000 members, only 2,000 are 'individual' Labour Party members – but the vast majority pay the political levy, and expect their cash to be spent on furthering their interests.[140]

He also wrote to the *Independent*:

> Presumably, Patricia Hewitt had not heard the Speaker [Michael Martin's] statement to the House of Commons when she made her allegations about my union. [He stated that] he had found no evidence to refer RMT to the Standards and Privileges Committee. We have never made 'unacceptable demands upon MPs' … The new members of our parliamentary campaigning group have neither asked for nor received any money. Our recent AGM did decide to put money it would otherwise have paid to constituency parties into a political campaigning fund.[141]

(*Stoke Sentinel* 27 June 2002), who had previously been in agreement with the RMT and worked with it in her capacity as chair of the House of Commons' Transport Committee (1997–2008). The RMT also donated £1,500 to a website for Dunwoody as she was a 'critic of privatisation' (*Guardian* 1 March 2002). Indeed, the *Telegraph* (16 February 2002) reported that: 'Gwyneth Dunwoody MP is his role model'. Upon her death, Crow commented: 'Transport workers have lost a good and true friend in Gwyneth Dunwoody … [she] was a straight-talking, no-nonsense and fearless individual whose powerful and principled leadership of the Transport Select Committee helped to expose the utter failure of transport privatisation. [She] was her own woman who would always look you in the eye, and regardless of differences she had an unswerving loyalty to the Labour movement' (RMT press release, 18 April 2008). At this point, Labour MPs gaining the RMT endorsement were Diane Abbott, Joe Benton, Harold Best, Helen Clark, Ann Cryer, Brian Donohoe, Bill Etherington, David Hamilton, Alice Mahon, John McDonnell, Jon Trickett and Robert Wareing. MPs from whom RMT support was withdrawn were John Prescott, Gwyneth Dunwoody, Keith Hill, Robin Cook, Hugh Bayley, Ivan Henderson, John Hepple, Ian Lucas, Tam Dalyell, Tom Watson, Frank Dobson and Donald Anderson (*The Independent* 26 June 2002). Crow noted that the new RMT-supporting MPs 'had already tabled a motion opposing Tube privatisation, which was more than the likes of Mr Prescott had done in five years of government' (*Morning Star* 26 June 2002). Robin Cook subsequently joined ASLEF 'in a move which asserts his old Labour credentials' (*Sunday Mail* 11 August 2002), while Prescott joined Amicus (*Independent* 19 July 2004).

139 *Guardian* 10 April 2002.
140 *New Statesman* 15 July 2002.
141 *Independent* 13 July 2002.

Looking back on the allegation of being cast into the political wilderness, Crow argued:

> Nearly a decade on nothing could be further from the truth. By freeing ourselves from the shackles of automatic Labour support, RMT's political influence is thriving with political groups established in the British, Scottish and Welsh parliaments and assemblies that involve a base of supportive Labour representatives, Greens and SNP. The condition for joining is that elected members must sign up to the core political priorities laid down by the union.[142]

The relationship with Prescott took a particular turn after the RMT sought to end his tenancy of a flat on a peppercorn rent in an RMT building in south-west London.[143] The process was lengthy, leading to one of Crow's best witticisms: 'Reclaim the Labour Party? We can't even reclaim our flat!' at the aforementioned Socialist Campaign Group conference.[144] The reorganised parliamentary group of Labour MPs was led by John McDonnell and operated by putting down early day motions, asking questions in the House, lobbying and hosting meetings. By the time of Crow's death, it numbered 21 and became a model for how the FBU and PCS unions organised their parliamentary groups.[145] And, as Crow put it: 'We have more MPs in our parliamentary group since we've been outside the Labour Party than when we were in it. So it hasn't done us any harm.'[146]

Some on the Left expected – and hoped – that other unions would follow the RMT in breaking with Labour (especially after the FBU disaffiliated in 2004). They were wrong because both the RMT and FBU cases had specific roots that were not generalisable.[147] So while the anger

---

142 Crow (2013b).

143 The *Guardian* (2 July 2002) reported that: '[the] union has lodged a tribunal application to raise the [rental] rates after leaders discovered it is paying £60,000 a year on maintenance yet collecting just £34,000 in rent', and that while Prescott was paying £220 per month, the monthly rental value of the flat was £1600.

144 The *Guardian* (11 November 2003) reported that: '[Prescott has] abandoned his legal fight to retain possession of a two bedroom London flat provided for him by his union since 1970'.

145 The official RMT historian observed that the NUR parliamentary group was large and effective (Berlin 2006: 29–30). An RMT Scottish parliamentary group was established in 2010, with former RMT member Ann Henderson as the union's parliamentary liaison officer until 2008. She noted in this regard that 'Bob was quick to take all the political opportunities that came along'.

146 *Socialist Worker* 17 September 2005.

147 Instead, many of the unions that chose not to disaffiliate reduced the number of members they affiliated to. While this reduced the source of financial support, these same unions often gave one-off donations to Labour, so that the net effect was not as dramatic as it may have at first seemed. See also McIlroy (2011: 93; 2012: 253–254).

felt by both unions was patently anti-'new' Labour, in which there were many particular components like the Iraq invasion, there were specific dynamics involved: Labour's continued refusal to countenance rail rena-tionalisation and its handling of the 2002–03 fire brigade strikes (where a deal to settle the dispute was deliberately scuppered by Labour), respectively.[148] For the RMT, the sense of injustice was more keenly felt as its first forerunner, the Amalgamated Society of Railway Servants, was a prime mover in establishing the original Labour Representation Committee which led to the creation of the Labour Party. The sense of injustice was further compounded as it became clear that privatisation was more costly to the public purse than public ownership had been. The bravery of facing expulsion was further emphasised by the RMT affiliating to other political parties (unlike the FBU). There were internal RMT left-wing critics of the move – Alliance for Workers' Liberty members claimed that:

> Bob Crow's policy amounts to a variant of 'syndicalism', the doctrine that holds that trade-union action alone is enough to win socialism and the emancipation of the working class, without the systematic building also of an authentically working-class political party. Worse, it is 'single-union' syndicalism ... Bob Crow has directed the RMT's political affairs as if the RMT can go it alone, conducting its own industrial action, sponsoring various election candidates here and there, with scarcely any reference to other unions.[149]

Relations with Tony Blair

The relationship of Crow with Tony Blair continued to be a fractious one. While the divorce was messy, the aftermath was not much better. Crow's overall assessment was that 'He squandered a massive landslide from an electorate hungry for change, poured billions of public pounds into private pockets and accelerated the growing gap between rich and poor.'[150] At the 2006 TUC congress, and holding a 'Time to go now' placard, Crow led a walkout of RMT delegates when Blair spoke.[151] His rationale was 'What is the point of listening to someone when you can't believe a word they say? In opposition, Blair promised us a publicly owned railway, an ethical foreign policy and fair labour laws. He has delivered privatisation, illegal wars and the boast that Britain maintains

148 See Seifert and Sibley (2005).
149 'Rail Unions in Politics: the Future', 28 June 2004, http://www.workersliberty.org/story/2004/06/27/rail-unions-politics-future.
150 *Financial Times* 8 September 2004.
151 *Guardian* 13 September 2006.

the harshest anti-union legislation in western Europe'; 'Why should we sit down with someone who threw us out of the Labour Party?'[152] When Blair published his autobiography in 2010, Crow's response was typically critical:

> This book is the predictable wallowing in self-pity and self-promotion of a Labour leader who squandered a golden opportunity to tackle the inequalities in our society. Blair could have taken the side of millions of working people against the greed and corruption of the bankers and speculators. Instead he sided with the rich and his legacy will always be of a war-monger whose instincts are to follow the trail of cash.[153]

Conclusion

Former deputy Labour leader and self-proclaimed 'moderate social democrat' Roy Hattersley, in 2002, said that Crow showed 'every sign of becoming a major media celebrity before the year is out', predicting that he would make 'regular appearances on the [Radio 4] *Today* programme and *The World at One*'. But he also predicted that 'he will become the Conservative Party's favourite working-class hero'.[154] On all counts, Hattersley was proven right. By the end of his first term of office, Crow had become thoroughly well known for his regular and consistent – if predictable – pronouncements.[155] But this predictability was a virtue. The reasons for Crow's success and notoriety are not hard to find. He had already established with his politics, personality and members' potential power that he would become a leading figure in the union movement – it was patent strength in these areas when set against the relative weakness in these areas of many other union leaders that allowed Crow to flourish. But it was also because, when Labour endorsed neoliberalism, the Tories could gleefully attack Crow and the RMT. By ceding so much ground, Labour emboldened the Tories, which made being an outspoken and defiant left-wing union leader much harder. Under Crow's leadership, the RMT broke with Labour to adopt a multi-pronged political strategy of working with Labour MPs in its parliamentary group and a number of other left-wing forces.

152 *Independent* 12, 13 September 2006, respectively.
153 *Independent* 2 September 2010.
154 *Times* 12 September 2002. Labour MP Ian McCartney weighed in with the same line: 'The thing about Bob Crow is if he wasn't around, the Tories would have to invent him' (*Scotsman* 2 December 2002).
155 Being interviewed regularly on Radio 4's *Today* and *PM* programmes was important, as quite apart from the size of the audiences, the programmes helped set the news agenda of television and newspapers.

This showed more political nuance and acumen than was commonly recognised as well as two other factors – the continuing hold of labourism within the RMT and political necessity because of the radical Left's weakness.

Ironically, it was *The Times* that recognised Crow's industrial prowess: 'Grim throwback to Seventies confrontation he may be, but what an effective trade union boss: £31,000 for driving [on] the Tubes.'[156] His old adversary the *Evening Standard* added: 'Bob Crow's Tube workers have shown that militancy pays.'[157] The *Guardian* also noted that 'the confrontational tactics of Bob Crow's RMT ... [have] delivered some successes for his members'.[158] Unjum Mirza recalled that 'Bob's insistence [was] we're not just awkward, we deliver'.[159] Although Crow said his greatest negotiating triumph came in 2001 in gaining a long-term job security agreement on the Underground, what was achieved in further reducing the working week for these workers in 2004 was also noteworthy.[160] By the end of his first term of office, Crow had established himself a key figure in the wider union movement as well as on the radical Left.

156 *Times* 21 December 2002.
157 *Evening Standard* 14 November 2002.
158 *Guardian* 8 December 2005.
159 Unjum Mirza, email correspondence.
160 This was not without some controversy, as a planned strike was called off despite the London Regional Council setting a date. The strike was called off after what Crow said was an indication that the employer was prepared to 'negotiate seriously on all of our aspirations on pay and conditions' (*Solidarity* 10 June 2004).

4. Second term as general secretary

On 7 December 2006, Crow was returned unopposed for a further five-year term of office. In the process, he received nominations from 131 of the union's 225 branches, indicating the strength of his support and that the right wing of the union was in no position to challenge him (as had happened in ASLEF, with Mick Rix being defeated after serving one term of office). Crow began his second term in February 2007. Then president Tony Donaghey commented:

> In all my 46 years' membership I can never remember a time when the union was so united and so focused on the twin tasks of organising to win at the workplace and campaigning vigorously for a publicly owned, publicly funded and accountable integrated transport network ... Bob has had the nerve to stand up without compromise for the rights and interests of RMT members and working people in general, and for that he has been vilified by the right-wing media – but he has kept every promise he made to the members.[1]

Donaghey also ventured that 'the 100,000 [members] benchmark is now well within our sights'.[2] Crow himself said: 'I am grateful [members] have given me the honour of serving a second term. The priorities remain: fight for jobs and better pay and conditions at work and continue building RMT membership, campaign for public transport to be returned to the public sector, and fight for trade-union rights fit for the 21st century.'[3] Crow's second term of office indicated that he had reached a peak – on which he would continue – in terms of dominating the union with his personality, political authority and track record.

European Union

The RMT had a longstanding policy of leaving the EU[4] so Crow happily continued his and the RMT's attacks on the EU as a bosses' club and

---

1 RMT press release, 7 December 2006.
2 *RMT News* January 2007.
3 RMT press release, 7 December 2006.
4 For example, Gordon Martin, Regional Organiser for Scotland, stated that:

the vanguard of neoliberalism, turning public services into 'cash cows to exploit in the pursuit of profit'.[5] This was not just in words but also in deeds, for at the 2007 TUC congress he moved the RMT's motion for the TUC to back a call for a referendum and campaign for a 'no' vote. He argued that without a referendum there would be 'a further transfer of power to unelected mandarins in Brussels and undermine democratic advances fought for by working people over the centuries ... If a referendum is good enough for the people of Ireland it should be good enough for the people of Britain.'[6] The motion was defeated and represented something of a reversal of fortunes compared to the TUC 2004 congress, when Crow and the RMT played a role in establishing the position that the TUC would not support a 'yes' vote in a referendum on the European constitution.[7] Although he kept up his attack on the EU at the TUC and elsewhere, he began to take other concrete steps to prosecute his criticism in the form of the No2EU electoral initiative (see below). Under Crow, the RMT was a frequent organiser and attender of demonstrations in Brussels and Strasbourg against EU neoliberalism, and the RMT affiliated to the longstanding Campaign against Euro-federalism and helped launch Trade Unionists against the EU Constitution in 2004.[8] Some in the union movement and on the Left accused Crow of covertly succumbing to British nationalism – particularly with regard to supporting 'British' industry and especially train-building capacity – as a result of not just his stance on the EU but also his call for state protectionism.[9] In this regard, he stated in 2007: 'Other countries in Europe protect their manufacturing industries and there is no reason why Britain cannot do so';[10] in 2011 he said: 'This act of political sabotage to a key element of the remaining UK manufacturing base could leave the nation that gave the world the railways building nothing but a few basic components';[11] 'The fight to defend train building in the nation

---

'RMT policy since 1979 has been one of leaving the EU' (*Morning Star* 28 June 2016).

5 *RMT News* July 2008.

6 *Times* 13 September 2007.

7 *Telegraph* 16 September 2004.

8 See http://www.labournet.net/ukunion/0502/tuaeuc1.html (27 February 2005). This organisation became Trade Unionists against the EU.

9 Such accusations could continue to be levelled at the RMT since Crow's death, with regard to the RMT's response to Arriva trains placing an order for rolling stock with a Spanish company (see *Guardian* 23 January 2016; *Morning Star* 24 May 2016). It should be noted that unions such as Unite and the GMB have also advocated such a 'buy British' policy.

10 *Guardian* 17 November 2007.

11 *Guardian* 5 July 2011.

that gave the railways to the world, in the teeth of government inaction and EU diktat, remains well and truly on.'[12] He continued to make such statements when responding to developments.[13] He rebutted the 'little Englander' tag because, for him, it was a matter of retaining jobs, skills and capacity for those who lived and worked in Britain in order to maintain wealth generation and control over a key part of the economy, namely, the means of production of a rail transport infrastructure. This could hardly be characterised as 'British jobs for British workers' as then Prime Minister, Gordon Brown, stated in 2009, especially when it was an attack on both domestic and EU forces of neoliberalism.[14]

Further political initiatives

Under Crow's leadership, the RMT took a number of important political initiatives. Beginning with a series of conferences on the 'Crisis of Working Class Representation' from early 2006, three organisations were formed. The first of these was the National Shop Stewards' Network (NSSN) in 2007, the second was the No2EU political party in 2009 and the third was the Trade Union and Socialist Coalition (TUSC) in 2010.[15] All three stemmed from the analysis propounded by Crow that Labour no longer represented either the interests of working-class people or socialism. Even though the RMT supported John McDonnell's campaign for the Labour leadership,[16] Crow told the RMT 2007 AGM: 'Any hope of the Labour Party working for workers is dead, finished, over. I think all of you who are staying in the Labour Party are just giving credibility to it.'[17] Thus, steps had to be taken to establish a new political vehicle for workers because none of the existing left-wing

12 *Guardian* 6 September 2011.

13 One of his last comments on this matter was 'This is basically Siemens running up the white flag and admitting that if the dice aren't well and truly loaded in their favour, then they aren't interested. There is now no excuse for the Crossrail fleet not to be built in Britain, guaranteeing the future of train building in the nation that gave the railways to the world' (*Independent* 6 July 2013).

14 However, the SWP in its 2013 *Pre-conference Bulletin 1* (p. 69) accused Crow of advocating a form of 'national socialism'.

15 Previously, the Socialist Party had established the Campaign for a New Workers' Party in 2005 but it had failed to reach out to those beyond its own membership. It was wound up in 2009 and the broader vehicle of TUSC was established with the support of leading RMT activists. Nonetheless, Crow identified more with the Socialist Party than any other party once he became general secretary. In addition to his involvement with TUSC, he spurned the Convention of the Left initiative of the late 2000s (unlike Serwotka and Wrack).

16 *RMT News* May 2007.

17 In Darlington (2014b: 77).

political parties were either large enough or credible enough to do the job. For example, the SSP had split and imploded in 2006 over Tommy Sheridan's lies over his private life, with none of its MSPs returned in the 2007 Scottish Parliament elections.[18]

The 'Crisis of Working Class Representation' conference on 21 January 2006 saw some 300 attendees, most of them union activists, pack the Small Hall in central London's Friends Meeting House, while around 100 were turned away due to seating limitations. The conference took place after the RMT's AGM twice voted for such an event following its expulsion from Labour for supporting the SSP.[19] There were no resolutions to be debated or passed but there were seven platform speakers including Crow; John McDonnell; SSP convenor Colin Fox MSP; Jean Lambert, Green MEP; then Socialist Party councillor and former Labour MP, Dave Nellist; John Marek; and Liz Greene, SLP spokesperson. Tony Benn and Matt Wrack sent their apologies. George Galloway was not invited.[20] Crow put forward the idea of a 'new national shop stewards movement' as central to reversing union decline and being a prerequisite for establishing a new workers' party. *RMT News* reported:

> Rather than immediately setting up a new party, Bob said that what was needed now was 'a new national shop stewards' movement to strengthen popular demands of the labour movement. We've all got to get together to build these trade union workplace structures to put working-class policies in place. Then, we can take this process forward for a political party that can represent working men and women' Bob said.[21]

From the chair, Tony Donaghey pledged that the CoE would receive a thorough report of the day without promising any specific action. Subsequently, the NSSN was founded at a conference called by the RMT on 7 July 2007, with another that year to flesh out the idea.

18 In late October 2006, the RMT ended its affiliation to the SSP, with Crow saying: 'The atmosphere within [the SSP] is no longer conducive to comradeship and it is no longer in our members' interests to remain affiliated.' Crow supported the campaign to defend Sheridan from News International, with Colin Fox, the SSP leader, saying, 'The fact is that the RMT did not support the party's position regarding Tommy Sheridan's court case. I believe that we were entirely right and that subsequent events have entirely vindicated us on this' (*Times* 28 October 2006). This resulted in a loss of income to the SSP of around £10,000 annually in fees and donations. However, the RMT did not then affiliate to Sheridan's Solidarity party.

19 The original motion put to the first AGM came from the Bristol Rail branch.

20 Crow had been critical of Respect for being more communally than class based (see *Socialism and Left Unity – A critique of the Socialist Workers Party*, Socialist Party, 2008). The RMT did not support Respect even though a small number of branches did.

21 *RMT News* February 2006.

The NSSN sought to support and organise workers in a common fight against employers (without interfering in individual unions' affairs). It gained official support from the RMT, PCS, CWU, FBU, NUM, NUJ, POA, NAPO and BFAWU unions. At its founding conference, Crow closed proceedings by arguing that an 'alternative political party' was also needed and that the RMT might initiate 'a little political party' to contest the London mayoral and assembly elections, with this being a step towards a new workers' party in a few years' time. A year later, at the second Campaign for a New Workers' Party conference, organised by the Socialist Party in June 2008, Crow reiterated his call: 'What our members don't want to see is another Respect or Socialist Labour Party. They want to see a political party and we've got to move towards it.'[22] By his reference to Respect and the Socialist Labour Party, he meant a party dominated by one group and without roots among organised workers.

The NSSN held annual regional and national conferences, published weekly email newsletters and organised solidarity protests and lobbies. However, its challenges were several. First, it attracted support from the very unions that were most inclined to support and encourage their members to fight back – so quite what it added was unclear – and not from those that were seen as less likely to do so. Related to this, it explicitly pledged not to criticise existing unions, this being the price of gaining their official backing. Second, the NSSN never became a network of shop stewards because not only had their ranks become much depleted since the 1980s, but the network did not operate on the basis of credentials. In other words, it was open to anyone who supported its aims regardless of whether they held office. Third, strike activity (measured by days not worked per 1,000 workers, and excepting 2011) fell almost continuously, showing no signs of moving away from a period of very low levels. Fourth, the NSSN had rivals, primarily the SWP's successive initiatives (Organising for Fighting Unions (OFFU), Right to Work (RtW) and Unite the Resistance (UtR)). Such problems of sectarianism were compounded when in 2011 the NSSN suffered a split as a result of the Socialist Party majority insisting that the NSSN launch its own – and thus another – anti-cuts organisation (in addition to the Peoples' Charter, the Coalition of Resistance and others). This occasioned criticism from Crow.[23] Thus, the sense that the NSSN could

---

22 'Britain: Union leaders stifle growing militancy of London Underground workers', World Socialist website, 15 September 2008, https://www.wsws.org/en/articles/2008/09/tube-s15.html.
23 See *The Socialist* 12 January 2011.

act independently of unions and effectively so in the way the first shop stewards' movement had was never achieved. In practice, the NSSN existed as a ginger group, mostly calling upon others to do things and not being able to do these things itself. It was then displaced on the anti-austerity front by the People's Assembly against Austerity from 2013. All this must have been of great frustration to Crow and the RMT given the commitment, effort and resources they had put into the NSSN. Yet Crow remained upbeat, for he understood that any manifest revival had to take place across the whole union movement, with any advances the RMT made being ultimately limited by the poor health of the overall union movement.

It was for such reasons that Crow's – and thus the RMT's – political perspective also required action on the political front. A second conference on the 'Crisis of Working Class Representation' was held at the (London) Friends' Meeting House on 10 January 2009 with Crow speaking alongside Serwotka, McDonnell and the POA general secretary, Brian Caton; a third was held on 7 November 2009 with Crow again speaking alongside Caton, Wrack, then CWU deputy general secretary Dave Ward, and Jeremy Corbyn. Both conferences were, like the first, 'non-binding and non-resolution based ... [to] discuss the options for fighting back'.[24] Crow told the second conference:

> Labour is finished. It's over. Some say that the party can still be changed, but Labour can't be changed. Maybe there will have to be a new political party for workers' sometime down the road ... Let's go ahead with a People's Charter and win over the hearts and minds of workers to ensure better political representation for our class.[25]

The beginning of this new political formation was the founding of the No2EU electoral alliance in early 2009. Its slogan in the 2009 European elections was 'Yes to democracy', but it changed to 'Yes to workers' rights' in the 2014 European elections. No2EU was led by Crow (as convenor) and backed by the RMT,[26] the Communist Party of Britain, the Socialist Party and Solidarity among others.[27] The specific reason for its creation for the RMT was the EU's spearheading of neoliberalisation, namely privatisation and deregulation of public services. This affected transport

---

24 *RMT News* October 2009.
25 *RMT News* February 2009.
26 The 2009 AGM in June endorsed No2EU by 63 votes to nil, with three abstentions (*RMT News* July 2009).
27 On behalf of Crow, Brian Denny visited Tony Benn at his house to try to persuade him to stand as a candidate for No2EU (Benn 2013: 216–217). Benn toyed with the idea but rejected it, being ultimately a 'Labour man'.

in terms of transferring what still remained in the public sector and militating against returning privatised elements to the public sector. Allied to this were the general encroachment of market forces and the removal of the ability to regulate labour markets in order to protect workers. Crow's politics from his Communist Party days also took him in the direction of rejecting the EU as capable of offering social protection because it had become, he believed, a club for bosses. Writing in 2012, he said:

> The Social Europe agenda was always a smoke screen to fool the organised working class that we had something in common with big business. We didn't then [in the late 1980s/early 1990s] and we don't today when unelected EU institutions, directly representing Europe's biggest banks, are removing elected governments and imposing mass unemployment, social dumping and unending austerity ...[28]

Just before he died, he commented:

> No2EU wants to see a different Europe – one made up of democratic states that value public services and does not offer them to profiteers; states that do not put the interests of big business above that of ordinary people. We believe that EU structures and rules make this impossible.[29]

On the euro, he outlined the same basic position: '[it] will mean more privatisation, the destruction of our social services and an end to democratic control over our own economy – and ... it will result in massive industrial unrest'.[30] The position of No2EU was to contest seats but not take them up if elected, since it believed that the parliament was a talking shop and a gravy train, with the seat of power residing in the European Commission.

On its first electoral outing in 2009, No2EU received just 153,236 votes (1%) and finished eleventh behind the SLP. Crow headed the London list while fellow RMT officials and officers Craig Johnston, Brian Denny, Peter Pinkney and Alex Gordon stood for other regions, bringing the total number of RMT candidates to ten out of 69 overall.[31] Crow's assessment was:

28 Crow (2012b: 4).

29 *Morning Star* 6 March 2014.

30 *Evening Standard* 10 September 2002. Later, he wrote in the *Guardian* (18 May 2013): 'But governments do not have to carry out such EU policies: they could carry out measures on behalf of those who elect them. That means having democratic control over capital flows, our borders and the future of our economy for the benefit of everyone ... The only rational course is to leave the EU so elected governments regain the democratic power to decide matters on behalf of the people they serve.'

31 *RMT News* May 2009. The figure of 66 candidates was used in *RMT News* (June 2009).

We came into the European election just a few weeks before polling day on the basis that someone had to raise the banner for the Euro-sceptic left. Despite a media blackout and a campaign run solely on the energy and commitment of our local activists, we got over 150,000 votes. In some areas of the country No2EU was the only force on the streets directly challenging the BNP. I don't regret for a moment that we stood and I am proud of what we achieved, and we have also sparked off a debate on the future of working-class representation in the wake of the collapse of New Labour.[32]

He then stated: 'This campaign will continue and must reach out to other organisations and unions to decide the best way forward.'[33] Yet after the election, activity dwindled and No2EU was statutorily de-registered by the Electoral Commission on 2 November 2010, being re-registered on 16 October 2013. Crow was again to head its London list in 2014, with Brian Denny and Alex Gordon also standing, and with the RMT donating £35,000.[34] The results were abysmal. In London, just 3,804 votes (0.17%) were secured, nearly 14,000 less than in 2009, while nationally just 31,757 votes (0.2%) were gained. Standing in only seven of the twelve regions was a further indication of weakness. No2EU did not become 'a major political operation that will challenge both the neoliberal, pro-boss agenda of the EU and the cynical opportunism of UKIP head on' as Crow had prophesied.[35] Overall, the far Left (including No2EU) secured just 48,121 votes (0.29%), some 292,684 votes fewer than in 2009. The contraction in No2EU support reflected much more than the death of its star advocate and candidate. No2EU had failed to become a left-wing UKIP, that is, a new and sizeable popular political force. One RMT activist believed that 'the verdict must be that this has been a failure'.[36] Its failure was attributed by some on the Left to attacking the wrong target, namely the EU, and not capitalism, the Tories and austerity, because the latter were of more immediate relevance to workers.[37]

Meanwhile, in 2009, Crow provided his assessment of the outcome of the tumultuous political events of 2003–04:

32 *Independent* 29 June 2009.
33 *RMT News* June 2009.
34 *Times* 20 February 2014.
35 Crow (2013b).
36 Jeff Slee, then secretary, RMT South East Regional Council, in 'Bob Crow – a great trade unionist', 26 March 2014, https://labourbriefing1.wordpress.com/2014/03/26/bob-crow-a-great-trade-unionist/.
37 Nonetheless, the RMT affirmed its position of campaigning for a 'no' vote regarding Britain's continued EU membership at its 2015 AGM, stating its wish to be part of a progressive alliance arguing for a 'no' vote (*The Socialist* 30 September 2015).

Since we've been disaffiliated, there's not been one resolution from any branch to re-affiliate. Not one. In fact, there would be uproar if someone mentioned re-affiliation. We have doubled the MPs through the new representation [TUCG] group with the NUJ and FBU. We have more representation than we did before. I'm not saying we get listened to more – we don't. Nor does any other union.[38]

But this situation was not sufficient, so the third political project, TUSC, was launched for the 2010 general election on 12 January 2010, as a result of the agreement between leading RMT members (like Crow and Alex Gordon) and the Socialist Party. Following on the launch of No2EU and many meetings throughout 2009, TUSC was set up as a domestic electoral vehicle comprising a similar set of participating organisations (save for the Communist Party).[39] Early on in the discussions to form TUSC, Crow said: 'If we don't believe that any of the candidates are [any] good, there may be an alliance that comes together. We would be putting up policies that we believe people want. What [party] our members vote for is their democratic right, but certainly we can't just sit back and say vote Labour.'[40] However, there was a limit to what Crow could do, as 'my [union's] rules restrict me from standing at a general election'.[41] Instead, he campaigned for TUSC and spoke at its public meetings, saying: 'I would like to see taxes go up massively for the rich, I'd abolish all private education and all private medical care. I would do away with the Royal Family – that's not to say they'd be executed but why should those people have a privileged place in society?'[42] The RMT decided not to formally back TUSC in January 2010 for that year's general election but it subsequently supported 20 TUSC candidates upon receipt of local RMT branch requests (along with 17 Labour candidates).[43] Then in 2012 and 2013, the RMT endorsed TUSC at its AGMs, and took seven positions on TUSC's steering committee out

38 *Times* 9 May 2009.

39 Crow addressed several of the rallies of the Socialist Party's Campaign for a New Workers' Party. He also spoke at the Socialist Party's Socialism conferences, the last one being held in November 2013. One of his first public speaking engagements after becoming general secretary was to speak at the Socialist Party's 2002 national conference.

40 *Times* 12 September 2009.

41 *Times* 12 September 2009. Despite this statement, 'At the second ever meeting of the TUSC steering committee, in January 2010, Crow raised the question whether he should stand for TUSC in Barking against the British National Party's Nick Griffin in the coming general election' (*Socialism Today* December–January 2009–10, 184).

42 *Times* 12 September 2009.

43 *RMT News* March 2010.

of just over twenty places.[44] Although TUSC was promoted and sup-ported in the April 2010 edition of *RMT News*, no mention was made of its performance in the general election in subsequent editions. Crow's analysis of its 42 candidates receiving just 15,500 votes (0.1%), with no deposits saved, was:

> [It] is not the answer for everything that we need to do as a movement to resist the austerity measures that will come from this Tory-Liberal government ... But in my opinion, speaking in a personal capacity, TUSC should carry on, it should stand in future elections, and it should be at the forefront of anti-cuts campaigning as well. The votes for TUSC candidates were small on this occasion ... and a report will be presented to the RMT's annual general meeting listing the votes of all RMT-endorsed candidates. But I'm looking forward to having the argument with those who say the unions shouldn't be involved with election campaigns that get small votes. When do you start to offer an alternative? And what's the alternative if you don't stand, other than to back a New Labour party that has held down the working class in the interests of capital for 13 years?[45]

By May 2013, 100,000 votes had been secured in the 2010 gen-eral election, the 2011, 2012 and 2013 council elections and various by-elections and mayoral elections. In the 2014 council elections, 54 RMT members were candidates in TUSC's biggest campaign, with 561 candidates standing, gaining 64,098 votes.[46] But in the 2015 general election, when it put up 135 candidates, giving it entitlement to a party political broadcast, TUSC received just 36,420 votes.[47] In local council elections in May 2015, it put up 613 candidates, gaining 78,677 votes.

---

44 Prior to this, Crow sat on the TUSC national steering committee in a personal capacity. As of February 2013, the TUSC national steering committee comprised Crow, CoE members Daren Ireland, Sean Hoyle, Darren Procter, Steve Skelly and Sean McGowan; representatives from the Socialist Party, the SWP and the Independent Socialist Network; and, in a personal capacity, Steve Gillan, POA general secretary, Chris Baugh, PCS AGS, Joe Simpson, POA AGS, John McInally, PCS vice-president, Ian Leahair, FBU National Executive, Nina Franklin, ex-NUT president, Brian Caton, ex-POA general secretary, councillor Michael Lavalette and Nick Wrack. As of July 2013, the TUSC national steering committee comprised the same members plus councillors Keith Morrell and Don Thomas. Sean Hoyle was elected to be RMT president 2016–18 on the basis of support for TUSC.

45 *The Socialist* 16 June 2010.

46 These ranged from an AGS (Steve Hedley) through to regional council officers, branch secretaries, industrial reps and workplace activists. Yet the tone of Gordon and Upchurch's (2012: 262) assessment was still correct when they stressed that 'only a minority of RMT branches' were involved.

47 This number of votes was fewer than the Socialist Alliance (57,304, 0.2% of the vote with 98 candidates) and the Socialist Labour Party (57,497, 0.2% with 114 candidates) gained in the 2001 general election.

In the general election, 'one in twelve' candidates were members of the RMT.[48] This brought the total number of votes cast for TUSC to 'around 300,000' since its creation.[49] In the 2016 devolved assembly/ parliament and local elections, its 302 candidates secured 43,309 votes.[50]

Along the way, a handful of councillors were elected in the likes of Preston, Fleetwood, Maltby and Southampton.[51] While the RMT's involvement with TUSC was of a more advanced (socialist) nature than the PCS's 'Make your vote count' campaign[52] and Unite's political strategy of getting members selected as Labour parliamentary candidates,[53] TUSC failed to make a breakthrough to become a credible and popular force as the SSP and Respect had once been (albeit for short-lived periods). Clearly, Crow and the RMT were of insufficient political weight to break TUSC out of its marginalisation. TUSC represented a Catch-22 situation whereby until more unions joined, it would not become credible – but it would not become credible until more unions joined. Within TUSC, the RMT in the figure of Crow was a major force in determining its policies. This was not just because of Crow's forceful personality and the RMT being the only union affiliate but also because the RMT had seven seats on the steering committee, which operated 'by consensus', that is, without using votes.[54] Thus, Hannah Sell, Socialist Party deputy general secretary, recalled that TUSC was 'a coalition' and its political platform was a 'compromise'; hence 'Bob Crow didn't agree

48 TUSC (2015) 'Elections 2015: The TUSC results', 15 May. TUSC received a message of support on 27 April 2015 from David Wallis, Crow's cousin and RMT London Taxi branch member, saying he 'would be proud to know that you are all fighting for a democratic socialist society run in the interests of working class people … I have a picture at my front door of Bob. It's a copy of a portrait that was present at his funeral. I look at this when leaving the house every day which inspires me to be strong and fight for what we believe in. I hope the memory of Bob has the same effect for you all. I would like to wish you all the best and hope to meet some of you in the future. Let's have one last hard push for the late great Bob Crow.'

49 *The Socialist* 2 September 2015.

50 *The Socialist* 11 May 2016.

51 Many were existing councillors who left Labour and stood as TUSC-endorsed candidates, indicating that their pre-existing profile and personal appeal were crucial to their re-election.

52 Although the PCS had a policy to allow it to put up and back anti-cuts candidates, it did not do so (see also McIlroy 2014).

53 The target was 41 selected candidates as per its political strategy of 2011 (see http://www.unitetheunion.org/uploaded/documents/(JN4673)%20Unite%20 A5%20Political%20Strategy11-12984.pdf).

54 See 'How TUSC functions', http://www.tusc.org.uk/16861/14-11-13/How-TUSC-Functions.

[with an open borders policy]', with the effect that TUSC policy was not opposed to all immigration controls.[55]

While not part of the three initiatives authored by the RMT, under Crow the union was also a founding member in 2008 of the Trade Union Co-ordinating Group (TUCG). Now comprising ten left-wing, often smaller, unions (BFAWU, FBU, NAPO, NUJ, NUT, PCS, POA, RMT, UCU and URTU), it coordinates campaigning activities in Parliament and beyond through its chair, John McDonnell MP. The group lobbied on its key issues and worked alongside supportive MPs on a cross-party basis with the specific purpose of promoting its unions' policy objectives. One of these was the Trade Union Freedom Bill, which sought to repeal many of the anti-union laws. However, the TUCG remained a marginal player within the union movement for it was not able to form a counter-weight to the likes of Unite and UNISON in order to further a left-wing agenda over and above the activities of its own affiliates such as the FBU, PCS and RMT.

These same political instincts led Crow and the RMT to co-found the People's Charter for Change in early 2009. Along with the CWU, FBU, PCS, NUT, NUJ, BFAWU, POA and UCU unions, the RMT launched 'a set of six policy priorities [which] will resonate among millions of people who face the harsh realities of the present economic crisis, and which will help build a popular movement to support the new agenda'.[56] The charter called for a new model for the finance industry, with priority given to investment for new jobs and green technology, and to protecting existing jobs; public ownership and ending privatisation; and building new affordable social housing, among other measures. While it had success in gaining support from unions, it never attained the wider support that the People's Assembly did (see below). More importantly, it was unable – like the People's Assembly, Coalition of Resistance, Unite the Resistance and other such initiatives – to either increase popular resistance or unite existing struggles into a singular movement where the whole was greater than the sum of the parts.

Although there was criticism from established left-wing groups that Crow was too slow to act,[57] in all three initiatives Crow did not let the experience of past industrial and political retreats stop him from moving forward, and neither did he make himself beholden to other union lead-

55 *Weekly Worker* 29 January 2015.

56 *Guardian* 11 March 2009. The text is from the letter of the initial signatories. The Charter emerged from an initiative of the Communist Party towards a number of Left-led unions.

57 See, for example, *The Socialist* 26 January 2006, 27 July 2006; *Socialism Today* February 2006; and Darlington (2009b: 103).

ers by waiting for them to take action first (such as by setting up a new workers' party).[58] No matter the difficulties, Crow remained steadfast in recognising the need for steps to be taken to renew the union movement and the forces of socialism. He continued to excoriate Labour,[59] calling upon unions to disaffiliate from Labour to help establish a new party. While the NSSN gained support from the same type of unions affiliated to the TUCG, that kind of support evaded No2EU and TUSC, showing that there were limits to what a small specialist union could achieve even when led by an outstanding individual.

One of the political battles Crow fought was inside his own union against fascists. In 2006 Rodney Law, a rail worker and BNP councillor, was expelled from the RMT for conduct 'inconsistent' with membership, acting in a manner contrary to the interests of the union and its members, and acting in a threatening manner towards Crow when Crow campaigned against the BNP in Essex earlier in the year.[60] Law was charged with misconduct under RMT's rules and was expelled by the union's executive after twice failing to attend to answer questions as part of the disciplinary process. The battle to be able to expel fascists from their union was also fought by ASLEF.

58 This was, however, a criticism from one left-wing union leader, who said that rather than approach others to get their agreement for an initiative, Crow and the RMT would launch the initiative themselves and then seek support thereafter. This was believed to be putting the cart before the horse (personal recollection, 2009). A former RMT president also ventured that sometimes Crow would develop new political policy lines 'depending which way he fell out of bed that morning' and without first consulting with colleagues (personal recollection, 2007). The occasion referred to was the raising at the founding NSSN conference of 'the possibility of the RMT initiating "a little political party" to contest the London mayoral and assembly elections … that … could be a step towards a new workers' party in a few years' time' (*The Socialist* 12 July 2007).

59 For example, he said when commenting on the speech by the Chancellor, Alistair Darling, in 2007: 'The billions wasted on a new generation of nuclear weapons and hundreds of millions to fight oil wars would be better spent on declaring war on climate change through increased investment in Britain's public transport infrastructure' (*Independent* 10 October 2007); 'Blair will be remembered for carrying on where Thatcher left off, with a legacy of war, privatisation and lies' (*Times* 11 May 2007); and 'Today's living wage announcement is a cop out by Labour … the only solution is to raise the statutory minimum wage to the current living wage rate, making it legally enforceable … Offering employers a tax break to try and drag them into paying a decent rate just smacks of corporate welfare …' (*Evening Standard* 4 November 2013).

60 *Independent* 12 December 2006.

Relations with Ken Livingstone

Crow's relationship with the London Mayor, Ken Livingstone, was a difficult one. He voted for Livingstone on 10 June 2004 but within weeks had a major falling out with him.[61] In the run-up to the mayoral election, Crow said:

> He has certainly been better than any of the alternatives, and RMT will be backing his re-election campaign. We welcomed the transfer of the Tube to the Mayor. For Underground workers, one key benchmark will be the long-awaited improvement in industrial relations. Ken once remarked that senior LUL managers weren't fit to clean his toilet – but some have been allowed to continue pissing on long-suffering Tube workers.[62]

The *Guardian* reported that Crow was crucial to getting a proposed Underground strike on the day of the 2004 mayoral election called off: 'Had it not been for Bob Crow, putting his personal authority on the line the strike would probably have gone ahead.'[63] But Crow then resigned from the TfL board after Livingstone recommended that RMT members break a strike, saying he could not 'in all conscience' continue: 'I was brought up according to Labour movement principles and to believe that the 11th commandment is "Thou shalt not cross a picket line". To say I was shocked, saddened and disappointed to hear Mr Livingstone yesterday call on RMT members to cross their own union's picket lines would be a massive understatement.'[64] Livingstone's rationale for strike-breaking was explained (albeit in relation to a later strike) to the Greater London Assembly at Mayor's Question Time on 9 September 2007:

> Roger Evans: You did point out during the dispute that Bob Crow was making a very good case for legislation to limit the right of the union to go on strike and to limit their powers. Will you now join in with making that case to Government as well because it would be much more effective coming from you than from Bob I suspect?
>
> Ken Livingstone: I think that the right to strike is our second most important right after the right to vote. What appals me about the RMT is that by misusing the strike weapon, basically as a bullying technique rather than to resolve a genuine and irreconcilable difference, they undermine that. It

61 *Guardian* 2 July 2004.
62 *Independent* 17 December 2003.
63 *Guardian* 12 June 2004. The *Guardian* (3 June 2004) had previously reported that 'A leading rail union is planning to disrupt London's mayoral election with a tube strike on polling day likely to cause traffic chaos that could deal a blow to the re-election prospects of Ken Livingstone.'
64 *Guardian* 26 June 2004.

certainly would not be right, I don't think, to impose on people in Unite and the TSSA the loss of their right to strike because a small handful of people on the RMT executive are behaving rather more like a protection racket than a proper industrial union.[65]

This particular strike of 2007 was condemned equally vociferously by the *Observer*:

Last week, a trade union badly damaged the legitimacy of collective action – and achieved nothing. By going on strike after having won almost all its demands, the [RMT] closed down the London Underground for 48 hours ... If it had been over a vital matter of principle, Londoners might have understood. But by deciding to return to work for, essentially, the same promises over redundancies, rights and pensions that had been made beforehand, it has only confirmed ... people's doubts about unionism ... reminding [them] of the trigger-happy striking of the 1970s and 80s ... Bob Crow, leader of the RMT, is doing the same today.[66]

Management, injunctions and no-strike agreements

Crow's view of particular managements was not always quite what was expected, given that he said 'Some people seem to shy away from the "militant" tag. In the RMT, we wear it proudly.'[67] Of Network Rail's chief executive, he said: '[John] Armitt is a decent man. In all my dealings with him he has played it straight';[68] '[H]e talks with people. He's got a real care for the industry. He's a straight bloke to deal with. It's not many chief executives I can say that about.'[69] To some extent the compliment was returned, with Armitt saying: 'On the few occasions I have dealt directly with Bob, I have found him to have a clear understanding about what he wants and that he is willing to make a sensible assessment of what is achievable.'[70] Even though Armitt's deputy, Iain Croucher, played the 'bad cop' to Armitt's 'good cop', Croucher commented of Crow: 'He's a very reasonable and practical person.'[71] This relationship existed in the context of the RMT calling off a proposed signallers' strike in 2004 after Network Rail made it clear it would seek an injunction to stop the strike. The anger that Crow usually displayed

65 *Guardian* 11 June 2009.
66 *Observer* 9 September 2007.
67 *Tribune* 11 September 2009.
68 *Times* 2 October 2004.
69 *Observer* 4 March 2007.
70 *Guardian* 2 July 2004.
71 *Times* 4 October 2003. The compliment was not returned, as Crow later made it known that he had a very low opinion of Croucher (*Independent* 18 June 2010).

in the face of such actions was not present because Network Rail then agreed to re-open the final salary pension scheme to employees after five years of service, following Armitt's personal intervention to resume negotiations. Indeed, Crow said: 'We are very happy. We had been told we were living in a dream world and that we had no chance of getting this scheme reopened ... Someone told us that there was more chance of Hell freezing over ... Mr Armitt has acted very honourably and dealt directly with us.'[72] The deal prompted the *Guardian* to comment: 'In the light of all this, the RMT's small victory on behalf of one group of workers should be applauded by anyone who can see that this is not a question of the politics of envy, but the politics of equity. Crow has secured better working conditions for his members. All power to his elbow.'[73] Nonetheless, the relationship between Crow and senior Network Rail management was not always smooth. Before the conclusion of the aforementioned negotiations, Armitt said: 'Neither we, nor the public, can or will understand why they are threatening to bring the country to a standstill when we have offered concession after concession.'[74] Crow commented: 'The directors' decision to go ahead with awarding themselves telephone-number bonuses for financial efficiency will be seen by thousands of loyal employees as a grubby reward for pulling the plug on their decent pension scheme';[75] 'It is huge bonuses for the directors and P45s for the rest. We will resist any compulsory redundancies, with industrial action if necessary.'[76]

Network Rail's use of injunctions would be a recurring theme. Its application in 2004 concerned a slim signallers' vote for action where it alleged that information from the RMT contained workplaces that did not exist (having been closed down), workers who were not signallers and grades that no longer existed.[77] This was exactly the same basis as was given for an application for an injunction in 2010 which was granted. In 2004, the RMT responded by saying: 'Our database may not have been updated. People only contact their union when something is wrong and it is very difficult to keep track of people who may have

---

72 *Times* 25 June 2004. See also *Independent on Sunday* 2 May 2004. However, the *Guardian* (25 June 2004) reported that: 'Rail industry sources suggested Mr Crow had softened his position after facing defeat in a high court challenge to the RMT's strike ballot today.'
73 *Guardian* 1 July 2014.
74 *Times* 22 June 2004.
75 *Independent* 22 June 2004.
76 *Independent* 27 June 2003.
77 *Times* 24 June 2004.

been promoted or moved to other locations.'[78] Crow likened these legal requirements 'to painting the Forth Bridge'[79] because it takes so long that once finished it has to be started all over again. Keeping information up to date was, thus, practically impossible. But crucially in the case of the 2004 application, the RMT revealed that there was no obligation on employers to help unions maintain an up-to-date database: 'Network Rail is not prepared to give us the information on where members work.'[80] Nonetheless, in both the 2004 and 2010 Network Rail cases, and in the case of other injunctions gained by employers such as TfL, the RMT under Crow would not be bowed. It re-balloted, won a mandate for action, pursued the dispute (usually winning many of its objectives),[81] and sought to overturn any new precedents set by the injunctions.[82] Crow's stance of resolute defiance was matched by the RMT members concerned, whereby the one allowed and reinforced the other. Any victories employers won by way of injunctions were pyrrhic, because they did not demobilise the RMT (as they did some other unions).[83] As was to be expected given the effectiveness of its strikes, in relative terms the RMT experienced more injunctions (and threats thereof) than other unions, giving rise to Crow's quip that 'today's employers have been handed so many legal traps that any union standing up for its members' rights and jobs is hauled in and out of court like a yo-yo'.[84]

Crow's unexpected approach to Network Rail could also be found elsewhere. He told the *Guardian* 'I'm all in favour of co-operating with management'[85] and offered

the hand of collaboration ... [where he] insisted ... he was looking to work more progressively with HR on industrial relations and establish 'an open agenda' [saying]: 'We certainly don't want our members to join the union to go on strike; we want them to join to get the best possible pay and conditions. We want good industrial relations and a good relationship with the employer. And if we have to have a dispute, it's over a big principle – not a minor issue that should be resolved at local level.'[86]

78 *Times* 24 June 2004.
79 *Financial Times* 10 September 2004.
80 *Independent on Sunday* 2 May 2004.
81 In the case of the 2010 Network Rail dispute, the RMT won a 'deal worth about 7% between now and December 2011, plus a £2,000 lump sum for Christmas and a guarantee of no compulsory redundancies' (*Guardian* 11 October 2010).
82 Such cases were to be found with Serco (DLR) and Metronet.
83 See Gall (2006, 2016).
84 *RMT News* January 2007.
85 *Guardian* 13 December 2010.
86 'Bob Crow – a new age of mediation?', *People Management* 28 November 2012. The video address can be seen at http://www.youtube.com/

For Crow, it was the nature of partnership that was crucial. Clearly, he only wanted 'partnership' from a position of strength so the union, and not management, held the whip hand. On the Underground and elsewhere, Crow and the RMT vigorously rejected proposals to enter into 'no-strike' deals because they believed the right to strike was not only a fundamental human right but also an essential tool to right the imbalance of power between capital and labour. Indeed, asked 'Are there any circumstances in which you would negotiate a no-strike agreement?' Crow responded, 'No way. Workers' rights are human rights and the most fundamental of those is the right to withdraw your labour.'[87] However, matters were not necessarily so clear cut, since EWS, the rail freight operator, threatened to withdraw recognition from the RMT for reneging on a deal to introduce a 'no-strike' agreement:

> Bob Crow, the general secretary of the RMT and regarded as the country's most militant union leader, signed a letter allegedly agreeing to give up his members' right to take industrial action at EWS. But he has since withdrawn his approval of any deal, declaring he would never agree to such an accord. Under the framework all industrial disputes would be referred to arbitrators whose decision would be binding on both parties – in effect, a no-strike deal ... One senior source in the union movement said: 'It's not clear whether this is a deliberate breach of RMT policy or an example of shoddy workmanship by the union's officials'. An RMT spokesman said the company had unilaterally inserted the clause after a meeting in which a no-strike deal was not discussed.[88]

A triumph for the RMT during Crow's second term as general secretary was the Metronet dispute on the Underground in 2007, when following the threat of a three-day strike, the consortium that maintained most Underground lines ended its plans to outsource 250 maintenance workers and the contract was brought back in house by TfL. Of the Metronet dispute, one activist said it was 'probably one of the greatest testaments to Bob' (given that it was Crow's own branch).[89]

Industrial unionism

In its desire to become an industrial union, the RMT developed a closer relationship with the OILC union (originally the Offshore Industry

---

watch?v=2MVUzsiNT-Q. In the video, he lauded Darren Hockaday, London Overground HR director, as a straight-talking, no-nonsense manager to deal with.
87 *Independent* 29 June 2009.
88 *Independent* 28 March 2006
89 Unjum Mirza, email correspondence.

Liaison Committee) from 2002.[90] The RMT organised a variety of off-shore oil and gas workers (such as caterers), so some synergy existed, especially as both unions adopted more militant positions than the other offshore unions and were seen as pariahs for doing so. For example, in 2006 RMT organised divers to gain a 45% pay rise over two years, after threatening to strike in response to a 37% rise over three years.[91] The desire to merge with the OILC came to fruition in 2008 after OILC members voted 80% for merger.[92] This was very much the result of personal work and contact between Crow and Pottage and the OILC's general secretary, Jake Molloy. The OILC became the RMT's offshore energy branch. The RMT's involvement in the 2009 Vestas wind turbine factory dispute said much about it under Crow and its continued desire to be a militant industrial union. In response to the announcement of the closure of the factory on the Isle of Wight, some workers occupied the plant for 18 days to try to save their jobs and the capacity to generate green energy. The workers were mainly non-unionised. Through its energy branch, the RMT supported the occupation financially and organisationally, recruiting its participants. It became the workers' cheerleader because more than anything else the occupation symbolised what Crow and the RMT felt was needed in response to workers being made to pay the price for an economic crisis not of their own making. In Crow's words: 'The Vestas occupation ... show[s] that workers under attack can develop tactics that drive a coach and horses through the anti-union laws rather than just bending at the knee and accepting their fate ... Occupations are immediate, focused and high profile and can force a dispute right into the headlines at short notice.'[93] After the occupation ended, he argued: 'Every single one of them is a hero and the country should be proud of them. They've done more for the future of green energy and green jobs in the UK in two weeks than the government has done in 12 years.'[94] In addition to the Vestas dispute, Crow also made a point of supporting the struggle of other workers. Consequently, in 2009 he addressed the unofficial strikers at the Lindsey oil refinery and the Olympics construction site. Such acts of support and solidarity were carried out many times before and after these examples.[95]

90 *Morning Star* 9 November 2002.
91 See *Times* 2 November 2006; *Socialist Worker* 18 November 2006.
92 RMT press release, 23 April 2008.
93 *Guardian* 25 July 2009.
94 *Guardian* 5 August 2009.
95 Examples were the 2012 BESNA construction dispute and the Blacklisted Workers' Group campaign against victimisation in the construction industry.

New wine in old bottles

The change of Labour leadership after the loss of the 2010 general election and the arrival of David Cameron and George Osborne into Numbers 10 and 11 Downing Street was greeted by Crow as 'new wine in old bottles'. Saying that 'The Tories have always been the party of mass unemployment because that suits their class and keeps the workers under the cosh',[96] he also coined the new term 'fiscal fascism'[97] to describe the coming austerity. The Conservative–Liberal Democrat coalition's budget in October that year was met with 'This is all-out class war with its roots firmly planted in the playing fields of Eton.'[98] Crow claimed that 'Osborne has ratcheted up the class war and has made it clear through his attack on pay and employment rights that he wants the workers to keep taking the hit while the rich get richer';[99] Osborne's first budget was greeted with 'The champagne corks will be popping in the City tonight as the bankers and speculators realise they have got away with the biggest financial heist in history.'[100] Crow was equally scathing of Labour's new leader, who had, at least formally, repudiated 'new' Labour: 'Ed Miliband has to decide for himself whose side he is on – the working class or the ConDems and the bankers who created this crisis.'[101] This 'which side are you on?' approach to Labour would be regularly played out. Thus, before the 2011 TUC congress, Crow said:

> Labour is all over the shop because it wants to represent both big business and workers. You can't. It's got to make up its mind. Or the union movement has to cut ties with Labour and form a new party of labour … And the worst is that [Miliband] told those teachers and civil servants that they should work on 30 June. When it comes to a strike, you're either on the side of the bosses or the side of the workers. There's no in-between.[102]

Shortly afterwards, he told the *Guardian*:

> Ed Miliband needs to decide just whose side he is on. Criticising teachers and other workers taking strike action to defend jobs, services and pensions alienates core Labour supporters in their hundreds of thousands and is a

96 *RMT News* May 2010; *Guardian* 18 May 2010.
97 *RMT News* May 2010; *Guardian* 18 May 2010.
98 *Telegraph* 21 October 2011. He used the same turn of phrase earlier: 'This is class war in the raw, with its roots planted deep in the playing fields of Eton' (*Guardian* 13 May 2011).
99 *Telegraph* 29 November 2011.
100 *Socialist Worker* 22 June 2010.
101 *Times* 27 September 2010.
102 *Observer* 4 September 2011.

political suicide mission. You can't play political games when workers are facing the biggest all-out attack on their rights and their livelihoods since the war. A Labour leader who doesn't stand by the workers is on a one-way ticket to oblivion.[103]

This approach was interesting because Crow had already decided that Labour was not a workers' party as it was pro-business. Indeed, at the 2013 Durham Miners' Gala, he stated that 'clinging to the wreckage of a Labour Party ... is a complete waste of time. The time for an alternative party of labour is now.'[104] He was trying to deal with the challenge of most workers still looking to Labour to represent their interests by unmasking Labour in order to establish support for a new party of labour. The riders to this were that nothing good would come from dismissing those workers who still looked to Labour, and that a declaring a new party and expecting workers to flock to it was not going to happen imminently.

Crow was well versed in farting and chewing gum at the same time – to use Lyndon Baines Johnson's salty phrase – proffering that despite Labour's inadequacy, the RMT was capable of defending its members in the age of austerity:

> The pay award of 5.2% on South West Trains sets a clear benchmark for our negotiators and for the transport sector as a whole. At a time when the doom and gloom merchants ... are repeating the government line that everyone has to draw in their belts and accept cuts, job losses and austerity, RMT has shown once again that strong union organisation delivers the goods.[105]

> At a time when the doom and gloom merchants are telling working people that they must accept pay freezes [and] job cuts ... our Network Rail maintenance members have shown that if you stand together in a strong trade union you can win. The package [7% pay rise, £2,000 lump sum for Christmas and a guarantee of no compulsory redundancies] our negotiators have secured on the back of a solid mandate for strike action from our members is a testament to the results that can be achieved by trade unionists who refuse to accept they should take the hit for the banking crisis.[106]

The *Telegraph* commented on the former: 'At the moment Bob Crow wants to win most. So, by and large, he does. Deals like this make him look more and more like Britain's Jimmy Hoffa – and I mean that as a

103 *Guardian* 13 September 2011.
104 *The Socialist* 9 July 2013. See also the *New Statesman*'s 'Trade Union Guide', 14 September 2009.
105 *Telegraph* 6 October 2010.
106 *Guardian* 11 October 2010.

compliment.'[107] The breakthrough for Tube drivers – who would earn more than £50,000 as a result of a four-year pay deal with London Underground in 2011 – led Crow to comment: 'In these days of austerity we have shown that fighting trade unionism is the best defence from attacks on jobs and living standards. I doubt you will find a better offer than this anywhere else in the public sector.'[108] The same year, the RMT's campaign to prevent the partial privatisation of Merseyrail (following the McNulty report) was successful.[109] A year earlier, strike action by RMT (and ASLEF and TSSA) members increased a pay offer of 0.5% to 3.5% on National Express East Anglia. As examined in Chapter 7, Crow sought to lead from the front in resisting austerity, saying:

> it is that level of resistance [in Greece, Ireland, Portugal, Spain] that needs to be fostered here in Britain. That is why RMT has called for a summit of unions to discuss how best to co-ordinate industrial action to defend jobs, pensions and conditions, and for a broader conference uniting unions with community, service users', tenants' and pensioners' groups, to establish a broad alliance against the cuts.[110]

Conclusion

Crow's second term as RMT general secretary saw him become cemented as the 'go to' figure for scathing critiques of the government, mainstream political parties and capitalism. This was based upon his continuing ability to successfully lead the RMT in battling against employers, taking steps to forge new organs of political representation, and (via the RMT) his use of new social media to be able to speak to newer and younger audiences. It was, thus, evident that he spoke for a body of opinion far wider than just RMT members. Seasoned rail commentator Christian Wolmar was way off the mark to say that Crow's 'constant threatening of strikes and his very confrontational style of negotiation means ... no one is prepared to listen to what he says'.[111] While Channel 4's *Dispatches* programme concluded that 'Bob Crow's approach was highly effective in delivering results for his members',[112] it was important to recognise that he also perfected the public and

107 *Telegraph* 6 October 2010.
108 *Independent* 4 October 2011.
109 *Times* 1 July 2011.
110 *Federation News*, 10/2, summer 2010, GFTU/IER.
111 'Union and management should grow up', *Christian Says*, http://www.chris tianwolmar.co.uk/2009/06/union-and-management-should-grow-up/.
112 *Dispatches* 27 September 2010.

behind-the-scenes roles. Fronting the union, he frequently played the 'more militant than thou' card, which satisfied those in the RMT without hampering his pragmatic ability to strike a deal (albeit a tough one). Looking back on his first and second terms, Crow said: 'I think of the last ten years I have tried to get unity in our union. That does not mean not being able to have disagreements. But it does mean respecting other people's views you disagree with and uniting behind the decision of the majority.'[113] This was no more clearly evident than in the continuation of the RMT's multi-pronged political strategy of working with select Labour MPs while building alliances with forces to Labour's left. While labourism's continuing hold reflected more than just the influence of Crow's conception of socialism, the perspective of pursuing socialism through Parliament also reflected the weakness of the groups to the left of Labour that the RMT worked with. In all of these industrial and political matters, Crow's personality and persona were key drivers and enablers.

113 *RMT News* July 2011.

5. Last term of office

Crow was returned unopposed as RMT general secretary on 11 November 2011 for a third five-year term of office, beginning in 2012.[1] He again received 131 branch nominations, the then president, Alex Gordon, commenting that his 'unopposed re-election ... is a total vindication of the industrial and political strategy that has been developed by the union under [his] leadership'.[2] Crow should have served until 2017 but he was cut down in his prime by a heart condition on 11 March 2014. This last chronological chapter examines his final term and begins to lay out the themes for subsequent analysis and assessment as well as examining a number of issues such as growth in union membership and women's participation. Since this chapter deals with his last term in office, it is now appropriate to look back over his achievements as general secretary.

Industrial muscle

The 2012 London Olympics was a once-in-a-lifetime opportunity to wield old-fashioned industrial muscle. The last Olympics held in Britain had been in 1908 and 1948. Crow and the RMT had no embarrassment in using the opportunity to gain more remuneration from their members' employers. Partly, this was a case of compensation for the extra work that resulted from the huge numbers of participants and spectators; partly, it was a making up for the stagnation of wages due to the recession and public sector pay restraint. Just before the Games started, Crow stated that 'we have secured good deals on Olympics recognition and reward for the vast majority of our members'.[3] This was also the *Guardian*'s view: 'Unions win gold medal for Olympic bargaining ... scor[ing] a string of Olympic pay victories.'[4] The RMT played the big-

1 *Evening Standard* 14 November 2011.
2 RMT press release, 11 November 2011.
3 *Independent* 23 July 2012.
4 *Guardian* 25 July 2012.

gest role in gaining gold. But Crow also continued to be the champion of those without the same industrial muscle, encouraging them to fight back and supporting their actions in his own inimitable way. One example was the case of the Eurostar cleaners: 'The cleaners who mop up the spilt Bollinger in the St Pancras champagne bar are on poverty pay levels. This scandal is a blight on London's status as a world class city in the run up to the Olympics.'[5] However, industrial muscle was not much in evidence during the spate of accidents and deaths in the North Sea oil industry in 2012 and 2013. There were no walkouts or strikes. Crow did, however, give support: 'The entire Super Puma fleet must remain grounded until the causes of this latest event are established and dealt with thoroughly to the unions' satisfaction ... We will support any member who refuses to board any suspect aircraft type in light of this disaster.'[6] Of course, it was not just a case of the RMT lacking industrial muscle here. The situation was common elsewhere, with Crow criticising unions' mobilisation in merely marching but not mounting a general strike.[7]

RMT membership and inter-union relations

Well before his death, it was widely known that the RMT under Crow had bucked the trend by increasing its membership. Membership grew in new and existing areas of organising. While 53 new union recognition agreements were gained in 'greenfield' sites,[8] covering engineering and maintenance, cleaners, caterers, customer service staff and security staff, the largest proportion of new members came from traditional 'brownfield' in-fill recruitment (among drivers, guards, signallers, track workers and station staff). Pursuing greater membership was not an end in itself, but was consciously sought in order to increase union power and influence so as to be better able to advance and defend members' interests. As Table 1 indicates, prior to Crow becoming general secretary in 2002, the RMT's membership had contracted. Between 1995 and 2001, the union 'lost' around 10,000 members. This had a number of causes, such as falling numbers of workers employed in core areas of organising (especially on the railways after privatisation), the ending of check-off by British Rail and the sense of union drift in turbulent times. After 2002, significant growth was recorded, reaching a peak of one-third higher

5 *Guardian* 17 February 2012.
6 *Socialist Worker* 27 August 2013.
7 *Socialist Worker* 20 October 2012.
8 Author's own research. The overwhelming majority were not re-recognitions. Six new recognition agreements were gained in the two years following Crow's death.

by 2009 before falling back; numbers then rose again and overtook the 2009 level by the end of 2014. Crow's contributions to reversing the decline were 1) establishing the organising and recruitment unit in 2002; 2) generating an identifiable 'brand'; and 3) providing in himself the most easily recognisable figure for association with the 'brand'. Underlying this was, of course, the attitude and behaviour of a militant 'fighting back' union which resulted from the policies adopted and the actions consequent upon those policies. Early on, this was certainly Crow's view: 'RMT's willingness to stand up to dictatorial employers seems to strike a chord among transport workers';[9] 'Clearly we are doing something right: might that just be that we are already listening to what people want at work?'[10] This remained his view a decade later: 'These membership growth figures ... are a testament to the fighting, campaigning stance of this trade union ... The RMT has shown ... militant, industrial trade unionism is the only defence that working people have.'[11] A useful by-product of this was the restoration of membership pride in and loyalty to the union.

The RMT's organising strategy, based around employing specialist organisers, was more successful than that of many other unions because, in alliance with the promoted brand, it focused not just upon recruitment but upon engaging and deploying the energies, talents and knowledge of existing reps and activists to recruit and represent members, rather than requiring all members to be self-organised and to represent themselves, or by having employed organisers acting as shop stewards.[12] This did not mean that members were not called upon to play an active role – they were expected to support union balloting recommendations so that the union had bargaining leverage. As Pottage recounted, it was not a case of a new 'rocket science' but of using tried and tested traditional methods.[13] Crow acknowledged that the RMT's growth was down to the combination of an expanding industry and workforce, its activists and hard work.[14] This work, especially in signing up expired members and providing individual services to members, was aided by the set-

9 *Times* 25 May 2004.
10 *Guardian* 23 April 2004.
11 *The Socialist* 9 January 2013.
12 General Secretary's Report, 2006 and 2009 AGMs. The latter stated: 'Our strategy is constantly evolving but will continue to rely on our main strength – the active participation of our activists, reps and officers ... our strength comes from our local organisation. Without that we suffer and our members are denied a proper service and representation.' See also Darlington (2009b: 89–92).
13 Berlin (2006: 167).
14 *Socialist Worker* 17 September 2005.

Table 1 RMT membership, 1994–2015

Year	Membership	Male (%)	Political fund (%)
2015	83,854	86	95
2014	82,278	86	89
2013	80,105	87	88
2012	77,549	88	90
2011	76,093	88	89
2010	77,031	89	90
2009	79,499	89	90
2008	80,041	88	87
2007	75,906	88	87
2006	74,539	88	88
2005	73,347	89	88
2004	71,544	89	99
2003	67,476	89	97
2002	63,084	90	n/a
2001	60,001	90	n/a
2000	57,869	91	n/a
1999	55,037	91	n/a
1998	56,476	92	n/a
1997	56,337	93	n/a
1996	60,142	93	n/a
1995	59,250	93	n/a
1994	67,981	94	n/a

Source: RMT membership notified to Certification Officer as at 31 December each previous year. Figures for gender breakdown and political fund contributors also from the Certification Officer. The OILC, numbering some 2,500 members, joined in 2008 through a transfer of engagements. In 2009, the areas of membership were rail (76%), shipping (7%), bus (8%), offshore (5%), cleaners (1%), road transport (1%), taxi (1%) and others like catering and miscellaneous (1%).* In 2010, 11,000 members were classified as 'young members'.

Note:
* Figures from Geoff Revell (email correspondence 30 October 2009).

ting up of a union call centre in 2005, which re-signed 1,000 lapsed members in its first year. The RMT's brand was clearly manifested in words, deeds, images and associations. Its demonstrations and protests, and those of the wider union movement, were adorned with its flags, badges and slogans.[15] Of its slogans, the predominant ones were 'The

15 Alan Pottage was the officer behind giving the RMT such a visual identity. The

past we inherit. The future we build', 'Never on our knees' and 'Agitate, Educate, Organise'. The brand was responsible, reasoned and effective militancy. Indeed, success was the greatest recruiting sergeant and Crow was the figurative Lord Kitchener.

Crow suffered some criticism from within the RMT about organising workers such as cleaners, who had far less strategic leverage and whose employment turnover was greater than that of traditional RMT members. But he robustly defended the strategy because of his strong belief in industrial – and not occupational – unionism and in fighting low pay and poor conditions. Membership growth was no mean feat given that in some areas of the transport sector (over and above competition with ASLEF among drivers) the RMT faced other competitors. In road transport (storage and distribution) there were Community, GMB, Unite, URTU and USDAW while in engineering and track maintenance there was Unite. Many also expended considerable resources in recruiting, and the RMT was sometimes the victim of collusion between employers and these unions through single-union 'sweetheart' deals that excluded the RMT. Examples were found at Wessex Connect, Serco (Boris Bikes), Securitas and in the North Sea. Crow claimed that such deals were 'disgraceful class collaboration'.[16]

RMT membership growth was not all plain sailing. Crow's stated target of '100,000 by the end of the decade'[17] was never reached and would have required much greater economic growth (thus boosting the numbers employed) and an even more mobilised union. As it was, recession from 2008–09 onwards somewhat undercut the previous high rates of growth (even though some growth was maintained). But measured by criteria other than just membership growth, the RMT was renewed and revitalised under Crow's leadership by dint of increased organisational vitality, enhanced leverage with employers and effectiveness of outcomes through a militant approach. Some of the methods employed were relatively innovative such as using membership and sectional charters of demands. Reps and activists were schooled in the required industrial and political tasks at the residential centre in Doncaster, which held company-specific courses. The centre was able to take up to 1,250 students per year when extended in 2012 but

RMT used the Ethical Nation company to produce its merchandise and associated paraphernalia, believing that 'it's important not only to advocate ethical standards for those who produce RMT merchandise – but we also want to see that put into practice' (General Secretary's Report, 2009 AGM).

16 *RMT News* July 2009.
17 *Guardian* 23 April 2004.

worked at less than full capacity,[18] indicating limits to activism and politicisation.[19]

The proposed merger with the TSSA would have been boosted the RMT's membership – even if this was not organic growth. The prospect worried the Right, with Tory MP Dominic Raab saying that it would be 'a Gordon Gekko-style takeover by Bob Crow, not an act of fraternal solidarity'.[20] Despite some early promise in 2011,[21] by 2012 talks had foundered – from the RMT's standpoint – on the TSSA's affiliation to Labour, its practice of not electing all its senior officers and its attitude towards branches. Arguably, some of this might have been foreseen. There was also the not inconsiderable matter of the overall differences between the unions' political outlooks, despite convergence of interests arising from the McNulty Report on staffing levels, and work practices and cuts on London Underground. Crow recorded that 'It is a matter of regret that those talks have … failed to bring us that step closer to a single union for our industry … [because] the failures [of our union] often serve to highlight that the job of creating a single industrial union remains to be completed.'[22] The failed talks brought to an end any remaining hopes under Crow's leadership for further realising the RMT's longstanding policy of creating a single industrial union. At the outset as general secretary, he said he was in favour of 'mergers that give workers more muscle, more bargaining power. For example, I'd love a merger with ASLEF and TSSA. It makes obvious sense industrially to have a single union covering the rail industry. We organise seafarers and I'd like a merger with NUMAST, the ships' officers' union, for the same reason.'[23] Earlier, recounted Mick Rix, he and Crow:

> put in place joint union executive meetings and on a quarterly basis created
> other joint meetings between our unions. We instituted a policy, that if it

18 *RMT News* January 2013. Since 2010, annual enrolment has been around 500, with 'significantly' fewer prior to 2010 (Andy Gilchrist, email correspondence, 24 May 2016). The RMT funds its members through the courses, so gaining release (paid or otherwise) from work is not necessarily the problem that it might be assumed to be. The RMT continued its longstanding practice of predominantly using lay tutors, that is, RMT members to teach the courses (see *Trade Union Solidarity*, 3, summer 2012).

19 Andy Gilchrist alluded to some of the challenges of getting RMT reps to conceive of themselves as more than just *workplace* reps (*International Union Rights*, 19/1, 2012).

20 *Financial Times* 23 July 2011.

21 *Guardian* 23 July 2011.

22 Crow (2012a: 155). TSSA then tried unsuccessfully to merge with Unite in 2013.

23 *Socialist Worker* 17 September 2005. See also Crow (2012a).

was not possible for each other's union to assist in action, we would not hinder the union taking action. On an occasion we were unable to ballot members for action [at the same time], we issued letters instructing our members not to cross RMT picket lines ... Although we did not talk about it publicly, we jointly believed that we had to unite all railway workers into a single union [which had at its heart] a campaigning and organising agenda ... We discussed potential structures. This led to the TSSA union being invited into quarterly meetings with both unions.[24]

The failure to progress industrial unionism came about despite periods of leadership of ASLEF by Mick Rix (1998–2003) and Mick Whelan (2011–) and of the TSSA by Gerry Doherty (2004–11) and Manuel Cortes (2011–), which provided more auspicious conditions.[25] Short of merger, there was some limited joint industrial action organised with ASLEF, especially on the Underground, during Crow's leadership. The sectionalism of both RMT and ASLEF was at the root of this lack of progress. There was often good reason to act alone in terms of the specific nature and timeframe of disputes, but opportunities to act together by accelerating or decelerating disputes to facilitate common action were often not taken. In this regard, Whelan noted that while Crow 'preferred consensus on the staff side as he saw his natural opponents on the other side of the table ... [he] was never afraid to plough a lone furrow if the RMT's view was different'.[26] The National Union of Marine, Aviation and Shipping Transport Officers (NUMAST) merged with its Dutch counterpart in 2009 to form Nautilus International (having federated in 2006). During Crow's leadership, the RMT was most closely politically aligned with the PCS and FBU, but cooperation was limited because of the lack of industrial overlap and differing political strategies. So while the RMT initiated the NSSN and took part in the TUCG, only it supported TUSC.

Women in the RMT

Women comprised some 5% of NUR membership in the 1980s[27] with the union being slow to set up an autonomous organisation of women – its 1988 AGM established by only one vote the Women's Advisory

24 Email correspondence, 8 September 2014.
25 In 2007, relations between the RMT and ASLEF were at a sufficiently low ebb to require a joint statement signed by both unions that they would desist from any words or deeds that might be perceived as hostile or derogatory towards the other union (*RMT News* March 2007).
26 Email correspondence, 30 April 2015.
27 Maksymiw *et al.* (1990: 277).

Committee. This gives some flavour to the background for RMT membership becoming more feminised under Crow's leadership and his support for women's rights.[28] However, progress was not dramatic (see Table 1) and during this period the RMT had no women in its leadership (save Janine Booth's single three-year term as a CoE member),[29] in spite of women comprising around 10% of the membership.[30] Many new women members came from organising newer constituencies such as cleaners and caterers, for which Crow led the charge. Some commentators believed that the RMT was 'heavy with an air of exaggerated masculinity. Staff appeared to be blokishly protective towards their boss, but subtly deferential.'[31] The union was tinged with a machismo that sometimes turned into violence (either against managers, non-union members or fellow members and officials)[32] and Crow 'was not always a popular figure amongst the … union hierarchy. Many felt his macho style was somewhat outdated in an era when more women than men are trade unionists.'[33]

While there was no doubt some element of this, the paradox was that what some called a 'macho' RMT culture had two sides – one often militantly oppositional to management and the other often not progressive regarding women. Women benefited from the first but not the second. Personally, Crow supported campaigns for higher wages for women on the basis that they unfairly received less and that this brought down the wages of all workers (without men benefiting from the lower pay of women).[34] He was also said to be supportive of women RMT officials.[35] While it would be hard to say that Crow was 'in touch with his feminine side', he commented:

> Greta Garbo once said that the men who think they're macho aren't really macho at all. That's true. Some people go around puffing their chest out

28 See Berlin (2006: 168).

29 In early 2014, four of the nine industrial relations officers were women, but these are neither senior nor elected posts. See also Darlington (2009b: 103). Michelle Rodgers and Kathy Mazur were elected after Crow died, serving from 2015 to 2017.

30 The same point – to a lesser extent – can be made about non-white members.

31 *Guardian* 12 March 2014.

32 *Evening Standard* 5 September 2007 (headlined 'Inside the loutish and macho world of the RMT henchmen').

33 *Union News* 24 March 2014.

34 Selma James and Nina Lopez of Global Women's Strike (*Guardian* 13 March 2014).

35 Scarlet Harris, TUC women's officer, recounted: 'When I first started, I was the only woman in the industrial relations department. Bob Crow was really supportive. I was also well looked after when I was pregnant' (*Observer* 5 August 2012).

111

saying it's a man's world. I don't think that's the case at all. I'm very soft with my daughters, they're grown up now, but they can always work on my heart.[36]

In practice, there were examples of him taking to task those (like Shaun Brady) who he saw as being disrespectful of women.[37] But there were limitations to his vigour in promoting feminism and women's rights and the extent of culture change achieved under him.[38] Thus, criticisms of women activists were that *RMT News* did not give sufficient coverage and weight to women's issues,[39] that sexist imagery was used by the RMT[40] and that there was an unwillingness to take proactive measures to address women's under-representation. Hence, for example, at the 2007 RMT Women's conference, Crow argued against 'any kind of structural changes to guarantee women's representation, for example, at the AGM or on the Executive … [saying] he wants the 13 best people on the Executive'.[41] When asked 'Are you making progress in tackling equality issues in the RMT?', he responded by downplaying the need for dedicated measures to specifically help under-represented groups:

36 *Times* 12 September 2009.

37 Of course, this incident may also show two other aspects, namely, the very machismo that is criticised, and men doing something for women that the women should be doing for themselves (with men only playing a supportive role).

38 An example was that some RMT activists thought that having a women's newsletter was divisive for an all-grades union ('A Union Women's Newsletter: Is It Divisive?', AWL, 1 June, 2007, http://www.workersliberty.org/node/8560).

39 For example, Janine Booth wrote to the *RMT News* (June 2014), saying: 'I am disappointed by the report of RMT's women's conference in the last issue … Unlike the reports from several other conferences, which were double-page spreads, women's conference was tucked away near the back with just half a page [and] … did not mention any of the women delegates who spoke in the debates, any of the reports we received and discussed or any of the excellent guest speakers who addressed the conference. Sadly, it failed to capture the friendliness, spirit, camaraderie and enthusiasm of the event. The report also misrepresented one of the resolutions that the conference passed, stating that it challenged "sexualised images" whereas it in fact objected to sexist images.' The March and September 2008, April 2009 and April 2010 editions carried two-page articles on International Women's Day, organising women, and women's conference reports.

40 See 'Don't use sexist stereotypes', AWL, 7 May 2014, http://www.workersliberty.org/story/2014/05/07/don%E2%80%99t-use-sexist-stereotypes: 'Activists in the RMT union, and wider labour movement, were dismayed in March 2014 when a boxing tournament organised to raise money for the RMT's London Widows and Orphans fund was promoted with a poster including a stylised, cartoon image of a bikini-clad "ring girl" … The RMT Women's Conference on 7–8 March 2014 passed a motion condemning the union's promotion of the poster.'

41 'RMT Women's Conference: Day One', AWL website, 11 March 2007, http://www.workersliberty.org/node/7866.

Equality issues are not just about having black, women's and gay and lesbian committees for the sake of them, but trying to open up the union's structures as widely as possible with the aim of involving the widest possible range of members. It's about ensuring that the union pursues the interests of all its members.[42]

Ann Henderson recollected: 'I remember Bob as being supportive of women's structures and organisation in the NUR/RMT', while Pam Singer recalled:

Bob had a theoretical understanding of women's rights, but he was not always able to translate that into actions. [For example], we had quite an argument in 1990 when his branch members had a fund-raising event in a local club where someone invited an 'exotic dancer'. He could not see why our Women's Advisory Committee was concerned. He saw that as a social club event, not a formal branch event.[43]

Reflecting on the period of Crow's leadership, a former CoE member commented: 'I wouldn't suggest the position of women in the union got any worse ... It was just as bad before, if not worse. He took over a union in which women were marginalised and under-represented, and that did not change nearly as much as women activists would have liked it to.'[44]

Forever seeking socialism

Despite all the problems and setbacks, Crow retained his faith that socialism was not only desirable but necessary. The matter of what organisational form it should take continued to perplex him (as it did many others). Just before beginning his third term of office, he was interviewed by *LookLeft*, in which he commented:

I don't think [a new workers' party] is going to happen tomorrow or next week. There is a group called TUSC ... who are doing well in that they are giving people an alternative to the Liberals, Labour and Tories ... Some way down the line, there is going to have to be a new party because political parties represent classes of people and there is an under-representation of working class people. When that will be I don't know, but one thing's for sure, it's got to be rooted in the trade unions and the communities.

He added: 'To this day, there has not been one resolution at any of our general meetings to re-affiliate to the Labour Party.'[45] So while

42 In Murray (2003: 103).
43 Email correspondence.
44 Email correspondence.
45 *LookLeft*, 2/7, 23 September 2011.

TUSC was both a work in progress and a coalition, Crow continued to call upon other unions to break with Labour and set up a new workers' party. In typically blunt language, and trying to take advantage of Labour leader Ed Miliband's further erosion of union influence in Labour, he said:

> If others want to stick around and be insulted by those whose only interest is our money and not our ideas, then that's a matter for them – for the rest, there is a whole world of opportunity outside the constraints of the Labour Party and RMT would urge them to embrace it and join us in this new political project … The time for the alternative party of labour is now.[46]

> [T]he time is right to start building an alternative political party that speaks for the working people and the working class communities that find themselves under the most brutal attack from cuts and austerity in a generation. Clinging to the wreckage of a Labour Party that didn't lift a finger to repeal the anti-union laws despite 13 years in power is a complete waste of time.[47]

The *Guardian* noted that it was 'a call he has been in the habit of making for several years. Some people at the top of the big unions tend to respond to such talk with groans rather than serious interest. As they see it, even if such unions as the GMB finally split with Labour, the chances of them founding a new party remain slim.'[48] And echoing what he said to *LookLeft* two years earlier, in response to the question 'when [do you] think a new workers' party might materialise?', Crow replied:

> I don't think it's imminent, like next week. I think what it is, at the end of the day, you can't just go out and say, 'I'm forming a new party'. People are saying to themselves, they're not getting value for money from Labour … I think, eventually, people will turn around and say, 'Well hang on a minute – no one's representing our class of people.' And they'll come together and say, there ought to be a new political party – a new party of working people, unemployed, pensioners … That's the significance of it. They'll come together and form a political party that fights on behalf of working-class people.[49]

Asked where the Ken Loach inspired Left Unity fitted in, he said: 'Well, it's another group of people. Good luck to 'em. But there's not enough people on the left to start having two or three campaigns. There needs to be one party, speaking on behalf of workers.'[50] In noting that 'Beyond the insistence that any new force will have to grow out of the unions,

46 *Guardian* 13 July 2013.
47 *Evening Standard* 7 September 2013.
48 *Guardian* 10 September 2013.
49 *Guardian* 10 September 2013.
50 *Guardian* 10 September 2013.

exactly what Crow has in mind is unclear', the *Guardian* highlighted that Crow was trapped between a rock and a hard place.[51] The rock was the objective domination of Labour by neoliberalism and the hard place the subjective lack of will to create a new party. Consequently, despite all his prowess and influence, Crow was left saying, 'It will happen. When it's ready to happen, it will.'[52] Despite this limitation, he vehemently denounced those on the Left who continued to advocate a vote for Labour, telling a *Morning Star* conference in March 2012 of his frustration that these people criticised Labour 'but when it comes to an election you all go and vote Labour'.[53]

Class war in the classroom

Crow was not just an advocate of education[54] for raising workers' class consciousness but also specifically for increasing the capability of the most class conscious to fight capitalism practically, politically and ideologically. According to the then RMT education officer, Ray Spry-Shute: 'Last year [2005], Bob Crow suggested to the Council of Executives that they may wish to look into the feasibility of purchasing a new education centre. [They] agreed and the search … began.'[55] This resulted in the Doncaster centre being opened in 2006. When opening the refurbished and extended Doncaster centre in 2012, Crow said that the RMT was hereby 'sending a warning to both the boss class and the political class that this union is building for the future with plans to train up and tool up hundreds of new militant activists who will drive the RMT's brand of industrial trades unionism deep into workplaces the length and breadth of the land'.[56] Reflecting on this after his death, the then president, Peter Pinkney, wrote:

> Bob knew how important education is. If we want the best reps, we have to educate them to the highest standard. We need to equip them to be able to represent our membership to the highest standard. I was part of the executive, in 2005, that made the decision to open the school in Doncaster, and

51 *Guardian* 10 September 2013.
52 *Guardian* 10 September 2013.
53 'Bob Crow calls for new working class party', *Socialist Resistance*, 3 April 2012, http://socialistresistance.org/3371/bob-crow-calls-for-new-working-class-party
54 This included being supportive of 'union learning' through the Union Learning Fund and union learning reps.
55 *RMT News* October 2006.
56 The opening was on 23 November 2012 and was broadcast on 30 November 2012 on *RMTv*.

it was a very proud moment for all of us. We were expanding our education while other unions, and the TUC, were closing theirs. We have now spread the facilities out to the regions and we are reaping the rewards.[57]

The former CoE member Janine Booth commented: 'Bob was an advocate of reading and study. As General Secretary, he introduced book reviews to the ... *RMT News*, and significantly increased the union's education and training programme.'[58] In a ceremony on 31 July 2015, the RMT's Doncaster education centre was officially renamed after him.

Courting controversy

For some, Crow courted controversy when he ignored the convention not to speak ill of the dead. On Margaret Thatcher's death, he told BBC Radio London: 'I won't shed one single tear over her death. She destroyed the NHS and destroyed industry in this country and as far as I'm concerned she can rot in hell. She has got nothing in common at all with working people. She didn't die in a hospice, she died in the Ritz, somewhere no working people could stay for one night.'[59] The concrete action the RMT took was to back a campaign to 'Bury Thatcherism. Join a Union' which was launched on the day of Thatcher's funeral. Again Crow put the boot in: 'Margaret Thatcher, and the class interests she represented, hated ... unions. That's why she sought to destroy us and that's why her legacy has to be a resurgent union movement.'[60] However, those who found these remarks controversial did not find what he said about the railways to be so, even though it was expressed in the same blunt and colourful language:

This Government's rail plan isn't a recipe for efficiency, it's a recipe for exploitation with the train operators given the green light to rob passengers blind to travel on overcrowded and unsafe trains in the name of private profit. Axing ticket offices and guards will turn stations and trains into a criminal's paradise. For passengers it will mean the double scandal of being mugged by those who set the fares and then running the risk of being mugged by yobbos using the destaffed services as a cover for violence and assaults.[61]

The First West Coast deal is an exercise in casino franchising that lays bare the whole sordid enterprise which is rail privatisation. Companies promise the earth, jack up fares and slash jobs and services in a drive for profits

57 *RMT News* April–May 2014.
58 *Solidarity* 19 March 2014.
59 *Telegraph* 11 April 2013.
60 *Times* 13 April 2013.
61 *Telegraph* 8 March 2012.

and if the numbers don't stack up they throw back the keys and expect the public sector to pick up the pieces.[62]

Richard Branson and his shareholders are laughing all the way to the bank. Not only have they made hundreds of millions from the rail privatisation lottery but they have now scooped the rollover as well.[63]

International politics

Understanding the struggle for workers' interests and socialism to be global, Crow was a keen advocate of working with the organs of the international union movement such as the International Transport Workers' Federation (ITF), the European Workers' Federation, and the Trade Unions International of Transport Workers (TUI). In 2006, he attended the ITF's 41st congress in Durban where he proposed a successful motion on the Arab-Israeli conflict.[64] His ability to take part in ITF initiatives and protests was further aided by its headquarters being based in London.[65] Meanwhile, in 2012, he said at the World Federation of Trade Unions congress:

> There needs to be a global response of the workers against capital. Of course, our job first of all is to do the fight in our own country and to link that struggle with all the struggles of the workers around the world who are fighting for justice ... We are involved with a number of WFTU unions around the world, especially with the Brazilian comrades. We have always been involved in the expression of solidarity especially to our Cuban comrades who are part of the WFTU. We recognise them as great partners, true socialists and fighting trade unions who are prepared to roll their sleeves up for the struggle for the rights of the working people.[66]

Two years earlier, he told the *Guardian*:

> Quite clearly globalisation is about lowering pay and conditions. So therefore our job is to organise globally ... To organise globally to try to raise wages and help unions in other parts of the world for increasing their pay ... If there's not a strong trade union movement, the employers will get their way. They will drive pay and conditions down for the workers in this country, so who else is going to stand up for working people in this country except the trade union movement? Who else?[67]

62 *Independent* 17 August 2012.
63 *Guardian* 16 October 2012.
64 *Morning Star* 10 August 2006.
65 See, for example, *Morning Star* 7 March 2008.
66 'An Interview with Bob Crow', *Marxism-Leninism Today*, 9 May 2012, http://mltoday.com/an-interview-with-bob-crow.
67 *Guardian* 13 December 2010.

His support for workers' rights and progressive politics extended from Boliva, Cuba and Venezuela to Palestine, Egypt and Colombia, as well as including anti-imperialism, anti-fascism and anti-war positions.[68] To this end, he spoke at countless meetings, attended many demonstrations, wrote letters to the press[69] and raised the relevant issues as often as he could at conferences and congresses.[70]

Relations with Mick Cash

As with Jimmy Knapp earlier, Crow did not have the relationship with Mick Cash that might have been expected. Although Cash had stood against Crow in 1999 and campaigned against him in 2002, it was interesting to note, for example, that Cash was not challenged by the Left in 2007 and 2012 when he was returned unopposed to serve as senior AGS. This was despite

> his career ... not be[ing] without controversy; in 2003 there were calls for Cash to be ousted from his then-position as RMT representative on the Labour Party National Executive Committee [when he voted for the Iraq war]. Initiated by Workers' Liberty, members of the Bakerloo Line London Underground branch called for the union to remove Cash from his post and replace him with someone who would fall in with the union's policies. Cash kept his job after Crow spoke out against the motion.[71]

Cash also abstained on the Labour NEC vote to expel the RMT,[72] and was reported not to be part of 'the RMT leadership loop'.[73] However, even though they seemed to be politically poles apart and had differing industrial perspectives regarding the relationship between strikes and negotiations, Crow directly and indirectly defended Cash when he could have made use of various opportunities to take him to task and unseat him. The *Guardian* noted that Cash and Crow 'were said to be more similar in their outlook than early public rhetoric appeared',[74] indicat-

---

68 The RMT stance on such international issues under Crow was seldom criticised by members – such as via letters in *RMT News* on previous articles on these issues – suggesting either agreement or agnosticism. This contrasted with the situation Mick Rix found during his ASLEF general secretaryship.

69 For example, along with other general secretaries, he wrote to the *Guardian* (16 September 2005) against the renewal of Trident.

70 Under Crow, the fundraising RMT garden party for medical aid for Cuba was established in 2003.

71 *International Business Times* 17 April 2014.

72 *Independent* 2 May 2014.

73 *Evening Standard* 5 September 2007.

74 *Guardian* 1 October 2014.

ing there was more affinity between them behind closed doors. Cash had his own substantial powerbase as a result of being the lead officer for Network Rail and maintaining support – on a personal level through his continued membership – of Labour. So long as he did not challenge Crow for the general secretaryship, an amicable working relationship seemed to prevail. Some went further, with the current ASLEF general secretary, Mick Whelan, suggesting that Cash 'had Bob's untold trust'.[75]

The last big struggle

From late 2013, Crow engaged in what would be his last big struggle. This concerned redundancies, redeployment and ticket office closures on London Underground. The dispute was a start–stop one, as talks broke down, restarted, saw planned strikes called off, and other strikes take place. It looked as though the dispute had been settled just a month before his death, as a station-by-station review was agreed. But this was not the end of the matter and the dispute and strikes continued into the summer and autumn of 2014. This dispute saw the greatest scrutiny of Crow's personal life, more noise from the Tories on raising the industrial action ballot thresholds (which led to the Trade Union Act 2016), and was the closest Crow ever came to having a meeting with the London Mayor, Boris Johnson, on a radio phone-in programme. Despite repeated requests, however, Johnson refused to meet. In the battle with London Underground, Crow remained defiant and unrepentant. One victory gained before he died was in the longstanding campaign led by the RMT to have new trains built in Britain – in this case for Crossrail, safeguarding 1,500 jobs at Bombardier in Derby[76] – but this contrasted with the opposite outcome in the case of Thameslink in 2011.

Conclusion

Crow was in his element and riding high when he died, further testifying to the importance of the triad of his personality, politics and (members') power. He did not achieve his ambition of fostering a new socialist party, and his wider political influence was cut short, robbing him of the opportunity of playing his part in the battle for control of Labour under Jeremy Corbyn, the fight against full-blown Tory austerity from 2015, the Trade Union Bill and the EU 'in–out' referendum. These would have been tremendous challenges, but ones that he would no doubt have met

75 *Guardian* 13 August 2016.
76 *Guardian* 7 February 2014.

with his usual energy and élan. His voice would have been loud and interesting on whether Labour under Corbyn could provide a parliamentary road to socialism and whether the RMT should re-affiliate to Labour, thus ending its support for TUSC. Industrially, the battle on London Underground over jobs in 2014 and night working in 2015, and the numerous other disputes with TOCs, would have benefited from his high-profile, forthright and steadfast leadership. The next chapter, *inter alia*, considers in human terms how Crow was able to provide the personal embodiment of this kind of leadership.

6. Person and personal life

It is important to examine Crow's person, personal life and personal interests for four reasons. First, the personal was political with him. He made it this way, so this was not entirely a product of media manufacture. That is to say, the way he lived his life often epitomised what he was about and what he stood for. Second, the media used aspects of his personal life to attack and undermine him – as *Socialist Worker* commented: 'The media is gunning for Crow … they would vilify Crow even if he lived in a shed and had never taken a holiday in his life.'[1] Third, it is important to have some idea of the private person behind the public figure, given that his personality was such an important part of what made him. Fourth, his ability to work with people in order to exert influence in the RMT, the union movement and the radical Left was helped by his personality.

Two of the most obvious aspects of his personality were his lifestyle and leisure pursuits in relation to his salary, and his love of Millwall football club. Of the first, he firmly believed, using contemporary popular terms, 'I'm worth it and so are my members – workers, [myself] included, deserve nothing but the best.' Indeed, he used to say 'Why should the Tories have all the posh wine and peasants drink all the shitty beer?'[2] This was elevated into something of a personal philosophy and was as much a foundation of his wider politics as Marxism. Of the second, the supporters' chant of 'No one likes us, we don't care' became an armour for Crow, with him saying 'I'm like Millwall – a dog with a bad name'.[3] But equally significant was that Crow was not aloof from RMT members, with the RMT Morden Oval branch noting that he was 'amicable, modest and highly approachable to anyone who wanted a word with him'.[4] Paul Jackson recalled that 'He was approachable … and easy to get on with.'[5] Beyond this, many of the general secretaries

---

1 *Socialist Worker* 8 February 2014.
2 *Camden New Journal* 13 March 2014.
3 *Times* 18 November 2003.
4 *Branch Newsletter* 17 March 2014.
5 Email correspondence.

of other unions he worked with testified to his friendly, down-to-earth nature. One was Billy Hayes of the CWU.[6] He called Crow a 'one off', having the rare commodity of charisma as well as being likeable, genial and approachable. He felt, sounded and looked, Hayes said, like a real person with no side.[7] Crow was a self-styled 'man of the people', choosing to be this way because of the influence of his upbringing but also because it was compatible with his personal politics and the outside perception of these. Culturally, he remained working class. 'I have no time for snobbery of any kind. I like to be in the pub having a pint with my members, not [being] in a cocktail bar looking out at them';[8] 'Personally, I like watching a football match and having a couple of pints.'[9] However, his affection for certain aspects of the high life seemed to jar with this. This chapter begins by examining his family and personal interests before considering his demeanour and lifestyle.

Football, family and fun

Crow was a keen football fan and a well-known supporter of Millwall (which he called his 'passion').[10] He also followed his local club, Dagenham and Redbridge, and was a lover of boxing.[11] He also watched

6 *CWU TV* 12 March 2014.

7 Email correspondence.

8 *Telegraph* 4 September 2003. See also Alex Gordon's comment in Chapter 8 on Crow's lack of airs and graces.

9 *Independent* 17 February 2004.

10 When the *Guardian* (20 June 2009) asked him who his sporting hero was, he instantly pointed to a framed picture of Millwall legend Terry Hurlock on his office wall: 'He's a friend of mine. Absolute hero. He was a very, very hard player, but a very, very intelligent player.' Serwotka recounted (*Huffington Post* 11 March 2014) that: 'We shared a love of football and he used to rib me ceaselessly about Millwall's supposed superiority over Cardiff. I have fond memories of him baiting me by text message as I stood in the away end in the bear-pit that is the Den.' The Saturday after his death, the programme for the Millwall game against Charlton included a tribute to him (*Daily Mail* 12 March 2014). Prior to this, the *Sunday Telegraph* (25 September 2004) had alleged that Crow cut short his time on a picket line to watch Millwall: 'Crow's comrades were even more surprised when their inspirational leader vanished after just a couple of hours spent giving TV interviews. It turns out he was overcome by his passion for Millwall FC and relocated the revolution to the New Den, where he saw a one-nil win against Reading. Keep the red flag flying, boys (or is it blue and white for the South London Lions?)'

11 On his office wall he had a glove signed by Joe Frazier after the 'Thrilla in Manila' fight with Muhammad Ali (*Observer* 17 February 2002) and a pair of Alan Minter's boxing gloves on display (along with a moose's head, a bust of Lenin, tributes to Fidel Castro and Che Guevara, a brick from the house of Jim Connell who wrote 'The Red Flag' and a framed newspaper front page headline, 'Last stand of

his local pub football team every Sunday.[12] But he was also a keen sports-man himself, with many journalists remembering his fast bowling at the pre-TUC congress General Secretaries versus Industrial Correspondents cricket challenge. Crow also worked out six days a week, and played five-a-side football as part of an RMT team.[13] On a typical Saturday, he ran and lifted weights after rising early: 'If I do stay in bed [after 6.30 a.m.], it's to read a book. I'll go downstairs and bring up a mug of tea and read. Then at seven I'll go to the gym for an hour and a half.'[14] He claimed to be able to bench press 'one hundred and twenty kilos'.[15] Despite all this he carried excess weight (which his sister commented on and which he tried to control with an annual Ramadan-type fast).[16] Photographs of him on a picket line at Leytonstone Tube station in 1995 and on Rio's Copacabana beach in 2014 showed that this continued throughout his life. While he told the *Mirror* that he looked like a 'Greek god' on Copacabana, others said he looked more like a 'beached whale'.[17] Crow also had a full head of hair in 1992 when he was elected to the CoE but he started to go bald just before he won the general secretaryship in 2002. After this, his shaven head was often taken by the media as a sign of his aggressiveness and militancy rather than as a way of dealing with baldness. Although he was the best-known union leader in Britain, Crow was also patently normal: 'I like TV. Even if I get home at one in the morning I can't go straight to bed. I relax with a cup of tea and watch the telly. I like a pint with my mates at the weekend.'[18] Somewhat unusually, he had a meteorological fascina-tion: 'I'm mad about the weather. I get a fix from watching forecasts on television – sometimes, I'll watch the weather four times an hour. I read books about tornados [and] I've got a barometer at home.'[19] He told the *Financial Times*: 'It just amazes me how they can tell where low pressures are coming from, high pressures are coming from. On Wednesday, they said, "There will be heavy rain." Thursday, they said, "The temperature could change overnight" – and it was spot on.'[20]

---

the dinosaurs' [*Times* 12 September 2009]). He wore a necklace featuring a golden pair of boxing gloves (*Guardian* 20 June 2009).

12 *Independent* 12 January 2002.

13 *Independent* 13 September 2007. Playing football led to the odd injury as in late 2008 (*RMT News* November 2008).

14 *Financial Times* 10 September 2004.

15 *Financial Times* 25 March 2011.

16 *Financial Times* 10 September 2004; *Financial Times* 25 March 2011.

17 *Mirror* 9 February 2014; *Daily Mail* 4 February 2014.

18 *Mirror* 15 April 2002.

19 *Telegraph* 16 February 2002. See also *Observer* 17 February 2002. Later, it was two barometers (*Times* 12 September 2009).

20 *Financial Times* 25 March 2011.

Crow married Geraldine Horan in 1982, and had a daughter with her, Kerrie Anne, in 1983.[21] He also has a son who worked on the railways.[22] He then divorced, beginning a long-term relationship with Nicola (Nikki) Hoarau in 1993, with whom he had one daughter in 1994 and a son in 1998 (Hoarau also had another daughter, Natasha, from a previous relationship).[23] According to Crow, he saw Hoarau in Woodford, got hold of her telephone number and phoned her, saying: 'I know where you live but I'm not a stalker. I'm going to stand under the lamppost outside your house and if you don't like what you see don't come down and I'll understand.'[24] He admitted – on his part – it was 'love at first sight'.[25] Although they were not married, he often referred to her as 'the missus'[26] or 'wife'[27] rather than as his long-term partner.[28] She did the shopping as 'she's got a car. I give her the money, she spends it';[29] he did not drive and would frequently work long hours, including weekends. Hoarau managed the RMT credit union. When accused of nepotism, Crow responded that she was the only applicant and that he had formally interviewed her as part of the interview panel.[30] What was not so widely publicised was that she was a member of the steering group involved in setting up the credit union, and had previously worked for Marks and Spencer in its administration department, completed an AAT course in accounts in 2007 and then a Credit Management Diploma in credit control in 2008.[31] When Crow's estate was settled, he left £106,000 to Hoarau and their three children, after liabilities.[32] This was 'mainly made up of savings and investments'.[33]

21 *Mail on Sunday* 1 February 2015. She gave him two grandsons, called Daniel Atlee and Jamie Atlee.
22 *Independent* 13 September 2007.
23 *Guardian* 20 June 2009.
24 Radio 4 Profile, 4 April 2010.
25 When asked by the *Independent* (17 February 2004) 'Do you believe in love at first sight?', he replied, 'I suppose there's something in that. It was certainly that way when I met my wife.'
26 *Independent* 13 September 2007; *Mirror* 9 February 2014.
27 *Independent* 17 June 2004, 26 June 2004; *Mirror* 9 February 2014; Radio 4, 10 March 2014. This may explain why some newspapers wrote of him being married – see, for example, *Evening Standard* 1 October 2002; *Observer* 17 February 2002; and *Telegraph* 4 September 2003.
28 *Financial Times* 12 March 2014; *Guardian* 9 June 2009, 20 June 2009, 12 March 2014; *Independent* 12 March 2014; *Observer* 4 September 2011; *Sunday Times* 2, 9 February 2014; *Times* 12 September 2009.
29 *Independent* 13 September 2007.
30 See *Guardian* 2 July 2004, 20 June 2009
31 See http://www.rmt.org.uk/about/credit-union/personnel/nicola-hoarau.
32 *Daily Mail* 25 June 2014.
33 *Mail on Sunday* 1 February 2015.

Because his first daughter, Kerrie Anne, was omitted from the will, she contested it. As Hoarau was the sole executor and the trustee of Crow's estate, Kerrie Anne lodged a writ against her, saying that she could not believe her father would have ignored her and his grandchildren, and claiming that the will was riddled with errors.[34]

To his children and step-children, Crow offered support in whatever they wanted to do. Asked what he would do if they wanted to go into banking, he said: 'Good luck to them. I have never interfered, I have never said to them do this or that ... They have to live their lives.'[35] He also proffered: 'I have tried to be a good father. I am not there for my children all the time but I show them love and affection and that is what counts.'[36] This seems to have been the case, for when addressing the crowd as 'fellow Bob-ists',[37] his 30-year-old step-daughter, Natasha Hoarau, told the 2014 London May Day rally that he was 'an amazing family man that has left such a huge mark on all our lives. When recently reminiscing about his character, one huge part of his personality shone through, he was a man who loved to laugh, loved to see others laughing too'; she said that he was 'inspirational and courageous ... caring and gentle ... always there for us' and that she would 'think of her father every time she sees someone in a flat cap'.[38] The family set up the Bob Crow Gift of Hope fund through the British Heart Foundation, to which Natasha left a tribute: 'A soul mate, loving dad, amazing granddad, baby brother, uncle, friend and comrade. Always full of life, living every day to the fullest.'[39] Of all his children and step-children, Natasha was the one who followed in his political footsteps, for example by standing on the London list in his place for TUSC in the 2014 European elections.

Of his brother, Richard, Crow said: 'I have differences with him. He's made a lot of money; he's stock market, dividend first and the rest comes after. We're good mates but we're chalk and cheese'; he added: 'I hate him much more for supporting Arsenal.'[40] Crow's family also extended into the animal world. His beloved dog, a mainly black Staffordshire bull terrier named Castro after Fidel Castro, was (symbolically) bought on 1 May: 'He wouldn't fight, if somebody broke in he'd lick them

34 *Mail on Sunday* 1 February 2015.
35 *Financial Times* 25 March 2011.
36 *Financial Times* 10 September 2004.
37 *Evening Standard* 1 May 2014.
38 *RMT News* April–May 2014.
39 A number of sponsored bike rides and walks were undertaken by RMT members to raise money for the fund.
40 *Financial Times* 25 March 2011.

to death';[41] 'he's part of the family. When he dies I will be absolutely heartbroken, I have to admit. He's a lovable oaf.'[42] The cat was simply called Candy: 'I couldn't get away with naming it after a political hero, and the fish has got no name.'[43]

Musically, Crow had diverse tastes. When asked whether he like Britney or Beyoncé, he responded: 'Britney ... My kids listen to her all the time, so I can't help but know her music. But I prefer bands such as Oasis, REM and The Police.'[44] He also liked the Rolling Stones.[45] He reputedly sang 'Fly Me to the Moon', made popular by Frank Sinatra, at an RMT Christmas party in 2011,[46] and while on a cruise for his partner's fiftieth birthday, he 'was the first up to sing at Monday's karaoke night and serenaded guests with Neil Diamond's Sweet Caroline, which includes the apt line: "Good times never seemed so good"'.[47] Crow was not much of a train enthusiast, as many RMT members were. Asked what he thought about trainspotters, he said: 'I've got nothing against them. I think other leisure pursuits are just as strange, such as sitting in front of a computer all evening when you have just spent all day in front of one.'[48] But he did appreciate train journeys, so when asked for his favourite train rides, he responded: 'Glasgow to Fort William, Fort William to Mallaig, Inverness to Glasgow, Plymouth to Par, Epping to Ongar (closed)'.[49]

Humour and wit

Whether directed towards friend or foe, Crow's sense of humour and wit were essential in making him not just a larger than life character but also an effective operator. According to the *Financial Times*, it was his 'flash of wit that made him a media star',[50] while *UnionNews* commented: 'Crow gave his members confidence and he gave them hope. He also

41 *Independent* 13 September 2007. His love of dogs had obviously got the better of him, as a few years earlier he had said: 'I'd love to have a dog, but, because I work so much, I feel it would be unfair. I'd have a golden Labrador' (*Independent* 17 February 2004). And when asked 'Bull dog or Labrador?', he responded: 'I've got a Staffordshire bull terrier' (*Times* 12 September 2009).

42 *Financial Times* 25 March 2011.

43 *Guardian* 20 June 2009. The fish died in 2010, with Crow getting 'all sentimental about [it]' (*Times* 21 June 2011).

44 *Independent* 17 February 2004.

45 *Guardian* 11 September 2007.

46 *Sun* 11 January 2012.

47 *Daily Mail* 1 February 2014.

48 *Independent* 17 February 2004.

49 *Independent* 18 August 2004. He had a fondness for the Western Isles of Scotland (in preference to Spain) (*Times* 12 September 2009).

50 *Financial Times* 12 March 2014.

gave them laughs.'[51] To others his 'pugnacious wit [was] a weapon of class struggle'.[52] Crow utilised aphorisms, adages, clichés, maxim, quips and witticisms, making him not just entertaining but also influential.[53] In 2002, a pay offer with conditions from Scotrail had, according to him, 'more strings than a puppet theatre'.[54] At the RMT's 2004 AGM, as a diehard republican, he complained that he was portrayed as a 'Little Englander' for opposing the euro. To this he said: 'They say I want to see the Queen's head on a fiver. The Queen's head? I don't care if it's the Queen's arse. The euro is still undemocratic.'[55] Of 'new' Labour, he said: 'We already have one Tory party – we don't need another';[56] the takeover of a rail franchise in northern England by the Dutch state railway was greeted by 'It is deeply ironic that this franchise is now at least partly back in state hands – it's just the wrong state';[57] allowing the Governor of the Bank of England to address the annual TUC congress was 'like Christians inviting Satan to preach their Sunday sermon';[58] he said of Labour's then Shadow Chancellor, Ed Balls, that he would 'give an aspirin a headache'[59] because his policies were so awful. And, in a tirade against Trident and its supporters' job-creation arguments, he said: 'What about when we used to hang people? We had chief executioners – we had to diversify and find new jobs for them.'[60] When these quips worked well, he used them repeatedly; hence at the 2012 TUC Tim Lezard reported: '[D]uring a debate on the EU, he was accused of nationalism, of wanting to keep the Queen's head on our currency. To much laughter, he replied: "I don't care if it's the Queen's head or the Queen's arse on a ten pound note."'[61]

The *Guardian* noted that

He can transform abstruse one-liners into an art form. When he said he wanted Tony Benn elected president of Britain because he is a 'true

---

51 *Union News* 24 March 2014.

52 MacUaid (2011).

53 This applied to his family too. He once commented: 'In the afternoon I had to push my daughter's bike two miles to her school so she could ride it back home again. She then tried to negotiate a trip to the cinema or ice skating. It makes a change, someone else doing the negotiating' (*Independent* 12 January 2002).

54 *Daily Record* 9 March 2002.

55 *Guardian* 2 July 2004.

56 *Independent on Sunday* 14 September 2003.

57 *Guardian* 2 July 2004.

58 *Evening Standard* 16 September 2010.

59 *Times* 4 October 2012. GMB general secretary Paul Kenny, when using the saying, claimed that Crow had stolen it from him.

60 MacUaid (2011).

61 New Left Project 12 March 2014, http://www.newleftproject.org/index.php/site/article_comments/a_tribute_to_bob_crow.

representative of working people', an interviewer pointed out that Benn was born with a silver spoon in his mouth and had renounced a hereditary title. 'Just because you go to the Virgin Islands, it doesn't make you a virgin, does it?' was Crow's baffling response.[62]

Occasionally, his humour did not come off at all. He attempted to invert capitalist 'fat cats' into workers as 'thin cats' who should start standing up for themselves.[63] And, responding to a TfL poll indicating public support for Tube ticket office closures when the RMT's commissioned poll showed the opposite, he said: 'The thing is figures can't lie, but lies can figure.'[64] He also saw humour in the antics of opponents: after being called 'demented' by Boris Johnson, he told the *Guardian* that 'he was recently interviewed on *Channel 4* news and Johnson was on a video link-up – when the mayor was told Crow was in the studio he said it was a set-up, and left. "He walked away with all these wires hanging from him. He looked like Frankenstein! Hahahaha!"'[65] Of the *Evening Standard*'s redrawn Tube map, he said: 'Absolute classic, this one. Look, you got the Militant Line, the Far Left Line, Bolshy Line, Greedy Fat Bastards Line, the Blackmail Line. Hahahaha! Brilliant!'[66] Oliver New recounted: 'Indeed, there were a couple of derogatory newspaper cartoons of him up on the walls at Unity House in frames.'[67]

Temperament, demeanour and self-image

To many, Crow came across as bolshie, even angry. Other than defiantly defending RMT policies and actions, according to Christian Wolmar, he 'talked aggressively on television and radio as a way of ramping up support for his cause and ensuring that the bulk of his members were behind him'.[68] But rarely could Crow be accused of being genuinely aggressive. He told *The Times*: 'I don't think I'm aggressive, except when it comes to negotiating.'[69] One such occasion was the meeting with the head of London Underground recounted in Chapter 3. It was noteworthy that the way Crow operated within the RMT and the union movement was

62 *Guardian* 2 July 2004. In the original interview with the *Independent* (19 April 2004) from which the quote emerged, it said Crow was 'a man known for occasionally abstruse one-liners'.
63 See, for example, *Sentinel* 4 November 2001; *Guardian* 11 January 2002.
64 *Mirror* 9 February 2014.
65 *Guardian* 20 June 2009.
66 *Guardian* 20 June 2009.
67 Email correspondence.
68 *Guardian* 12 March 2014.
69 *Times* 12 September 2009.

not quite how he was seen in public. Bluntness rather than aggression was his hallmark. Rix commented: 'the one thing you get with Bob is that he's upfront and is straight and is honest'.[70] Unjum Mirza recalled a conversation about leaving the RMT to become solely an ASLEF member (having had dual RMT–ASLEF membership):

> In fact, Bob and I had a good 'ding-dong' about it the Tuesday before he died [when] he addressed his own branch, LU Engineering that night. Bob was very upset with me but understood my viewpoint (though he didn't agree). The last words between us that night relating to my ASLEF membership were: 'Unjum, you're a cunt'. I replied, 'But Bob, you know I'm right, we've lost too many members'. Bob finished the conversation with: 'You're still a cunt' and we finished our pints and shook hands. That's what I loved about Bob. With me he was always plain, blunt and to the point.[71]

Les Harvey found the same quality: 'what struck me most was that when asked a direct question he gave a direct answer whether popular or not'.[72] Phil McGarry remembered that Crow 'never shirked from making hard choices', suggesting a certain steeliness, and he 'always had an opinion about things'.[73]

Others commented on Crow's ability to take criticism. According to Janine Booth, Crow 'could take criticism and disagreement from within our movement: he did not hold grudges or demonise critics';[74] 'He was open to criticism and generous to his friends and colleagues.'[75] Former CoE members remembered that 'One thing that made it quite easy to work with Bob is that he was not one for holding a grudge. You could have a fierce argument ... one minute and he'd be full of his usual bonhomie towards you the next';[76] 'He didn't get bitter if he was criticised.'[77] Paul Jackson remembered that 'You could have a debate with him on many issues, stand up rows, but once the decision was made by us all, he got behind it. There was never a grudge or anything like that carried over.'[78] Phil McGarry also recalled that Crow took 'criticism on the chin but could give as good as he got',[79] while past president Tony Donaghey

70 *Guardian* 2 July 2004.
71 Email correspondence.
72 Email correspondence.
73 Interview.
74 *Solidarity* 19 March 2014.
75 Report of Booth's book launch on 23 April 2014 at Housman's, London. Crow was due to speak as he had written a foreword to the book. Peter Pinkney spoke instead.
76 Email correspondence, anonymous CoE member.
77 Oliver New, email correspondence.
78 Email correspondence.
79 Interview.

remembered that Crow 'would support people when they were doing something right, but he would also constructively support them when they were doing wrong in a comradely fashion. He would say it's nice to be told what we've done right, but I'd rather be told what we're doing wrong so that we can learn from our mistakes.'[80]

Recalling his power of memory, Christine Buckley commented that Crow was 'absolutely on top of his own brief [having an] incredible attention to detail ... He could talk you through every small step of a dispute with total recall and no recourse to notes.'[81] She also noted: 'For someone of such uncompromising views, he was willing to engage and not put dogma before dialogue.'[82] Mick Whelan also observed that Crow had 'the talent to surprise [because] he could do data driven discussion and diplomacy that would take those that had not dealt with him by surprise or fall back on his vast repository of industry knowledge'.[83] Explaining the operation of the new RMT parliamentary group, its chair, John McDonnell, recalled:

> Bob attended the group meetings every 6 weeks, working through an agenda set by the RMT executive. He briefed MPs in detail on every aspect of the issues facing the different industrial sectors in which RMT organise. There wasn't a subject of interest to his members that he didn't have a thorough knowledge of. At these meetings we agreed a strategy for each issue to complement the union's industrial campaigns with interventions in Parliament. Often the strategy would include meetings with ministers and civil servants. Bob won the respect of even Tory ministers for his sharp judgement and negotiating skills, plus his absolute dedication to his members. With his knowledge and experience, he was able to argue the union case with decisive effect and respond to any challenge or question thrown at him. He employed his wit and sharp sense of humour to secure a point from some of the hardest nosed ministers. By investing his time and energy in the setting up of the new RMT Parliamentary Group, Bob ensured that even though the union was no longer affiliated to the Labour Party it had a strong and formally acknowledged voice in Parliament.[84]

These were good indications of Crow being an extremely competent and professional operator who was dedicated and hardworking.

Crow also had a well-developed sense of empathy, taking time out to visit Phil McGarry in hospital when he was in Scotland, or asking after

80 *Morning Star* 13 March 2014.
81 *Guardian* 12 March 2014.
82 *Guardian* 12 March 2014.
83 Email correspondence.
84 Email correspondence.

the well-being of Peter Pinkney after his father died.[85] It was for this type of behaviour that Alan Pottage said that 'Bob was one of the softest guys I have ever known, with a heart of gold.'[86] Whelan commented that Crow 'was generous with his time, humour and advice, powerfully aware of his public image but one of the kindest men it has been my privilege to know'.[87] Part of Crow's charisma was that he 'made a point of always remembering people's names, so although he must have known and worked with thousands of people he always made you feel special, valued for your contribution to the union'.[88] Les Harvey recounted that 'He had a common touch and once he met someone, somehow he remembered them the next time he saw them.'[89]

Crow was also gratified and affirmed by what he had achieved at the helm of the RMT: 'I'm proud when workers come to me and say they've been on a cruise, and they have a nice house. That is better than people sitting around on social security';[90] 'Dead right, I actually get pleasure when I see one of my members get a pay rise. That's another one we've had over them. Yeah, I admit to that.'[91] This pride was also evident when he was interviewed by the *Guardian*: 'Is it true that drivers earn a basic £40,000? He looks at me, wide-eyed, as if he can't quite believe the question. "Yeah! But we've got people on far more than that. Technical officers and signal workers are on £54,000. Basic. For a flat week. All pensionable."'[92]

Relations with the media

For his leadership of RMT strikes, especially on the Underground, Crow received a media battering. The *Evening Standard* led the way with front page headlines such as 'Man who Stopped London in its Tracks'[93] and 'Most Hated Man in London'.[94] These then mutated into 'The Most Hated Man in Britain'.[95] Others weighed in too. In an attempt to stir

---

85 Interview and *RMT News* April 2014, respectively. Crow also offered help and advice to Whelan when he was settling in as the new ASLEF general secretary. He offered to be 'only a phone call away' (email correspondence).
86 *Herald* 14 May 2014.
87 Email correspondence.
88 Martin Eady, email correspondence.
89 Email correspondence.
90 *Financial Times* 10 September 2004.
91 *Guardian* 13 December 2010.
92 *Guardian* 20 June 2009.
93 *Evening Standard* 4 September 2007.
94 *Evening Standard* 3 September 2007.
95 See, for example, the *Guardian* 12 March 2014, 1 October 2014: 'the

up hostility, London's LBC Radio presenter, James O'Brien, told his listeners that Crow was 'inflicting misery on millions of Londoners so let's give him a flavour of the havoc he and his union are wreaking. If Bob Crow turns up at your shop, pub, cafe or minicab firm, don't serve him.'[96] Crow did not take these attacks lying down. Most obviously he replied to them by writing letters and articles. But he also threatened and used legal action. This contradicted the belief of his hero, Arthur Scargill, that socialists should not seek justice in the capitalist courts (ironically, one case involved a comparison with Scargill).[97] Thus, Crow's lawyers wrote to the *Evening Standard* in 2002 warning that he would seek a high court injunction and damages unless it ceased its 'unlawful harassment' of stalking him.[98] In 2005, he won damages and legal costs from *The Times* over its 2003 article alleging that he had influenced a ballot for industrial action.[99] The same year, he won further damages and costs from *The Times* over its allegation that Crow had interfered in the ballot to elect the president by attacking one of the candidates.[100] In 2007 and 2008, he gained an injunction against offensive material about him on a website – the material was removed and costs awarded against the defendant.[101] Crow also sought damages in 2012 from Boris Johnson in a libel case concerning Johnson's campaign leaflet for the mayoral election, in which Johnson linked Crow with Ken Livingstone. The action was unsuccessful, as the judge deemed the text to be 'within the latitude permitted by the law'.[102]

The uncovering of phone hacking by News International shone a light on the degree of surveillance and harassment Crow was put under. Consequently, the Metropolitan Police was asked to investigate whether his phone had been hacked, with Crow saying: 'RMT has had suspicions that journalists may have had access to private information about my movements and my union's activities that date back to 2000. We are now asking for the police, as part of their renewed investigation, to dis-

---

rightwing press ... regularly called him "the most hated man in Britain"' and also commented 'headlines describ[ed] him as Britain's most hated man'.

96 *Telegraph* 5 September 2007.

97 *Guardian* 2 October 2002. It should be noted that his approach here had rather more in common with that of Galloway and Sheridan.

98 In this regard, he commented: 'I do object to what the *Evening Standard* has been doing, saying we are going to follow you and we can make it easy or make it hard, and then talk to my fifteen year old son about his parents' activities. I don't mind it personally, but not for my kid' (in Murray 2003: 99).

99 *Times* 16 August 2005.

100 *RMT News* November 2010.

101 *RMT News* March 2008.

102 *Telegraph* 17 July 2012.

close to us any evidence or information that they may have uncovered in respect of the *News of the World*.'[103] Writing in the *Telegraph*, he commented: 'One thing that Leveson has uncovered is the level of collusion between press, politicians and the state to do over anyone seen as a threat to their interests and that includes the trade union movement ... no stone has been left unturned in vilifying and slandering those with the guts to stand up and fight back.'[104] Giving evidence at the Leveson inquiry into the culture, practices and ethics of the media,[105] Crow revealed that he had won a libel claim against the *Sun* for wrongly accusing him of having a union car and a union-subsidised house; he said that a freelance journalist working for the *Sunday Times* had taken material from bins outside an RMT AGM after being refused a copy of the agenda – with the comment that they 'might not go on fishing trips, but they certainly go on refuse trips – because the man had his head in his bin like the character Top Cat. I know local councils are making cutbacks on bin collections, but never thought journalists would step in to help out'; he mentioned a case against Thomson Cruises, alleging that a staff member had divulged information about him to a private investigator; he said that News International had confirmed that he was under surveillance from 11 January to 14 January 2011 while on holiday in the Caribbean; he said he was 'doorstepped' by *Sun* reporters and photographers who attempted to stop him going to work by blocking his way with a double-decker bus because the paper wanted to give him a taste of his 'own medicine' after a Tube strike;[106] and he reported that information about the ownership of a scooter (belonging to his personal assistant) on which he was given a ride when the Tube was not running because of an accident was inappropriately obtained from the DVLA and used by the *Mail on Sunday* on 2 February 2003.

Lifestyle

Inevitably, the media (especially the *Sun*, *Star*, *Express* and *Daily Mail* but also the *Mirror* and the *Guardian*) and his political opponents sought to use Crow's lifestyle to attack and undermine him – especially to try

103 *Evening Standard* 31 January 2011. It was unknown at the time of writing if Crow was monitored by undercover police officers (as Steve Hedley and Mick Lynch were for being blacklisted [*Morning Star* 6 June 2016]), given the complicity between them, the media and employers.

104 *Telegraph* 29 November 2012.

105 *Guardian* 25 January 2012.

106 See also Carrier (2012) on the treatment that the *Mail* and the *Sun* subjected Crow to.

to paint him as a hypocrite. The underlying narrative was that he lived it up at his members' expense, that he was an uneducated, ignorant and uncultured 'chav' getting above his station, and that he had no genuine concern for working people. They duly concentrated upon his salary, house, holidays and socialising. Other than Scargill during the miners' strike, no other union leader has experienced the same degree of constant, hostile scrutiny. Crow was steadfast in refusing to bend, believing that he was worth his salary and had the right to spend it how he saw fit. Given the *Guardian*'s comment that it was 'baffling that someone so dedicated to the socialist cause could be so deaf to the political impact of his own personal choices [on housing and holidays]',[107] and that some other union leaders might have taken measures to avoid such attention, his choices and defiant defence of them said much about him. When asked whether he had considered moderating his profile in the interests of bigger political goals, Crow said: 'Well what do they expect me to do. Instead of going to Millwall, play croquet? Or go have a game of polo? At the end of the day, you are what you are.'[108] For one journalist, 'his strength was his absolute refusal to modify his behaviour and lifestyle to some bourgeois ideal'.[109]

Whenever his RMT remuneration was used against him – as it frequently was – his total package of salary, pension and employer's national insurance contribution was invariably quoted rather than his pre-tax take home pay.[110] He pointed out that this was a case of one rule for him and another for everyone else.[111] For his last years, the figure of £126,942 was quoted for 2010, £131,330 for 2011 and £134,547

107 *Guardian* 7 February 2014. Christian Wolmar (*Guardian* 12 March 2014) said: 'Crow's weak point was his lifestyle'.

108 *Guardian* 13 December 2010.

109 Suzanne Moore (*Guardian* 13 March 2014). Another view was that of Christine Buckley: 'Where he did perhaps fall down was in not projecting that professionalism sufficiently, leaving him too open to the accusations of his detractors of being a firebrand' (*Guardian* 12 March 2014).

110 See, for example, *Daily Mail* 3 April 2011, 26 November 2013; *Evening Standard* 12 August 2010; *Guardian* 12 March 2014; *Independent* 28 November 2013; and *Sunday Times* 3 April 2011. This also included the *Mirror* 2 January 2014, 9 February 2014. In one further twist, the *RMT News* (November 2010) reported that: 'Some [newspapers] also claimed Bob Crow had been given a 12 per cent pay increase – but the truth was rather different: because the first pay-day of the new year fell on a bank holiday, Bob – like other members of RMT staff – was paid a few days early. But that early payment had to be included in the previous year's figures, artificially inflating the salary declared to the Certification Officer. That of course means that next year's figures will show a pay CUT – but it remains to be seen if that will be reported as keenly – or at all.'

111 *Mirror* 9 February 2014.

for 2012, when the figures for his salary were respectively £84,086, £86,730 and £89,805.[112] To the year end 31 December 2013, his salary was £92,344 and his employer's pension contribution £35,585.[113] Occasionally some, such as the *Guardian*,[114] pointed out that if he was compared to a chief executive of a private company on performance-related pay, then the equivalent of increasing profits was increasing membership, and on that basis he was worth his salary and the rises. Compared to unions overall and unions of RMT's size, his remuneration was neither over- nor under-generous.[115] Of his salary, Crow said: 'Look, my salary is voted for every year by the members. I take what I'm given. And whatever they give me I give them 100 per cent back';[116] 'My pay is democratically decided by our union structures, and they award me what they think is right for the job and we've never had a single complaint.'[117] There is no doubt that he was a well-paid general secretary, although far from the highest in absolute or relative (i.e., proportional to member-ship) terms. His salary rose from £60,327 in 2004 to £97,747 in 2009. He never contemplated taking a 'worker's wage' – that is the average salary of his members – which would have been something like a third of his salary and was a key demand of socialists within unions (like the Socialist Party). And, unlike his contemporaries at the FBU (Wrack) and the PCS (Serwotka), Crow was not known for donating proportions of his salary to union strike funds or left-wing causes.[118] In the RMT, Crow was not the only well-paid officer. For example, Cash was paid a salary of £69,510 and total package of £95,656 in 2012. The day before he died, Crow was questioned by BBC Radio 4 about his salary, responding: 'I am worth it, yeah. Our members, in the main, have had pay rises every single year right the way through austerity.'[119]

112 All figures from the Certification Officer. Its annual reports do not cover calendar years and the figures for union general secretaries' pay is comprised of salary and benefits (primarily pension), while the annual returns from the unions comprise a full calendar year and show salary, employer's national insurance contribution and pension at the year end.

113 *RMT News* October 2014.

114 *Guardian* 13 December 2010, 13 March 2014. Those commentators did not know that Crow's salary did not increase year on year. There were at least three years when his salary fell significantly.

115 See Certification Officer data derived from unions' annual returns.

116 *Mirror* 9 February 2014.

117 *Independent* 29 June 2009.

118 For example, Matt Wrack did not take any more than the average rise in his salary, contributing the excess to a fund from which he made donations to labour movement causes including a £7,000 donation to Jeremy Corbyn's Labour leadership re-election campaign (*Morning Star* 21 September 2016).

119 Radio 4 *PM*, 10 March 2014.

Although his home became an issue of contention, the media also expended large amounts of time and effort on taking Crow to task for his love of winter sun, especially during strikes by RMT members on London Underground. Thus, his cruise in 2010 was widely reported upon, as were his holidays in Egypt in 2005[120] and the Caribbean in 2011. But by far and away the biggest media battle he fought concerned his cruise to, and subsequent stay in, Brazil in the run-up to a Tube strike in February 2014. The strike was against the closure of booking offices to make way for commercial outlets at a cost of about 800 jobs. Crow was photographed on Copacabana beach sunbathing.[121] Quite apart from making it clear that he was available to return to London for negotiations aided by ACAS if need be and speaking twice a day to the RMT negotiators while away,[122] Crow pointed out that Boris Johnson, the London Mayor, had refused to meet him (keeping up his policy of never meeting Crow).[123] Indeed, he said: 'I could have been at home, in Rio or Kilimanjaro – it makes no difference because the Mayor won't meet me anyway. Manuel [Cortes] hasn't been away and the Mayor hasn't met him.'[124] Then he displayed his wit by pointing out at a press conference, while holding the advertisement aloft, that the cruise had been advertised in the pages of the *Daily Mail*, which – along with the *Evening Standard* – was his most vehement critic. He recounted that he had seen the advert because free copies of the paper were available at his gym, then pointed out the hypocrisy:

> They're the ones that were advertising it, so they're saying to people 'go on holiday' but when you go on holiday, you shouldn't go on it. So why are they advertising it in the first place? ... I'd love to see what the bill was to send a guy [a photographer] out to Rio: it must have cost more money than my holiday did.[125]

120 The *Sunday Times* (1 January 2006) reported: 'Celebrations in the capital were, however, marred by a Tube strike that threatened to cause chaos for revellers. Bob Crow, the general secretary of the RMT union, which had called the strike, suffered no personal inconvenience, however: he was sunning himself at a Red Sea resort.'

121 After Crow's death, the likes of the *Sun* were hard pressed to find such 'stories' about leading RMT officials enjoying foreign holidays while rail strikes took place. One instance was on 11 August 2016 regarding the Southern trains dispute, and concerned the president, Sean Hoyle, and the senior assistant general secretary, Steve Hedley (see https://www.thesun.co.uk/news/1589742/fatcat-rail-union-bosses-sun-themselves-in-turkey-as-rail-strikes-hit-thousands-of-passengers/).

122 *Evening Standard* 4 February 2014.

123 Crow had earlier joked that he would eventually meet Boris Johnson at Johnson's funeral (*Financial Times* 25 March 2011).

124 *Evening Standard* 4 February 2014.

125 *Independent* 17 February 2014.

The holiday for himself and his partner, which reportedly cost some £10,000, was to celebrate her fiftieth birthday. It had been booked months in advance[126] and he questioned why it was that others queried his right to spend his salary how he wanted: 'If I'm going to spend £10,000 on a car, or if I'm going to spend £10,000 on a holiday, or £10,000 on cigarettes, that's up to me ... What do you want me to do? Sit under a tree and read books of Karl Marx every day?'[127] He also commented:

> [D]oes being a union boss mean I have to be told how I can spend my money? I don't smoke. I don't drive a car. So if I want to throw ten grand at a holiday, I will – and I won't apologise for it. Would it be better if I went on holiday in a caravan to make myself look more working class? Because you know what they'd say if I did? They'd say, 'He's tight. He's got all that money and he holidays in a caravan.'[128]

One of his lesser known foreign holidays was to Cuba in 1999 where, upon arriving at Havana airport, he was 'bundled into a car ... and driven to meet Raul Castro [Fidel's younger brother who] ... "knew all about the political scene in Britain, he knew the trade union scene. They thanked us for all the help we've given them – we do a big garden party for Cuba every year."'[129] Probably because he was not yet RMT general secretary, there was no media interest in 'boss Bob greets communist dictatorship in cosy Cuban meeting'.

Like the attacks on his holidays, the *Daily Mail* reported on the lunch Crow hosted at Scotts fish restaurant in Mayfair for his fiftieth birthday, which reputedly cost £650.[130] The newspaper, like many others,[131] used this to label him a 'champagne socialist', or in an innovation from Tory MP Dominic Raab, a 'caviar communist'.[132] It is not known whether Crow liked caviar, but he didn't like champagne so didn't

126 *Evening Standard* 4 February 2014. He told the *Mirror* (9 February 2014): 'That holiday was booked a year ago for my missus' 50th birthday.'

127 *Independent* 4 February 2014.

128 *Mirror* 9 February 2014.

129 *Independent* 13 September 2007.

130 *Daily Mail* 2 July 2011. It was reported that he was then banned from Scotts restaurant (*Independent on Sunday* 3 July 2011).

131 See, for example, the reports in the *Independent* (29 May 2004) of Crow attending a champagne reception, in the *Sunday Times* (2 February 2014) of his ordering wine and champagne while on a cruise, and in the *Daily Mail* (18 August 2012) of his ordering champagne while watching the cricket at Lords.

132 *Sunday Telegraph* 30 September 2012. The quote was 'We need stronger not weaker laws to prevent caviar communists like Bob Crow from holding Britain to ransom.'

drink it.[133] Another example was the £4,203 spent on Crow and 14 other RMT regional officials at the Corse Lawn House country hotel in Gloucestershire in 2004.[134] Here and elsewhere, Crow (and other RMT officials) was described as being raucous and uncouth.[135] Another such instance was when he was banned from the Somers Town Coffee House gastropub, in the same street as the RMT's headquarters. The *Telegraph* reported that he was banned after a 'rowdy drinking session with colleagues' in December 2005.[136] Another case was the *Evening Standard* reporting Crow as a football 'yob'. While watching a Dagenham and Redbridge home game in 2010, he was accused of rudeness and swearing, but an RMT spokesman played down the incident, saying: 'It was a highly charged match and there was some lively banter between the spectators and the Morecambe dugout. The result was a resounding victory for London which Morecambe took pretty badly.'[137]

With his partner and their children, Crow lived in an end terrace housing association property owned by London and Quadrant in a cul-de-sac in Woodford Green, north-east London from 2001 onwards, as reported by the *Sunday Times*. It was not a council house as such despite what the media (and sometimes Crow himself) said, although prior to this he and his family did live in a council house.[138] The tenancy was not registered in Crow's name and the family was transferred to the property after Redbridge council allowed London and Quadrant to build on the council-owned land. Housing legislation took no account of changes in the financial circumstances of occupants once a tenancy was signed. The weekly rent was estimated to be £150. In 2011, the RMT defended Crow, saying that he

> makes no apology for living in social housing at the heart of his local community. He was born into a council house and has lived in one all his life, and actually turned down a union mortgage in favour of remaining a tenant. He also turned down the right to buy his council house at a discount as he believes social housing stock should remain available for future generations.[139]

The offer of a union mortgage was a good one at a 3% interest rate.[140] In late November 2013, Crow was interviewed on LBC Radio on Margaret

133 *Mirror* 9 February 2014.
134 *Independent* 29 May 2004; *Sunday Times* 20 June 2004.
135 *Independent* 29 May 2004.
136 *Telegraph* 21 January 2006.
137 *Evening Standard* 17 May 2010.
138 This was provided by Redbridge council (*Sunday Times* 3 April 2011).
139 *Sunday Times* 3 April 2011.
140 *Mirror* 9 February 2014.

Thatcher's legacy. He bluntly stated that he had 'no moral duty' to move out of the property and purchase his own home, adding: 'I was born in a council house, as far as I'm concerned I will die in one.'[141] In a typically robust way, he argued:

It's not just me that lives there, it's my family. Yes I could buy my own place but why don't you ask the rest of my family who live at home with me whether they should have to move as well? Why is it just down to me to buy a house? Why should my family, who have lived there for 30 years with all the friends they've got, have to move because of the job I've got? If I moved out of my house tomorrow the first thing you'd say is Comrade Crow leaves his roots ... Where was it ever agreed that social housing was for people that are poor? ... Council houses is [sic] not just for poor people.[142]

Interviewed by the *Guardian* in February 2014, he again defended himself:

The real big problem here is not me living in a council house, but that both Labour and the Tories failed to build council houses, and sold them off ... where does it say that a socialist can't live in a council house then? Did Karl Marx write that in one of his volumes? ... Why can't all those Tories who've got three or four houses open up those houses to people who need them?[143]

Challenged right to the end over his decision to remain in the house despite his salary, he told BBC Radio 4 the day before he died: 'I'm the only person in my road paying the rent – everyone else is on social. Every single person down my road – because there are only nine houses – is on benefits. Who really is the mug?'[144] Despite these continual attacks, he found the ability to see the humorous side. After meeting the Duke of Edinburgh when he visited Bank Tube station, Crow tweeted: 'We laughed about both living in homes paid for by the state.'[145]

The media was less keen to report that Crow also enjoyed many rather more mundane and cheaper pursuits, like 'cooking curries and roast dinners', although he admitted 'I couldn't come in at 7 o'clock at night and

141 Recounted in the *Independent* 28 November 2013.
142 Recounted in the *Independent* 28 November 2013. He made the same kind of argument in the *Mirror* (9 February 2014): 'Why should I move my wife and daughter out of a home which is near all their family and friends?'
143 *Guardian* 7 February 2014.
144 Radio 4 *PM*, 10 March 2014.
145 *Evening Standard* 24 December 2013. It is not known what his view was of the left-leaning satirist Heydon Prowse placing a mock-up of a round, blue, commemorative plaque on the wall of his house as part of BBC 3's *The Revolution Will Be Televised* series on 5 September 2012. The plaque read 'Bob Crow – Fat Cat Council Tenant'. Official blue plaques mark the homes of famous or notable people.

start doing all that lark.' In addition to watching and playing sport and amateur meteorology, he read biographies and commented that, while 'the ballet's not my cup of tea ... if someone offered me a ticket I would go and have a look at it. I am not into flower arranging, but I do like gardening.'[146] He enjoyed a range of food from pork pies and pasties, Carling lager, bacon sandwiches and liver to cheese on toast, and egg and chips.[147] But he also enjoyed the rather more haute cuisine of Scotts, the Savoy,[148] the Inn at the Park[149] and Rules (where he was interviewed by the *Financial Times* in 2011).[150] All this made him somewhat sensitive to the expectation that he should live like the working-class cartoon character Andy Capp: 'is a working man supposed to walk around with a hankie on his head, eat chip sandwiches and drink pints of bitter to prove he's working class? I don't give two hoots what people say.'[151]

Sartorially, Crow was known initially as a jeans, polo top and baseball cap dresser, but as he was elected to senior RMT positions, he began to dress more formally, wearing suits 'out of respect to the members I'm representing'.[152] However, when attending early morning picket lines or speaking at meetings at the weekends, he continued to dress casually, saying: 'I can't win. If I dress in Levi's and a T-shirt, I'm a mess. If I wear a smart suit, I'm trying to be something I'm not.'[153] However, for Crow there was surprisingly something of a 'third way', that of 'smart casual', with the *Guardian* commenting: 'His summer shirt is loose and baggy, his trousers casual, and his sneakers carefully colour coordinated – a distinctive kind of dapper';[154] he was described as being 'immaculately groomed if slightly gaudy in a diamond-patterned cardigan and tie'.[155] When he made his turn to suits, the *Mirror* reported he had

> gone from picket line scruff to capitalist fat cat. Sartorially, at least. Angered by photographs of himself in a baseball cap and casual clothes, Crow obviously decided it was time for a change of image. Only he's taken things too far. This week he has been touring the TV studios wearing that favoured uniform of the City gent, a pinstripe suit.[156]

146 *Times* 12 September 2009.
147 Doncaster Brewery created 'Bob's Brew' in September 2014 in his memory.
148 *Mirror* 9 February 2014.
149 Where his last ever interview with Radio 4's *PM* was recorded (*Daily Mail* 12 March 2014).
150 *Financial Times* 25 March 2011.
151 *Mirror* 9 February 2014.
152 *Independent* 13 September 2007.
153 *Mirror* 9 February 2014.
154 *Guardian* 20 June 2009.
155 *Guardian* 13 December 2010.
156 *Mirror* 24 October 2002.

Crow never learned to drive, did not own a car and did not have a chauffeur[157] (which led to a successful libel action over the *Sun*'s claim that he had a union-subsidised 'luxury car').[158] This was as much about believing in public transport as it was about being served by a good public transport system – he professed that he was not 'anti-car'.[159] The *Evening Standard* reported that he 'commutes to his office ... every day on the Central line. ... When there's a strike he goes by bus.'[160]

Union bureaucrat

High salaries and cosseted lifestyles are often touchstones for the radical Left, implying that union leaders (most obviously, general secretaries) cannot be relied upon to lead consistent resistance to employers. Bluntly put, union leaders have a marked tendency to sell struggles short and work hard to avoid escalation by practising accommodation and moderation. This tendency is also attributed to the function that they perform, namely negotiating between workers and employers while not being workers themselves. They are held to be union *bureaucrats*. The conclusion drawn is that only the rank-and-file members can be relied upon to lead the fight because they have a material interest in doing so.[161] The case of Crow (along with the likes of Serwotka and Scargill) provides a challenge to this theory.[162] More especially, it is difficult to find cases when Crow did or did not advocate strike action or its continuation that were related, strongly or otherwise, to the aforementioned factors. It is much more convincing to suggest that how he acted resulted from his assessment of the balance of forces in any particular dispute. Moreover, he was a pretty consistent advocate of striking, often shoring up the RMT members' courage to take strike action and stand firm against employers and government. In this sense, he was ahead of members in their militancy. Former CoE member Janine Booth wrote that 'He was seen as the personification of the idea that the job of a trade union leader is to stick by and stick up for the union's members

157 *Guardian* 2 July 2004.
158 The offending article was published on 15 September 2010. The resulting £5,000 damages were paid into the RMT Widows' and Orphans' Fund and costs were awarded against the newspaper (*RMT News* November 2010).
159 *Independent* 13 September 2007.
160 *Evening Standard* 16 May 2001.
161 For examples of a recent exposition of this theory of trade union bureaucracy, see Darlington (2014a) and Darlington and Upchurch (2012).
162 As an aside, it does not appear to be the case that the likes of Bob Crow can be seen to be the exceptions that prove the rule.

– not apologise for, close down or slither away from their battles with employers'.[163]

Stress and his last days

There was popular speculation that a barrage of media scrutiny played a part in killing Crow at too early an age.[164] Being RMT general secretary, and doing job the way he did, undoubtedly affected his health. The long working hours, relentless travelling to address meetings and constant demand for interviews, allied to his high profile in disputes, indicated that Crow was a workaholic for the RMT and for socialism.[165] Oliver New recounted:

> During his day he would constantly flit from, for example, dealing with an industrial issue, fielding conversations and decisions with union reps, senior managers. He might flip over to union organisational or finance matters or jump to union employment issues ... There were legal issues of various kinds, requests to attend meetings, international matters etc etc. One issue after another, Bob seemed to work nonstop, around the clock. He rarely turned down a request to speak, especially to members and union branches and he had a prodigious memory for faces and people. He might be any-where in the country, go to a picket line, then speak to office staff on the phone, then speak at a funeral, then make more calls, then go to another meeting, on and on without breaking his stride.[166]

Crow did this and did it in this way because, as he said, he 'adore[d] his job',[167] despite the hostile scrutiny. Early on as general secretary, he said: 'I used to be demonised about twice a year. But now it seems like every day. But I put up with it.'[168] Yet this led to a sense of fatigue over a decade later. Just before his death, the *Guardian* journalist Decca Aitkenhead wrote of her interview with him that he had 'been giving back-to-back interviews for hours, and has the beleaguered air of a man worn out by relentless

---

163 *Solidarity* 19 March 2014.

164 See, for example, George Galloway (*Guardian* 12 March 2014). Martin Wicks, a former Network Rail RMT national clerical rep, also wrote after Crow's death: 'His premature death seems undoubtedly to be the result of the stresses of a job which he took as seriously as life itself' (*Facebook*, 13 March 2014).

165 *Independent* 14 February 2002. The *Guardian* (12 March 2014) reported: 'He was, those close to him say, a hard and dedicated worker'; and the *Morning Star* (11 January 2002) commented on him as a being 'hard-working, dedicated and com-mitted'.

166 Email correspondence.

167 *Guardian* 20 June 2009.

168 In Murray (2003: 100).

questions'.[169] After his death, she wrote: '[T]the first time I visited Crow … in 2010, he looked like a man in his element. The last time, just a month ago, he looked highly stressed and at the end of his tether.'[170] Aitkenhead's view of him in 2010 chimed with what he had said a year earlier when asked: 'What's the worst thing about your job?' He replied 'Nothing … I consider it an absolute privilege to be able to represent RMT members and to be able to work with such committed and energetic people as our staff and representatives. Genuinely, there is no downside and nothing else I would rather be doing.'[171] Aitkenhead also recalled: 'The last time we met he got properly angry with me for questioning the socialist ethics of continuing to live in a council house … once Crow got wound up he was quite incapable of hearing anything. Red-faced and frustrated, afterwards he bolted in a huff before our photographer had a chance to shoot his portrait.'[172] Aitkenhead's interview also revealed that 'when he eventually explain[ed] why he thought it pointless to worry about how his [cruise and] holiday [in Brazil] might play with the media, it's the only time he allows a glimpse of how deeply Fleet Street has hurt him':

> Well, if it weren't the Rio holiday they'd be saying something about 'Bob comes to work in jeans and a Fred Perry top.' If I'm walking around in a suit they go: 'Look at him, he's done well for himself walking around in a Savile Row suit, he should be wearing a Fred Perry.' They will use any argument they want to try and humiliate me, and try and make me basically look bad, and try and make me small.[173]

Alluding to the stress and strain, Cash commented: 'I don't know how Bob dealt with some of the stuff he [did].'[174] Early on, Crow admitted to walking and jogging so as to 'clear my head … shake off some stress'.[175] He also said:

> Well it would be nice to walk down the road and all the shutters and windows opened and people started throwing roses out, shouting: 'Morning Bob, how are you?' That would be nice. However, you've got to recognise that the job you do ain't about being nice. The job we do is about defending our members. And as far as I'm concerned, if I can get job security and decent pay for my members I couldn't give two hoots about being unpopular.[176]

169 *Guardian* 7 February 2014.
170 *Guardian* 12 March 2014.
171 *Independent* 29 June 2009.
172 *Guardian* 12 March 2014.
173 *Guardian* 7 February 2014.
174 *Guardian* 1 October 2014.
175 *Independent* 12 January 2002.
176 *Guardian* 13 December 2010.

In what turned out to be one of his last media interviews, he expressed the possibility that he would not necessarily continue being RMT general secretary, since they were other things he wanted to do in his life. For example, he told the *Mirror*: 'I don't want to be doing this job too much longer. There are so many things I still have to do.'[177] These included spending more time with his grandchildren, watching Millwall play, going to every football ground in Britain and hill walking.[178] Yet the situation was not clear cut, since he also said: 'I haven't made up my mind yet when to go but won't stay too long because I think people get stale. I'm not ready just yet – but I'll know when it's time.'[179] Similarly, he told the *Guardian* in February 2014: 'I mean, I might not even stand for election next time [in 2016].'[180] When he died, Decca Aitkenhead re-examined her interview notes, finding that he had alluded to the reason why he might not continue:

> I asked Crow if he would be standing for re-election in 2016. 'Well at the moment I am. But that may change. I'm not going to be hanging around forever.' When I heard the news of his death I remembered that he'd said he might stand down ... It wasn't until I checked my notes that I saw the first reason he gave for why he might not run again. 'My health.'[181]

This chimed with former TSSA general secretary Gerry Doherty's recollection:

> The news of his all too early, sudden demise came as a shock but not, to be honest, as a huge surprise. I remember, a number of years ago he and I were returning to London on a late night train from some engagement or other when he confided to me that he regarded the job of general secretary as being 'a young person's game' given the amount of travelling and the stress involved. He confided that it was his intention to leave the job before it took its toll on his health. Sadly, he never got there.[182]

Indeed, Crow's last public engagement was typical of him. The Saturday before he died he travelled to Brighton to speak at a miners' strike thirtieth anniversary event. The *Evening Standard* reported that on 11 March 2014, Crow was taken to Whipps Cross hospital in Leytonstone by

---

177 *Mirror* 12 March 2014, from material for an interview published on 9 February 2014.

178 *Mirror* 9 February 2014, 12 March 2014. *RMT News* (October 2014) reported: 'Following a charity trip up Snowden in 2013, Bob Crow planned to climb England's highest peak Scafell Pike this October.'

179 *Mirror* 9 February 2014.

180 *Guardian* 7 February 2014.

181 *Guardian* 12 March 2014.

182 *TSSA Journal* April 2014.

ambulance at about 7 a.m. and that 'medical staff spent an hour trying to save his life, but he had suffered critical heart damage as a result of an aneurysm and could not be revived'. The next day the *Daily Mail* reported that 'An RMT colleague yesterday said the union boss "wasn't feeling well yesterday afternoon" but had put it down a case of flu … He is said to have been unwell in recent weeks and to have visited the hospital where he died yesterday for treatment.'[183]

Conclusion

A plethora of adjectives were used to describe Crow as he was seen in public. Tenacious, steadfast, uncompromising, tireless, blunt, unashamed, fearless, inspirational, passionate, unapologetic, pugnacious, outspoken, bolshie and brash were among the most common. They were used of him in life and in death. His personality and consequent public persona were the vehicles that allowed him to express his politics and carry out his job in such a forthright manner. But it was the potential power of RMT members that made the vital difference, providing Crow with the confidence to be the leader that he was. He could afford to be defiant and pugnacious because he was able to put words into deeds. The psychology of being a leader critically involves self-actualisation and self-affirmation. Whether he saw himself as a self-styled class warrior or just a hardworking general secretary for his members, in carrying out his duties and tasks as he did – because of his politics and personality – Crow clearly achieved self-actualisation and self-affirmation.

183 *Daily Mail* 12 March 2014.

7. Politics and practice

This chapter and the following one provide an analysis of Crow in terms of his person, politics and members' potential power. Left-wing radicalism provided the viewpoint from which Crow looked at the world, guiding his actions and defining his role as a union leader. Indeed, this intellectual framework attributed a crucial role to unions as agents for radical ends. This chapter begins by looking at his intellectual worldview before moving on to examine how it played out in practice and the conditions that facilitated this.

'Communism/socialism'

Just as with the term 'militant', Crow was not shy to use the word 'socialism', deploying it as a defiant badge of honour: 'Some people are scared to use the word socialism, but I am not. We are opposed to the capitalist order and want a socialist society';[1] 'In the RMT, we are proud to have continued fighting our corner industrially and politically, with our eye on the socialist transformation of society that will ensure a decent life for all';[2] 'I'm proud to be a militant and I'm proud to be a socialist.'[3] Along with representing RMT members' interests, prosecuting the case for socialism was his key other objective, as this encompassed furthering the interests of the working class as a whole. Ironically, it was the *Evening Standard* that recognised this: 'No, the general secretary of the RMT has only two interests at heart: the wallets and general wellbeing of his members, and the class war which will one day bring about the socialist utopia he so fervently prays for.'[4] This recognition made the *Independent*'s comment somewhat strange: 'Mr Crow is very much a political animal although he has no discernible attachment to an ideol-

1 *Morning Star* 26 June 2002.
2 *Morning Star* 24 June 2002.
3 His speech to the Durham Miners' Gala in 2013 (see http://www.tusc.org.uk/17300/10-07-2016/from-the-archives-but-so-relevant-bob-crow-at-the-durham-miners-gala).
4 *Evening Standard* 1 October 2002.

ogy. Arguably he is more a devotee of Robin Hood than Karl Marx.'[5] Crow never hid his politics, making it one of the few issues the *Evening Standard* could find to praise him for: 'The one thing that can be said in his favour is that he is admirably straightforward: what you see is what you get ... he has never made a secret of his hard-Left politics.'[6] Crow's politics, and his openness about them, mattered for three reasons. First, he became a major figure on the Left in Britain, so what he did and said had a bearing on the struggle for socialism. Second, the RMT was committed to achieving socialism in accordance with its rule book – 'to work for the supersession of the capitalist system by a socialistic order of society' – and more than most other unions, it took practical steps towards doing this. As a senior figure in the RMT since 1994, Crow played an important role in guiding and shaping this. And lastly, the RMT was a union that punched well above its relative weight in the labour and union movement, solidifying Crow's influence.

So, as Crow described himself as a 'communist/socialist',[7] it is worth exploring what he meant by this. Coming from a political training in the Communist Party, followed by the SLP, Crow did not have a Trotskyist or anarchist approach to socialism and communism.[8] Although he recognised that Soviet state socialism was far from perfect, to him it was still preferable to western capitalism (whether of the social democratic or neoliberal variety). Therefore, his conception of 'communism/socialism' was not based on the self-activity of workers in the form of workers' councils (soviets) as is the case with revolutionary socialism, where the working class emancipates itself. Rather, his conception came from the Communist Party's 'British road to socialism' perspective of socialism being achieved by the working class leading other subservient classes in a popular democratic alliance against monopoly capital, and implementing a left-wing programme of socialist construction through Parliament. This involves capturing and reforming the capitalist state, as opposed to abolishing it and creating a new one, through winning Labour and the unions to a left-wing position. Notwithstanding the issue of whether the Labour Party was the party of labour, the key measure of this type of socialism was state ownership and control. For example, Crow believed that the nationalisation of Northern Rock and AIG by governments in Britain and the USA, respectively, in 2008 was 'a socialist impulse for nationalisation ... show[ing] socialism is not dead after

---

5 *Independent* 19 April 2004.
6 *Evening Standard* 1 October 2002.
7 *Guardian* 20 June 2009.
8 The *Daily Mail* (12 March 2014) wrongly called him a 'Trotskyite'.

all'.[9] Emphasising that he did not prioritise workers' self-government, his version of state socialism as applied to railways meant 'The railway has to be run like an army ... a command and control situation. You must have a general board with a general that can give a decision that is relayed straight away to the front line.'[10] And his favourite motto was thoroughly social democratic or state socialist: 'You pay tax and you buy civilisation',[11] as his hero, Tony Benn, believed.[12] All this suggested that he was in favour of a representative, indirect body like a parliament under the control of a socialist party instituting socialism by nationalising the commanding heights of the economy.[13]

In referring to 'actually existing socialism', Crow commented:

> Joe Slovo, the great South African communist leader, said the Soviet Union may have failed with communism, but capitalism has failed mankind. I think that's what it's all about. People are going to say this system ain't working, it's not providing me with jobs, it's not providing me with homes, it's breaking down socially, it leads to wars.[14]

He continued: 'I'd say [communism/socialism is] based on a society of people's needs.'[15] In his last interview, he stated that communism was based on 'need not greed'.[16] Elsewhere, he insisted upon a very practical aspect to his view of socialism: 'Retire as soon as possible – life isn't about working, it's about enjoyment.'[17] And during the campaign to prevent Britain's involvement in invading Iraq, *Time Out* reported that he 'waxed nostalgic for those halcyon days when a truculent Soviet Union might have kept America in check'.[18] In other interviews, he proffered:

> I've never seen a true communist state, so I don't know whether it would work ... I don't think communism failed – the problem was the lack of democracy. They had far better hospitals, far better education. I went to Cuba and they may not have had satellite dishes or DVD players, but they had a doctor on every corner, they had good schools, the basic fundamen-

9 *RMT News* September 2008.
10 *The Journal* (Newcastle) 1 January 2002.
11 *Telegraph* 16 February 2002.
12 *Times* 12 September 2009.
13 This was why he admired China (as the Communist Party of Britain did), speaking at a Maoist Communist Party of Great Britain (Marxist-Leninist) celebration of such forms of communism on 7 November 2009.
14 *Guardian* 20 June 2009.
15 *Guardian* 20 June 2009.
16 BBC Radio 4, 10 March 2014.
17 *RMT – Your Union*, Platform Films, 2005, London.
18 *Time Out* 3 April 2002.

tals in life were far better than they are here. If the communist regimes had got more people involved in democratic decisions, they would still be there now.[19]

Later he reiterated this, with *The Times* reporting that 'he loves the idea that he might retire to Havana. [He said] "I think communism is working well. If you go to Cuba you might not get everything you want in the shops, but if you drop down with a heart attack you will get first-class medical treatment."'[20] Elsewhere, he expanded on his ideal:

> I'm not looking for Utopia. In my view, everyone should have the chance of a job at a decent wage; to have the opportunity to buy or rent a house. There should be a decent National Health Service and good schooling for everyone.[21]

> In a socialist society you would have jobs, decent housing, a decent NHS, education, living in a world of peace.[22]

> [A] socialist society where the main aspirations of people are given: they have a job, a decent wage, a house, healthcare, good education and no wars.[23]

But the *Financial Times* reported that his version of socialism would not comprise total equality: 'A "utopian society" where everyone is earning the same amount of money would be unrealistic, he admits ... Brain surgeons deserve more than general secretaries, he says. He just wants everyone to have a chance to be a brain surgeon.'[24]

Crow never questioned that the regimes he favoured were not communist and that popular democracy is an inherent part of communism (as per workers' councils). So what he advocated sounded more like social democracy and labourism, however left-wing, being brought about by Parliament and not workers directly. Quintessentially, social democracy (or labourism) is state intervention in the operation of the market to ameliorate its outcomes (without abolishing it), and this intervention is directed by an 'old' Labour-type party in government. Social democracy – or state socialism as some prefer to call it – seemed especially to be Crow's ideal because there was no place for revolutionary insurrection of the Bolshevik kind in his worldview: 'I'm not into

19 *Telegraph* 16 February 2002.
20 *Times* 12 September 2009. Crow wrote in the *Big Issue* (8 May 2012) that 'we need our own Cuban revolution' in Britain.
21 *Independent* 19 April 2004.
22 In Murray (2003: 102).
23 *Times* 12 September 2009.
24 *Financial Times* 25 March 2011, 10 September 2004, respectively.

smashing things up';[25] 'I believe in peaceful civil disobedience, that's the kind of extra-Parliamentary action I'd like to see. I don't believe in going round smashing things up.'[26]

Delving a little deeper, Crow made clear that his understanding of Marxism was of a more practically orientated kind. Asked '[Do you] often discuss Marxism?' he responded: 'No, this happens only when [I see] journalists.' In rather self-deprecating terms, he told the same interviewer: 'I'm not an intellectual. I haven't read and understood all of Marx's volumes.'[27] The *Financial Times* reported that 'one quote was burnt into his brain from these [earlier] days: "The higher the profits, the lower the wages, and the other way round."'[28] He later said:

> No need to wade through all of *Das Kapital* – just a quick read of the little pamphlet *Wages, Price and Profit*, which lays bare the mechanism by which bosses extract surplus value from the labour of working people. It should be in the pocket of every trade unionist. In it, Marx demolishes the idea that wage rises cause inflation and that it is futile for workers to fight for higher pay. Marx's great achievement was understanding capitalism, and in understanding it he came to the conclusion that it could and must be replaced with something better. As long as there are capitalists Marx will remain relevant.[29]

Of course, Crow did not abide by the point that it was 'futile for workers to fight for higher pay', believing that it not only brought workers material benefit but also had a role to play in raising their socialist consciousness. It would be hard to say that Crow believed in historical or dialectical materialism when he responded to the question 'Do you believe in karma?' with: 'I don't believe in reincarnation ... I believe in understanding the world through facts ... But I do believe that what goes around comes around in this life. If you cause distress to others, it will come back to you.'[30]

Bearing in mind this and his view on the emergence of a new party of labour, it is clear that Crow did not have a coherent understanding of the relationship between his industrial and his political work in pursuit of socialism, or how trade union consciousness transmogrified into socialist consciousness. This was despite the TUC smear document which reported

25 *Financial Times* 25 March 2011.
26 *Independent* 19 April 2004. In the same interview, it was also reported that, while he deeply deplored the Iraq war, 'he would not support violent demonstrations against it'.
27 *Financial Times* 10 September 2004.
28 *Financial Times* 10 September 2004.
29 *Independent* 16 June 2006.
30 *Independent* 17 February 2004.

that he believed that 'strike action raises the class consciousness of the rank and file',[31] and the *Evening Standard*'s allegation that he was 'the most strike-conscious official' in the RMT,[32] and that the RMT under Crow 'was determined to use strike action as a consciousness-raising weapon'.[33] For example, since he did not have a 'transitional' approach, he did not consider what types of strikes (political or economic, continuous or discontinuous, sectional or mass) in what situations and with what outcomes could lead to heightened consciousness.[34] Indeed, he generally over-estimated the impact of strikes upon consciousness and, recalling his belief in spontaneity, he showed little understanding of how the processes that inform consciousness (such as cognitive liberation) unfold, especially as it was not self-evident under his leadership of the RMT that strikes did raise consciousness. Of course, the same could be said of other left-wing union leaders too.[35] And in arguing that, 'If I were a worker and my union leader was a communist and he was getting me good pay rises, [I'd say] bring on more communists',[36] Crow showed little concern that members could support leaders despite their politics, and that this would not advance communism's cause.

Echoing the absence of an effective combinination of industrial and political struggles was the same problem over combining the fight for reforms and the fight for socialist revolution (however defined). While having a certain view of what socialism looked like (notwithstanding that communism was thought of as a higher form), Crow believed, like the rest of the far Left, that revolutionaries are the best reformers without being reformists. Yet putting this into practice was harder than the dictum suggested, especially because any revolutionary appetite might be satiated by achieving reforms, thus reinforcing a reformist consciousness. Crow was not alone in facing this challenge – the same was true for Serwotka. Infrequently and ironically, Crow sometimes recognised the challenges he faced here, saying: 'I want all my members at Network Rail to have the same terms and conditions. There's nothing revolutionary about that.'[37] Part of the explanation for Crow's weakness

31 Quoted in *Evening Standard* (10 January 2002). The phrase was widely used in newspapers such as the *Telegraph* and *The Times* in subsequent months.

32 *Evening Standard* 10 January 2002.

33 *Evening Standard* 23 June 2004. See also *Evening Standard* 15 July 2002, 13 May 2003, for the same allegation.

34 See Kelly (1988: 85–128) for a discussion of the salient issues.

35 Nor did he consider how and why gaining reforms would lead to the eventual achievement of socialism in the manner of capacity building and encroaching control.

36 *Guardian* 20 June 2009

37 *Independent* 19 April 2004.

here was that he, like other left-wing union leaders, was not a writer of any great depth, so he was not compelled to think through the strategic issues. In his *RMT News* column, he provided summaries of what had happened and what would happen regarding the RMT and, in doing so, brought up bigger issues of capitalism (including profits, privatisation and EU neoliberalism) and socialism (based on nationalisation), and linked them to the battles that the RMT and workers more widely were fighting. But these and his other writings were of a propagandistic and agitational nature, and this style carried over into his speeches. Writing to greater length than he did would have allowed him to move beyond the basic paradigm he operated from. Yet in an era of retreating working-class power and consciousness, the more pressing, immediate need *appeared* to be for this steadfastness and motivational style of exhortation. Similarly, in the fight for better material conditions and against neoliberalism, it mattered little that Crow was from one far Left background rather than another, or that his view on transforming workers into agents for socialism was underdeveloped. It might have mattered had the radical Left been much stronger, if the struggle for socialism was at an advanced stage or if society had been in a pre-revolutionary situation. For Crow – given that none of these were the case – what was more important was his steadfastness of belief and his professing them widely and frequently, and that they motivated him to work and fight hard for his members and for the Left in general. Moreover, his intellectual framework chimed with the consciousness of activists and active members who were not of revolutionary socialist consciousness.

Political heterodoxy

Whatever the weaknesses, contradictions and inexactitudes of Crow's political worldview, it was a key part of what kept him going. The same was true of what can be termed his unexpected range of heterodox views. For example, he favoured the death penalty[38] (although not for the 'crime' of crossing a picket line as Paul Routledge quipped),[39] believed that MPs should be given pay rises[40] and cooperated with the Murdoch press.[41] His definition of the working class was idiosyncratic to say the least, and he did not believe in the workers' wage policy[42]

---

38 *Observer* 17 February 2002.
39 Routledge (2003: 64).
40 *BBC News*, 10 March 2014.
41 In the person of Christine Buckley.
42 See Chapter 6.

or that all union officials should be elected.[43] This heterodoxy did not displease everyone on the Left, with George Galloway opining that his views on MPs' pay showed his 'creative and counterintuitive line of thinking'.[44] Such views certainly made Crow refreshing and interesting for the media. On the death penalty, he was asked 'Should we bring back the death penalty?' and responded:

> No. But I only say that because I have no confidence in the judicial system. In principle, I think that if someone has killed someone else, the public shouldn't have to pay to keep them in prison. I'm not talking about manslaughter, but if someone has committed premeditated murder, I think they do deserve the death penalty.[45]

In his last interview, he told BBC Radio 4:

> I do believe [MPs] should have a pay rise. Some people like to think that MPs should live in a tent, they should have four to a room. I want my MP, particularly those who don't live in London and have to travel down to work in London, to have decent accommodation to go home to. I want them to have a proper meal. I don't want them to scramble around the place, but I do believe that the MP should be paid adequately. Or what we will get in my view is a lot of people not going into parliament because they will say 'We are going to lose out' … Anyone in the public sector, we are all civil servants, we are serving civilisation. That is what a civil servant does, and they should be paid accordingly.[46]

It seemed that this was more important to Crow than there being more MPs from working-class and union backgrounds, especially as he commented: 'It doesn't bother me if they have a privileged background. Tony Benn is one of my heroes. Fidel Castro was born with a silver spoon in his mouth.'[47] Maybe this was linked to his wide-ranging view of who was working class, since he believed that anyone who worked was working class.[48] The *Guardian* reported:

---

43 While many RMT officials were elected, not all were, especially the industrial relations officers, and there were no plans to change this. This reflected Crow's view that bringing in the necessary expertise and experience was more important than implementing the principle that members should elect all officials, because democracy is no guarantee of the quality of elected officers.

44 *Guardian* 13 March 2014.

45 *Independent* 17 February 2004. Earlier, the *Observer* (17 February 2002) reported: 'Crow says he still is, in principle. Killers should be killed, he says, but adds that he has too little faith in the criminal justice system to support the death penalty in practice.'

46 Radio 4 *PM*, 10 March 2014.

47 *Times* 12 September 2009.

48 This included well-renumerated footballers, whose wealth allows them to own property and businesses, to become businesses through sponsorship and have a

Crow calls himself a Marxist, and as such is typically maddening. A lot of what he says makes sense – but then he goes and spoils it by saying something that bears almost no resemblance to reality. His commitment to the working class is passionate, but when I ask him to define the working class, he says 'Those who have to go to work and sell their labour to their employer' which would apply to practically everyone, including multi-millionaire bankers. As he himself earns £133,183 a year – 'I'm working-class, absolutely' – you can't help wondering if this might explain the breadth of his definition.[49]

In a later *Guardian* interview, Crow defined 'a rich person as anyone earning more than £100,000',[50] a figure to which he came perilously close. This threatened to make a mockery of his claim to still be working class and displayed a strain of 'workerism', namely the idealisation of workers and working-class culture.[51] Upon his death and referring to his salary and lifestyle, the *Guardian* observed that 'his clarity regarding the class struggle between "them and us" vanished when it came to looking at himself'.[52]

Any Marxist definition of class begins by examining which people own and control the means of production, distribution and exchange, and benefit from this ownership and control. Workers are those who do not own and control these means. They are, thus, bound to sell their labour and they gain less than the value of it because they are exploited, with this exploitation providing the basis of surplus value (profit). This excludes many who do work but gain more than the value of their labour, most obviously senior managers such as directors of companies and chief executives of organisations. But just as importantly, workers are also those who do have control over other workers, since they do not direct their labour as managers do (especially regarding hiring and firing, discipline and performance). So members of elites work and there are larger numbers below them of capitalist functionaries, whether in private companies or the state. Yet in an interview with Radio 4's *Report* in 2009, Crow said: 'There's two classes – either you own pro-

lifestyle that is very different from that of workers: 'The fact that they are well-paid entertainers makes no difference. They are icons, but they are workers as well' (*Guardian* 10 October 2003).

49 *Guardian* 12 December 2010.

50 *Guardian* 7 February 2014.

51 Partly as a result of his belief that he was still working class, he said: 'Any shop steward or general secretary not doing his or her job properly can expect the order of the boot from those they represent' (*Guardian* 30 June 2003); he also said 'I've got more in common with a Chinese coolie than with Princess Anne' (*Telegraph* 16 February 2002).

52 *Guardian* 12 March 2014.

duction or you work for an owner of production – there's nothing in between.'[53] This was his longstanding view: 'My view is that there are two classes of people out there, those that go to work and those who own the means of production'; 'At the end of the day you are a worker or you are an employer. Either you own the production, or you work the production.'[54] He muddied the definitional waters even further, telling the *Financial Times* (in reference to the nearly one hundred RMT officers and staff):

> I would be upset if 90 per cent of RMT staff didn't say I'm the best employer they have worked for. I say: 'You can't call me Mr Crow, that's a disciplinary offence!' They don't have to make an appointment to see me, just knock. I've never sworn at staff in my life. I like to treat people with dignity and respect.[55]

He was involved in the process of interviewing for RMT jobs such as the manager of the RMT Credit Union. Being a general secretary also meant having to manage and direct an organisation of considerable resources, even if this was subject to some degree of membership control through the CoE. One does not have to subscribe to the aforementioned analysis of union leaders as 'union bureaucrats' to recognise that union leaders cease to be workers when they become general secretaries. So, rather than Crow being a 'working class hero' (as some such as the *Financial Times*,[56] George Galloway,[57] Christine Buckley[58] and the *Mirror*[59] thought), he is best characterised as a 'hero *for* the working class', not a 'hero *of* the working class'.

Crow's erroneous definition of the working class may have mattered in another place and time, but it had little practical importance for leading the RMT and being a leading socialist critic of neoliberal capitalism. Indeed, it reinforced his interlocking politics and personal identity, backing up the sense he had of himself. His defence of his salary and

53 Replayed on Radio 4's *Profile*, 4 April 2010, http://www.bbc.co.uk/pro grammes/b00rq2kx.

54 *Independent* 14 September 2002; *Times* 12 September 2009, respectively.

55 *Financial Times* 10 September 2004. Of his style of management, Cash said: 'That door was always open. He had a great way of communicating with people and getting them involved ... very pragmatic and very principled at the same time' (*Guardian* 1 October 2014).

56 *Financial Times* 12 March 2014.

57 *Guardian* 12 March 2014.

58 Her intended biography of Crow was to be entitled *The Last Working Class Hero*. Setting aside the issue of a general secretary not being able to be a 'working-class' hero – a hero currently in and of the working class – there were other contenders who were not yet dead, like Scargill and Serwotka, so Crow could not be the last.

59 *Mirror* 9 February 2014.

housing association tenancy are just two examples of this. Moreover, it spoke to a major characteristic of his, namely that he was an independent, free thinker prepared to go against orthodoxies even if it sometimes meant that subjective considerations outweighed objective considerations. The *Observer* reported that 'Crow's friends, and even those who campaigned against him, say that for all his socialist politics, he is too shrewd for doctrine.'[60]

Practically, this heterodoxy had two significant outcomes. First, he was a hardened optimist who was not taken in by the pessimism and defeatism that affected much of the Left, so he did not accommodate and acquiesce to social liberalism (the social democratic version of neoliberalism). Thus, he could sound convinced of the need to fight capitalism even when few were actually doing so or doing so successfully. Yet intriguingly, he did this without joining those perennial optimists on the Left who, in believing that two swallows make a summer and that revolution was always just around the corner, made themselves ridiculous. Second, he could on occasion call things as he saw them and not as he wanted them to be, despite working closely with many who could not (such as the Communist Party, the Socialist Party and the SWP). For example, he recognised that he could not simply launch a new workers' party in a top-down manner as Scargill had done, or expect activists to join it with its pre-existing rules. Instead, he recognised that the task of creating such a new party would be slow and difficult, and would ultimately come out of the unions and not from the Left outside the unions.[61] Yet he had no idea of how this would happen, nor a strategy to achieve it.[62]

His heterodoxy originated from his being a member of several political parties and none, so that he was not governed by one party canon and benefited from an independent political status (through the RMT), which allowed him to be freer thinking. The RMT's break from Labour enhanced this. Moreover, being a powerful and successful leader meant that his views seldom came under serious scrutiny within the RMT.[63] Something of a cult of personality along with a culture of deference within the RMT to Crow accentuated the tendency towards lack of critique. On some issues, however, Crow was perfectly orthodox for the Left. One instance was his republicanism: 'I think the royal family is very privileged. I wouldn't like to see any harm coming to them, but I do

60 *Observer* 17 February 2002.

61 *Guardian* 9 September 2013.

62 *Guardian* 9 September 2013. See also *LookLeft* interview, 23 September 2011.

63 Unlike the situation of his co-traveller, the ASLEF leader Mick Rix, who was defeated by the right-winger Shaun Brady in the 2003 general secretary election.

believe they lead a very privileged life. Why should they be able to start out in the world with far more benefits than other people?'[64] Indeed, this orthodoxy often led him to be accused of being contradictory. For example, Christian Wolmar argued that:

> I do not generally have much sympathy for [him]. He runs a union as a political project, and therefore much of what he says is obviously contradictory. He wants renationalisation and an end to private sector involvement, yet his constant threatening of strikes and his very confrontational style of negotiation means ... the last thing any government would want to do is to give his union more power by bringing transport more into the public fold ... Crow, by being so obdurate, negates his own case. His militancy is giving the government every possible reason to avoid bringing in any more services in house.[65]

Industrial and political, class and section

Crow was frequent and forthright in stressing that his members' interests came before all else: 'I don't care if the government is Tory or Labour, I only care about getting a good deal for my members';[66] 'Our organisation is purely to look after our members. Our job is to represent our members';[67] 'The only poll I'm concerned about is our members.'[68] This was recognised when the *Guardian* said: 'The RMT is a stroppy outfit with a bruisingly basic commitment to looking after its own.'[69] In making these points, Crow was concerned to stress the industrial side of his members' interests, for he was often accused of making the industrial 'political' by using industrial disputes to settle so-called political scores. Thus, the *Independent* reported: 'He insists he does not believe in using industrial action for political ends', with Crow telling it: 'We are concerned about purely industrial issues.'[70] The rub was that for the leader of a transport union where public transport was still publicly subsidised, still partly in public ownership and essential to the functioning of the economy and society, any industrial action – even in the private sector – inevitably had political ramifications. Thus, economic strikes against TOCs had significant political dimensions as well, while London

64 *Independent* 19 April 2004.
65 'Union and management should grow up', *Christian Says*, http://www.chris-tianwolmar.co.uk/2009/06/union-and-management-should-grow-up/.
66 *Scotland on Sunday* 13 January 2002.
67 *Times* 31 January 2012.
68 *Guardian* 7 February 2014. See also *Sunday Times* 17 March 2002; *RMT News* April 2010.
69 *Guardian* 12 May 2011.
70 *Independent* 19 April 2004.

Underground political strikes had significant economic dimensions. Hence RMT strikes often produced combined and usable economic and political effects. This influenced the RMT led by Crow to practise both political as well as industrial unionism, even if political expediency required that he deny it.

These statements also testify to the sense of sectionalism prevalent in the RMT. Sectionalism as an obstacle to working-class unity is often berated as narrow-mindedly self-serving, but to move towards a class-based approach, unions, whether trade or industrial, must begin with the defence of sectional interests. This was not, of course, the whole picture, as Crow and the RMT sought common cause with other workers and citizens. But even when asked if RMT members might want to control their 'own' industry, Crow's response was not as expected: 'Our organisation is purely to look after our members. It's not our job to run the railway network, our job is to represent our members.'[71] And, in response to a similar question about whether he would like 'the chance to run London Underground, rather than just represent the workers', he said:

> You couldn't do two jobs, not full time. I would like, however, an opportunity to sit on a board sometimes, not as a board member but just say four times a year or something, Network Rail or London Underground, and just give the view on how workers might be able to help run the system better. There's ideas that workers come up with every day that are never taken into account. There's no input, no process. You've got thousands of consultants for free here – workers who do the job every day. And passengers. They should talk to us more.[72]

This testified to a more conventional perspective whereby unions seek to negotiate between capital and labour over the wage–labour bargain rather ending the wage–labour bargain (even though for the latter they must in the first instance seek to negotiate over it). For Crow – as for others – these types of statements show the difficulty of understanding how sectional consciousness is transformed into (working-) class conscious, and how to influence this through active intervention. After his death, the *Guardian* reported: 'According to a manager who frequently negotiated with him: "Yes, he wanted to change the world, but he saw his first task as bettering the lot of his members rather than encouraging some kind of revolution."'[73]

What was evident in Crow's worldview was that he neither placed his members' interests in contradiction to those of others nor placed

71 *Guardian* 13 December 2010.
72 *Observer* 4 September 2011.
73 *Guardian* 12 March 2014.

their interests above the interests of other workers. This was because he believed that the best way to help non-RMT members to fight was through the example of RMT members fighting (and winning), even if this was to ignore a number of important differences in the power resources available to different workers. He saw no sense in which his well-paid members were an aristocracy of labour because in his view all RMT members – along with workers in general – were underpaid. The only difference between them was by how much. When he was on a picket line during a 2002 London Tube strike, the *Daily Mail* reported: 'Crow was quoted as saying he would like to see drivers' pay "doubled, if not trebled"';[74] he also said: 'When I see Ronaldo earns half a million quid a month and he gets a signing on fee of £8m, and people say train drivers are greedy working nine hours downstairs in them kind of temperatures all day long. Nah. I think it's the rate for the job.'[75]

Skill shortages, strategic leverage and bargaining strategy

Under Crow's leadership, the RMT sought to exploit skill shortages and increased rail passenger numbers to better its members' wages and conditions.[76] In 2002, the government recognised shortages of 900 drivers, 800 signallers and 1,200 track-layers.[77] These had developed since privatisation as companies cut staff and, rather than train new staff, poached staff from competitors. The RMT strategy was to target particular TOCs and contractors in order to engage in 'pattern bargaining' – essentially, driving up pay and conditions by threatening one company with industrial action (and taking it if need be) and then, once successful, moving on to another, using the deal just gained as a precedent by which to leverage the same deal or a better deal. With the threat of losing staff to rivals due to inferior pay and conditions and/or suffering industrial action, the strategy was successful overall. Crow put it this way: 'We've used the break-up of the industry to leapfrog other people. We go to the most sympathetic company and then to the others saying, "If it's good enough for them, what about you?"'[78] Given that the RMT did not organise the majority of train drivers – who are the most strategically placed workers – this was no mean feat and made a good fist of a difficult

74 *Daily Mail* 26 September 2002.
75 *Guardian* 20 June 2009.
76 *Sunday Telegraph* 13 January 2002; *Guardian* 16 January 2002. The increase in passenger numbers, in terms of developing leverage, offset the decline of freight traffic as it migrated onto the road network.
77 *Times* 15 February 2002.
78 BBC Radio 4 *The Report*, 8 October 2009.

environment.[79] This structure of decentralised bargaining – which led to many disputes – resulted from the ending of national or industry-wide bargaining. For the RMT, Crow pushed unsuccessfully for the return of national pay bargaining in order not only to augment leverage but also to put all its members on a level playing field.[80] Short of achieving this, if disputes could be coordinated in order to maximise pressure upon employers and government, this was done, as the strikes over protecting guards' duties showed. With hundreds if not thousands of separate companies, bargaining and industrial relations were 'messy', with Crow saying: 'We are involved in one negotiation a week with companies so if we wanted to manufacture disputes, we could. But we have come to agreements with more operators than not.'[81]

To appreciate and understand Crow's bargaining skills, recognition is required of the foundations of the potential power of transport workers (especially over- and underground workers), and that this potential power is only translated into usable power (strategic leverage) through the use of particular tactics concerned with the nature of the action and windows of opportunity. Under Crow, the RMT developed this into a fine art, targeting high-profile public events such as international football matches, mayoral elections, rugby cup finals, horse races (such as the Grand National), the Olympics, the Commonwealth Games and so on, as well as other times of peak usage associated with holidays (Christmas, Easter, New Year, bank holidays). This led the *Independent* to comment that 'the Bob Crow technique … is carefully timing your strike to cause the maximum disruption [and] discomfort'.[82] The technique also coordinated London Underground and overground rail strikes (especially rail services feeding into London). This was less reinventing the wheel or innovation, and more renewing and re-applying earlier practices that had fallen into disuse.[83] But limited confrontation – through consecutive one-day strikes on a weekly rotation[84] – was

79 Seldom has the RMT organised the majority of London Underground drivers (and it does not organise significant numbers of train drivers outside London). Although the proportions changed and there was some dual membership, the *Evening Standard* (29 September 2014) suggested that ASLEF had 60% of members and the RMT 40%.

80 See *Sunday Times* 17 March 2002.

81 *Scotland on Sunday* 13 January 2002.

82 *Independent* 27 October 2010.

83 For example, coordinated ballots and strikes were used under Knapp, such as the successful and coordinated rail and Tube strikes over the summer of 1989 and the 1996 strike against TOCs for a shorter working week.

84 Such as those by West Coast overhead line workers in 1990, signal workers in 1994 and Scotrail members in 1997.

modified in important respects. First, 24-hour strikes were held over two days. Second, one-day strikes were held closer together, such as one on a Friday and one on a Monday. Third, two-, three- and four-day strikes were held. All served to increase levels of disruption and, thus, leverage. Under Crow, the RMT had no significant problems in mobilising members for this greater level of confrontation. Indeed, loss of wages was often reduced, as more infrequent instances of widespread action brought quicker results than a greater amount of lesser action. Sometimes there was debate inside the RMT about whether the public should be targeted less and businesses more, because of the varying impact the actions had on these interests. For example, the proposal for a strike on New Year's Eve was countered by proposing to strike on the first day back to work in the New Year.[85] But whatever days were chosen, the decision was taken on the basis of 1) high levels of RMT membership density; 2) high levels of membership participation; and 3) insignificant availability of strike breakers such as managers. Understanding the foundations of this potential power requires the recognition of several components.

First among the components that give rail strikes strategic leverage is they have immediate impact upon large numbers of citizens by stopping a service's operation where alternative means are not readily available; journeys cannot be stockpiled and most journeys are of a perishable nature (they must be made on a particular day). Second, public transport remains a public good despite privatisation and given continuing public subsidy. Consequently, deliberate disruption can be used to generate political leverage over employers and government. It is not merely that public transport is used by millions of citizens but that it is also central to operating a capitalist economy (which governments are still held responsible for). So when a strike takes place, it affects not only the employer but also the public and the economy. It also helps that there is a special place for railways in the psyche of British society in terms of what it means to have a decent and civilised society. Third, the sector has experienced a long period of expansion in passenger numbers and investment (which is akin to an expanding or buoyant product market elsewhere). Fourth, the connection between members and their union (the 'union identity') is both persuasive and pervasive, partially arising from the industry identity of which the RMT is part. So overall, when a rail strike takes place, it can generate both economic

85 *Tunnel Vision*, AWL pamphlet, available as 'The fight against Tube privatisation reviewed', http://www.workersliberty.org/story/2004/07/02/fight-against-tube-privatisation-reviewed-part-1.

and political leverage, confirming the fundamentals of Batstone's schema.[86]

It is not only rail workers – and others like fuel tanker drivers and postal workers – who hold this kind of potential leverage; other workers and their unions can locate the sources and points of potential leverage in terms of the fragility of the work systems they operate (whether as a result of just-in-time production techniques or particular events). For example, workers whose jobs are being outsourced can refuse to help train their replacements, office workers can threaten to slow down the flow of work in the run-up to audits and lorry drivers can disrupt finely tuned delivery systems with short, selective action. Not all of this requires striking. Just as rail workers can refuse to work rest days, so too these types of workers can work-to-contract or refuse overtime. In the 2012 dispute over the Buildings and Engineering Services National Agreement (BESNA), construction workers and supporters blocked site entrances, stopping time-critical deliveries of material. Other workers and their unions also have to contemplate several other dimensions. One concerns using the process of moving towards industrial action as a form of escalation (notice of dispute, notice of balloting, notice of result, notice of strike and so on), and whether employers and governments become inured to such action if it is used too frequently. Another is forming alliances with other workers as citizens and consumers (see below). Public sector strikes are essentially political strikes as they do not seek to financially hurt employers. When Labour did not support such strikes and even condemned them, thought was needed on how such striking could still generate political heat. Crow's leadership of the RMT showed an advanced understanding of these issues even if he did not resolve the challenges for the RMT's non-strategic members such as caterers and cleaners, or for its bus transport members.[87]

Strikes, industrial action and injunctions

The ability to generate effective economic and political leverage through traditional techniques explains why there was relatively little innovation in industrial tactics under Crow's leadership. As Pottage put it, Crow's talent was to unearth 'our militant tradition that had lain dormant' and

---

86 Batstone (1988).

87 With regard to the latter, the *Telegraph* (4 October 2010) reported: 'In a fascinating Radio 4 documentary on pay Bob Crow told Danny Finkelstein that it was all down to the balkanisation of bargaining units. Because bus routes are tendered individually the unions can't bring London to a stop.'

have it 'gradually brought back'.[88] The one attempt to innovate was a form of industrial action short of a strike called a 'no fares day'. Tickets would not be sold or checked so that passengers were able to ride for free, a tactic that had been employed elsewhere (in, for exanmple, Buenos Aires, Chicago, New York, Adelaide, Vancouver and Dublin). This tactic was tried in 2004 on South Central Trains, but when the company threatened to seek an injunction against strike action that was also part of the overall action, the industrial action short of a strike was also stood down.[89] In 2007, and following strike action, Central Trains conductors who were RMT members planned to take the same action[90] but cancelled this after they were threatened with losing half their pay.[91] Although these actions were part of an overall package of industrial action, it was surprising that they were used, since in 2002 Crow had stated:

> [W]e've looked at the situation where our members come to work and refuse to collect tickets and give tickets free and let people go up and down. But what would happen is that our members would be breaking their con- tract of employment and could be sent home and dismissed. So we couldn't have that situation because we'd then have to end up having a dispute to protect the people that were dismissed. So [striking is] the only course that we've got at the end of the day.[92]

In the South Central Trains case, Crow said: 'To ensure that we do not fall foul of potentially damaging legal action the RMT executive has decided to call off the action.'[93] The decision not to collect fares was used just once more before Crow's death, when in early February 2014 an instruction 'not to carry out revenue duties' was given in the London Underground dispute over job cuts.[94] The caution displayed here with regard to the 'no fare' action echoed Crow's and the RMT's consist- ent response to employers' use of anti-union laws. For example, in response to Network Rail being granted an injunction in 2010 which also saw the calling off of intended action by Network Rail maintenance

88 *Scottish Left Review* May–June 2014.

89 *RMT News* June–July 2004. See also Lyddon (2009: 333).

90 RMT press release, February 13 2007.

91 'RMT climb down on Central Trains', 15 March 2007, http://www.workers liberty.org/node/7908.

92 BBC Forum, 9 September 2002, http://news.bbc.co.uk/2/hi/talking_point/ forum/2234265.stm.

93 *RMT News* June–July 2004, p. 6.

94 'RMT Tube Revenue Action Explained', RMT memo, 6 February 2014, http://www.rmtlondoncalling.org.uk/node/4793. The action was suspended after two episodes, and was not judged to have been effectively carried out (see 'Support and build the "revenue action"', AWL website, 9 February 2014, http://www.work ersliberty.org/blogs/tubeworker/2014/02/09/support-and-build-revenue-action).

workers, Crow wrote to branches and officers on 1 April 2010 saying:

> The matter has been considered by an emergency meeting of your full Council of Executives and they have made the following decision:– 'That we note the Court injunction granted against us today in regard to the signal workers action due to start on 6th April 2010. We instruct the General Secretary to inform our members and Network Rail that the action is called off'. In regard to the infrastructure ballot and the action due to take place on 6th April 2010, as a result of today's injunction we note that this ballot may also be unsafe in legal terms. The General Secretary is, therefore, instructed to call off all industrial action and inform our members and Network Rail.[95]

While Crow frequently condemned the anti-unions laws and their use, urging unions to break and defy them, he never led the charge for this to happen in practice, calculating that the RMT on its own would not be able to easily withstand the consequences of defiance. Thus, at a meeting of his branch (LU engineering) in 2007:

> Asked if the RMT would break the law, [Crow] answered that it would do so when the rest of the TUC did so ... The General Secretary explained that the anti-union laws were too vicious to break given that individuals could be picked out and sacked ... and that the union's funds could be seized.[96]

This was the same position taken by other Left-led unions (with the exceptions of the NUM, SOGAT and NGA in the 1980s).[97] The only examples since of unions sanctioning unballoted – and thus unlawful – action were the CWU at the Royal Mail in the 1990s[98] and the TGWU

---

95 'Network Rail industrial action called off for both signalling staff and engineering members', general secretary's office. At the end of the letter to branches and officers, Crow noted: 'Accordingly, the General Secretary is instructed to re-ballot all of our Operations and Infrastructure members as soon as practically possible ... We are still in dispute and are determined to fight on in defence of jobs, terms and conditions and for a safe railway. The General Secretary is to inform Network Rail that we remain available to negotiate a settlement to both disputes.' It is, therefore, important to note that later in October that year, 'the RMT said that after months in dispute it had secured a 7 per cent pay deal for Network Rail maintenance workers and defeated plans to lay off 1,500 maintenance workers' (*Times* 13 October 2010). The details were that maintenance workers would also receive a £2,000 lump sum for the implementation of the restructuring, equivalent to a one-off 8% of salary for a rail worker on a basic salary of £25,000, and that any future redundancies would not be compulsory.
96 'Campaign for a fighting democratic union', *Off The Rails*, 6 November 2007, http://www.workersliberty.org/node/9511
97 Their defiance led to fines and sequestration.
98 Gall (2003).

at Gate Gourmet in 2005.[99] Crow did not encourage RMT members through a 'nod and a wink' to take unofficial action as a means of getting around the anti-union laws. For this contradiction, he was criticised for hypocrisy.[100] Instead of unlawful defiance, he preferred promptly re-balloting when strikes were subject to injunctions or refraining from calling upon RMT members not to cross RMT picket lines. Indeed, in some cases he advocated that RMT members should cross picket lines,[101] casting an interesting light on his criticism of Ken Livingstone.

Power and growth

Crow often referred to the labour market within which RMT members (and other workers) existed as a 'jungle',[102] meaning that in a 'dog eat dog world' the generation and application of collective power was the only way to defend and advance their interests. Thus, 'whoever has muscle at the end of the day gets what they want ... That is why I make no excuses about taking industrial action to look after our members';[103] 'Whoever's strongest is going to get their way';[104] '[Union recognition] doesn't mean anything unless there is density and you have power.'[105] This indicated a firm understanding of the role of argument in putting members' case to employers but that, without mobilising members, this was necessary without being sufficient to win. Indeed, he understood that strikes had to cause disruption to be effective, with not striking causing damage to RMT members' interests and influence. To gain demands, leverage had to be exercised: 'We didn't do it with balloons, we didn't do it by being nicey-picey, hoping they will feel sorry for us and take pity on us. We did it by threatening industrial action';[106] 'We've made more progress in the last 24 hours than we have in the last three months. Because they haven't listened to us. Now suddenly they're taking us seriously. And the only reason they're taking us seriously is because we've got a strike.'[107]

---

99 *Guardian* 18 September 2006.

100 See *Socialist Worker* 11 January 1998 and 9 January 1999 (regarding the infrastructure and Underground strikes, respectively).

101 Instances were on London Underground in 1996 when he instructed RMT members to cross ASLEF picket lines until they were able to strike themselves following balloting (*Socialist Worker* 20 July 1996) and the infrastructure strike in 1998 with regard to signalling workers (*Socialist Worker* 11, 18 July 1998).

102 *Guardian* 20 June 2009; *Times* 12 September 2009.

103 *Times* 12 September 2009.

104 *Guardian* 13 December 2010.

105 *Times* 9 May 2009.

106 *Financial Times* 10 September 2004.

107 *Guardian* 7 February 2014.

Disruptive capacity was allied to labour scarcity, with the political leverage (gained from a combination of disrupting a public good and economic strikes having a political dimension) also utilised.

Notwithstanding the fact that Crow did not directly call action or decide its length and nature, his attitude towards striking was important. It was this ability not only to fight collectively but also to win collectively that was crucial for union growth. This is the context in which to set his statements:

> People join us on the basis that we're prepared to have a fight. We might not always win, but they do like someone having a go. Now our job, by the way, is to get what we want without going on strike. Our members don't get up in the morning going: 'What can we have a strike about?' But our brand is that we're out there, punching away.[108]

> Why was it that in 1978 we had 12 and a half million union members in this country compared to now where we've got six and a half million? Why did people join in '78? 'Cos the unions had teeth. The last few years you wouldn't even have known the TUC [conference] was on, but the TUC this year was probably the best publicised TV event in 15 or 20 years. Why was it? 'Cos they was talking about taking action, defending their members and so on. So it demonstrates the fact that if you've got teeth, and you're a force to be reckoned with, then people join you 'cos they see you can do something.[109]

> Trade unions have lost influence because they have lost density in the workplace ... If a trade union ain't gonna fight, there is no point in joining.[110]

Did this mean that all unions could easily fight and consequently recruit and retain members? At the 2014 London May Day rally, the TUC general secretary, Frances O'Grady, said, 'if all ... unions across the movement built their unions like Bob Crow built the RMT, the unions would collectively have 10m members instead of their present 6m';[111] George Galloway claimed that '[Crow] proved that workers can win if they are organised, determined and well led';[112] and Labour MP John McDonnell commented that 'Bob's most significant role was to demonstrate by example to every ... union member that the ... union movement could be as effective today in securing better pay and conditions of employment as at any time in its history.'[113] Yet unions have

108 *Guardian* 13 December 2010.
109 *Guardian* 13 December 2010.
110 *Times* 9 May 2009.
111 *The Socialist* 7 May 2014.
112 *Guardian* 12 March 20114.
113 *Independent* 14 March 2014.

both grown and declined while fighting, most notably the PCS. Under Serwotka's leadership since 2002, membership increased from 281,000 to 313,000 in 2006, falling back to 247,000 by 2014.[114] During this period, the PCS was a quintessential 'fighting back' union with frequent national and departmental strikes undertaken. Moreover, while utilising an organising approach within the ambit of partnership with employers, membership of the right-wing union USDAW rose from 310,000 in 2002 to 341,000 in 2006 and 433,000 in 2014 (although unlike the PCS it seldom had over 50% union density among the major employers it organises within).[115] And, as suggested above, particular account needs to be taken of the strategic work position of RMT members and the potential leverage afforded by this. Occasionally, Crow recognised this when saying: 'It's not the same playing field, I will accept [– that is] working on the railway compared to working in a call centre.'[116] Moreover, and compared to others, the nature of the transport system meant that for many RMT members, power was easy to demonstrate and measure, as well as their strikes' economic (to train companies) and political (to government and economy) impacts.

The ramifications of new technology for RMT members' power were not quite as deleterious as many made out in the case of driverless trains, automated ticketing on London Underground and automated signalling on overground lines.[117] Fewer workers would be employed, affecting RMT membership levels, but the other ramifications were not straightforward. Automated work still requires care and maintenance, so the issue becomes whether these workers are unionised, providing greater concentration of potential power into fewer hands. Moreover, human intervention is always needed with technology because, for example, not all passengers are capable of using it unassisted. In the case of driverless trains, not only were they not planned to be introduced until 2028 and not operational until 2030,[118] but they would

114 *Annual TUC Directory*. See also McCarthy (2009).

115 *Annual TUC Directory*. In a biography, it is not possible to definitively state what specific influence a particular leader had in increasing membership. Nor is it possible to make much in the way of useful comparison with leaders of other unions with regard to membership levels (not least because to do so would also require a study of these other leaders).

116 *Guardian* 13 December 2010. The more apposite cases for the RMT would have been in shipping where competition with other means of travel and crewing through 'flag of convenience' arrangements undermined bargaining power.

117 On signalling, the *Financial Times* (23 July 2011) reported: 'Network Rail ... propos[ed] clos[ing] nearly all 800 signal boxes and replac[ing] them with computerised centres, which the RMT says would cut 4,000 jobs over the next decade.'

118 *Evening Standard* 29 September 2014.

be staffed.[119] And, if the RMT was to get its way, as Crow wanted, the headcount reduction would not be as drastic because 'We are not opposed to new technology but we are clear that any changes that may arise should be accommodated through a shorter working week, additional annual leave and the right to retire at 55 on full pension entitlement.'[120] For the period of Crow's leadership, new technology did not undermine the RMT's bargaining power on over- and underground rail transport.

Provider–user alliances

Unions, as associations of workers providing services to citizens, have an interest in creating alliances between themselves and the citizens using those services. For a union, these alliances can bind industrial and political interests together in effective ways, and this is particularly so for privately owned transport which is publicly regulated and used *en masse*.[121] The profit imperative and government austerity endanger the interests of both workers and citizens, whereby lower levels of staffing lead to poorer standards of service. Crow recognised these linkages, saying for example: 'Overcrowding is a major source of the frustration that passengers all too often take out on our members, who face the constant threat of verbal and physical assault.'[122] On a number of occasions, he argued that:

> Health and safety is the number one concern for workers in the transport industry. The need to eliminate unnecessary risk and to ensure the safest possible working conditions for our members – and safer transport systems for the travelling public – is the one issue that overshadows all others ... the constant tendency to undermine safe working conditions [is] brought [about] by employers' drive to minimise costs and maximise production and profits.[123]

> Privateers love the market – until it works against them ... The private sector is in this first and foremost to make profits, not to run trains ... Return the industry to the public sector and you'll do away with the parasites ... Our

---

119 *Guardian* 31 December 2013. The *Evening Standard* (29 September 2014) reported that trains would be staffed at least 'initially', and the *Guardian* (10 October 2014) put this at 'at least a decade'. This made a mockery of Boris Johnson's dig at Crow 'for saying that his members would not test-drive new driverless trains for the London Underground' (*Independent* 9 October 2012).

120 *Times* 21 July 2011. The issue of resisting management's terms for the introduction of new technology led to the *Telegraph* (5 February 2014) labelling Crow a 'chubby cockney Canute'.

121 See Tattersall (2010).

122 *Guardian* 16 October 2003.

123 Crow (2007: 3).

aim for the railway industry is clear – we want a publicly owned, publicly accountable, reintegrated railway. All our experience as rail workers tells us that that is the only way to run a safe, efficient railway system.[124]

Few people, outside the government and private shareholders, would argue that rail privatisation has been anything but a failure. For passengers it has delivered Europe's most expensive railway, poorer services and massive overcrowding as investment in new capacity lags behind demand. For rail workers, privatisation has brought constant attacks on jobs, pension rights and working conditions, and for all concerned it has undermined safety, with tragic consequences … For the economy it has meant waste on a grand scale as subsidy is diverted into shareholders' pockets, work is duplicated and investment money is borrowed expensively on commercial markets. It has meant massive asset stripping, the squandering of a huge property portfolio, the dismemberment of Britain's train-making industry, the loss of vital skills and immense damage to communities.[125]

Although there was no formal alliance with public transport users, since passengers are not collectively organised,[126] ASLEF, RMT, TSSA and Unite established in 2012 the 'Action for Rail – people before profit' campaigning group, and RMT ran its own 'RAP – rail against privatisation' initiative during the 2005 general election campaign, consisting of marches and rallies in major urban centres, led by Crow, along with the publication of reports and studies. Participation in RAP outside the RMT was limited, indicating difficulty in mobilising citizens even though most supported rail renationalisation. The RMT sought with RAP and other campaigns before and after to press for renationalisation, and in the case of RAP the demands also included an immediate windfall tax on TOCs' 'excess profits' and legislation to end PPP on the London Underground.[127]

Beyond this, Crow was the best-known, most relentless and most effective advocate of passenger safety and well-being.[128] He was not the first to deploy the safety argument[129] but he did so more forcefully than Knapp and extended the repertoire of passenger-focused concerns

---

124 *Morning Star* 15 March 2002.

125 Crow (2008: 19).

126 Representatives of passengers on various transport bodies are not elected in popular ballots and so do not constitute genuine representatives.

127 *Independent* 29 April 2005.

128 He seldom overlooked an opportunity to promote this agenda – one occasion for which he was criticised was a demonstration on rail safety in 1999 (*Socialist Worker* 30 October 1999).

129 Knapp did so in 1997 during a dispute.

so that they ranged from fare rises[130] and safety (unstaffed level crossings,[131] derailments, poor maintenance and so on) to cuts to time-tabled services, overcrowding, delays and breakdowns. He consistently harassed and harangued those responsible (TOCs, maintenance companies, rail regulators, government) for passengers getting a poor, expensive and, sometimes, unsafe service.[132] Using colourful language, on fare rises in 2002 he said: 'This is the great train robbery that would make Ronnie Biggs green with envy ... He only nicked £2.5m';[133] on further privatisation: 'The most modern section of the UK rail network has been sold off for a song in what amounts to nothing more than a fire sale of the family silver to prop up the financial deficit caused by the bankers and speculators in the first place';[134] on corporate accountability: 'Seven years on, this is yet another sick legal farce that highlights the utter lack of accountability for corporate killers. Even if they are hit with a massive fine, it will only be recycled public money when, frankly, it should be spent on safety improvements, like the automatic train protection we are still waiting for';[135] and the effect of sub-contracting: 'We have contractors who use sub-contractors, sub-contractors who use agencies, agencies who use casual labour – and they're all in it for profit';[136] 'The RMT is seriously concerned that following the fragmentation of the industry the left hand does not know what the right hand is doing.'[137] Later on Crow opined: 'All of this debt burden increases the pressure on Network Rail to cut corners. People are doing safety-critical work on our railways on zero-hour contracts. Our fear is that safety standards that should be applied won't be, and we'll be back to the bad old days of

---

130 Crow also spelled out the environmental consequences of higher train fares: 'Talk about the need to reduce carbon emissions is just so much hot air if the privateer train operators are allowed to impose another round of rip-off rail fare rises. The private franchises are interested only in lining their shareholders' pockets, yet the failure to impose a sensible fares policy is having a direct effect on the environment, as more and more people who should be on trains take to their cars' (*Guardian* 1 December 2007). Earlier, he said that a £2.4bn programme of works was 'a good start towards the massive increase in capacity that our railways need if we are to meet the climate challenge and get people out of cars and aeroplanes and on to trains' (*Guardian* 4 April 2007). See also Crow (2008: 20).

131 The alternatives were to build bridges or tunnels or staff the crossings.

132 Some examples are to be found in the *Morning Star* 2 August 2002; *Evening Standard* 22 August 2002; *Mirror* 29 August 2002; *Independent* 21 June 2003; *Times* 7 September, 18 October 2005; and *Telegraph* 23 January 2007.

133 *Morning Star* 20 December 2002.

134 *Guardian* 6 November 2010.

135 *Telegraph* 1 November 2006.

136 *Mirror* 18 May 2002.

137 *Guardian* 17 February 2004.

Railtrack.'[138] Crow's self-selected role of passenger advocate and guardian was not uncontested, with the Strategic Rail Authority saying: 'Every time that Bob Crow appears passengers and taxpayers should be afraid, they should be very afraid.'[139]

The RMT under Crow did not just spout its concerns, but it also took action to prosecute them. So, for example, the RMT took industrial action in 2003 to try to bring London Underground maintenance back in house.[140] In 2005, the RMT threatened industrial action if drivers on the Northern Line were disciplined for refusing to take trains out over safety concerns[141] and then did the same to gain guarantees on staffing levels and safety equipment.[142] Later, RMT members at South Eastern Trains undertook to strike for a day over plans to replace booking office staff with machines and cut opening hours.[143] Finally, a New Year 2006 strike was held over rosters and redeployment and implications for safety.

The effect of strikes on citizens

Creating alliances with citizens was often fraught when industrial action sought to cause disruption in order to generate economic and political pressure on employers to gain demands.[144] Crow well understood this, without making a necessity into a virtue as was often suggested.[145] He believed that strikes were a means to an end: 'No-one likes going on strike and strikes are not the aim. The aim is getting just settlements for working people and, sometimes, it takes strike action to get there;'[146] and

> We know very well the disruption caused by our members striking ... and believe me we never take action lightly. But of course, we also know that there are times when we are pushed into a corner and it's either roll over and get trampled on or stand up for what you believe in ... So yes, there are occasions when we are left with no option but to close down sections of the transport system, but it's always a last resort.[147]

138 *Guardian* 15 July 2013.
139 *Times* 22 June 2004.
140 *Independent* 21 November 2003.
141 *Independent* 14 October 2005.
142 *Guardian* 29 July 2005.
143 *Telegraph* 28 November 2005.
144 Of course, strikes do not always cause 'misery' for commuters because they provide opportunities to work from home or not work at all.
145 The *Sunday Times* (13 January 2002) quoted him as saying (in a reference to Lenin) that 'one strike is worth 10 election victories'.
146 *Morning Star* 15 March 2002.
147 *Independent* 29 June 2009.

But he also made clear that 'I don't shirk from taking industrial action. Our job is to negotiate the best pay and conditions. Industrial action is the last resort and you don't take it lightly – but when you start you don't finish until you have won';[148] 'We don't want to hurt the travelling public, but if we don't take strike action, no one's come up with a solution yet about how to solve our problems.'[149] Arbitration was not seen by Crow as a magic panacea as it could not guarantee to fulfil union demands.[150] There were also times when he made it plain that management intransigence had led to strikes going ahead: 'Obviously we regret having to resort to strike action but passengers should know that LU's approach to these negotiations has been utterly shambolic.'[151]

That being said, Crow varied the emphasis he placed upon public apologies. Although he was often defiant, he was not always so. Examples of defiance varied from

I'm not one of those union officials who continually say they regret the inconvenience caused by industrial action. People would say I was crying crocodile tears. Our job is to represent working people. Management is refusing to negotiate. We either accept that or do something about it. You cannot have a dispute without inconvenience to the travelling public. It's not selfish. Our job is to defend and improve our members' terms and conditions.[152]

to

Last week a journalist asked me if I slept well knowing that if we did take action it would cause disruption to millions of people. The answer was simple: I will lose no sleep at all knowing that Tube workers and the people they serve will not run the risk of a minor incident turning into a major disaster because we failed to act.[153]

The extent of his apologies varied. For example: 'Our plans will clearly cause disruption to members of the travelling public, which we deeply regret, especially in the run-up to Christmas, but the messages we have received in recent days from members of the public indicate that the overwhelming majority of people share our concerns.'[154] This was

---

148 *Guardian* 14 February 2002.
149 *Telegraph* 16 February 2002.
150 Whether of an ordinary or pendulum nature (where in the former the difference is often split and in the latter the arbitrator must choose one or the other of the union or employer positions).
151 *Independent* 28 September 2001.
152 *Independent* 19 April 2004.
153 *Evening Standard* 10 September 2002.
154 *Independent* 25 October 2003.

because he blamed management, but they were messages of apology nonetheless: 'It's diabolical, they shouldn't have to go through this disruption … If London Underground had observed its agreement with the unions to go to independent mediation, the strike would simply not have happened';[155] 'I absolutely 100% regret what is happening to the travelling public, but blame for this dispute lies fairly and squarely on LU's doorstep';[156] 'I sincerely apologise. We are public servants and will be serving the public tomorrow. This is London Underground's fault';[157] 'Course I feel sorry for them. But they know our fight isn't with them. It's with Transport for London. And what do they expect a union to do?';[158] 'I'm sorry passengers will suffer. But I am sure they will sympathise with us when they know it is a safety issue';[159] 'We send our apologies to travellers and these are not crocodile tears.'[160] Of the divergence, the *Guardian* stated:

> Crow said in April [2004] that he would not keep apologising for inconvenience caused by industrial action because people would accuse him of crying crocodile tears. Ahead of this week's tube strike, he said he regretted the industrial action and insisted his were not crocodile tears. The two positions may not be contradictory, but the earlier statement is thought by those who claim to know him best to capture the authentic Crow.[161]

The ramifications of the disruption caused by the RMT strikes was a significant issue for Crow, not least because he was once attacked by what was likely to have been a disgruntled traveller: 'Several years ago Mr Crow was beaten up when the union chief said he was recognised by his attacker on a Tube train.'[162] Campaigns were also organised against him. The *Independent* reported after a Tube strike:

> In a nod towards the growing world of virtual activism, there were, last night, more than 30 groups on the *Facebook* website expressing the feelings of disgruntled commuters about the RMT and its … general secretary … Among the less explicit titles for the groups were 'Bob Crow and the RMT need a good shoeing' and 'Disrupted by the RMT strikes? Show your support and post them a turd'.[163]

155 *Independent* 3 October 2002.
156 *Guardian* 26 September 2002.
157 *Evening Standard* 1 October 2002.
158 *Mirror* 9 February 2014.
159 *Mirror* 15 October 1999.
160 *Telegraph* 30 June 2004.
161 *Guardian* 2 July 2004.
162 *Evening Standard* 4 January 2002. This is not to be confused with the attack on him at his house on New Year's Day 2002.
163 *Independent* 6 September 2007. Six months after being set up (in March

Crow's responses showed that he was sensitive to the accusation of being unpopular, tersely remarking 'Of course, commuters are angry with me'[164] and 'I know how [personally] frustrating [the RMT's industrial action] is'.[165] But they also showed that he believed he was not hated and that he was even liked and respected. Asked 'What's it like to be known as the most hated man in London?', he told the *Guardian*:

> Well, number one, if anybody says it is nice to be known as hated, they're lying. But I'm not hated. They're lying. I'm not the most hated. I tell you what, I've been travelling around on the trains, and I don't get no aggro at all … people actually come up to me and say, 'Why are the trains running late Bob[?]' and I say to them 'I'm not responsible for running the trains. I wish I was, but I'm not.'[166]

Elsewhere he gave similar responses: 'I travel on the Tube every day and don't get any aggravation. Some people obviously dislike me and what we're standing for, I accept that. But 10 times that amount of people come up and shake my hand';[167] 'They are, actually [sympathetic] … people I speak to personally, they say "Good on you" … [I get recognised] pretty much all the time. But I never get any aggravation, honestly. People come up and ask questions about the railway, and if can answer them I do';[168] 'I've got to say I don't get no aggravation … I don't get nothing shouted at me. I use the train every day, I use the tube every day, I don't get people come up to me going: "Oi, what about this strike?" … when I walk along the platforms, I see people look at me and as I go past I hear them go: "You know who that is – that's him." I get that. But I don't get no aggro.'[169] Indeed, one of his frustrations with his

---

2015), there were over 1,400 members of the invitation-only 'RIP Bob Crow … a union legend' Facebook group. There were also many others, such as 'Bob Crow's a C**T !!', 'Bob crow sod off', 'Bob Crow needs a damn good thrashing', 'Bob Crow Should be Castrated Just like his Dog "Castro"' and 'Get Rid Of Bob Crow'. All but one of these ('Bob Crow (and the RMT) are wankers', with 1,574 members) had less than 100 members. However, in total they outnumbered the 'RIP Bob Crow … a union legend' group, though only by a couple of hundred, and the 'Bob Crow (and the RMT) are wankers' group was started as long ago as March 2007. There was also a relatively popular 'I Bet I can find 1 million people who agreed with Bob Crow and Tony Benn' group, with over 2,500 members by mid-2015.

164 *Mirror* 12 March 2014.

165 *Times* 12 September 2009.

166 *Guardian* 20 June 2009. The same interview reported: 'When England played Andorra last week the tubes were on strike. One banner at Wembley read "Bob Crow is a ******". Did he see it? "Oh yeah, it had six digits in it."'

167 *Financial Times* 25 March 2011.

168 *Observer* 4 September 2011.

169 *Guardian* 13 December 2010.

exchanges with the travelling public was that they thought he ran the railways and was, therefore, responsible for them: 'People give me comments such as, "Oy, there was a signal failure yesterday, Bob, whatcher gonna do abaht it?" They think I run the railways!';[170] 'when people come up and complain about delays I say – "I don't run the Tube, I only represent the workers."'[171]

Against austerity: civil disobedience and general strikes

Crow believed that defeating the Conservative–Liberal Democrat coalition government's austerity and privatisation programme necessitated mass, coordinated strike action which, along with public demonstrations, would be reminiscent of the 1970s and 1980s. His approach varied between calling for a general strike and generalised strike action depending upon the tempo of struggle.[172] He also frequently called for mass civil disobedience. Recalling the actions of Fathers4Justice, at the TUC in 2010 he said: 'Maybe we need Batman climbing up 10 Downing Street, Spider-Man on Buckingham Palace as part of peaceful demonstrations of civil disobedience.'[173] In the light of the late 2010 London student protests, which he supported, Crow stated: 'Our immediate challenge is to link up all the different groups at the sharp end of the ConDem austerity measures into a united force of opposition that can turn the tide on Clegg and Cameron. The political and chattering classes have seriously underestimated the public mood and RMT will work with students, pensioners, communities and our fellow trade unionists to build the strongest possible co-ordinated and peaceful resistance in the coming months';[174] 'We need co-ordinated action, and a social and political movement that mirrors the anti-poll tax campaign if we're to turn the tide on the fiscal fascism of this ConDem government.'[175] In

170 *Financial Times* 10 September 2004.

171 *Times* 12 September 2009.

172 Following from his call at the 2010 RMT AGM for a 'sustained campaign of generalised strikes across both the public and private sectors and community direct action ... [and] general and co-ordinated strike action across the public and private sectors' (RMT press release, 30 June 2010), at the 2010 TUC for the RMT, he tabled a motion calling for 'generalised strike action' (*Times* 10 September 2010). This changed to a general strike by 2012 when the POA raised the demand. He repeated the call for a general strike in his 2013 May Day message to RMT members (*RMTv* 30 April 2013).

173 *Guardian* 13 September 2010.

174 *Guardian* 13 November 2010.

175 *Guardian* 21 December 2010.

doing so, he cited French citizens as a model to follow.[176] His New Year message for 2011 predicted that, while '2010 saw the initial skirmishes, 2011 will see those protests escalate into a popular movement that will match the success of the anti-poll tax campaign and RMT members will once again be right in the front line'.[177] Early in the New Year, he said: 'Cameron wants to give his big business supporters the chance to make a profit out of every section of our public services and he will have a bare knuckle fight on his hands as trade unions join with local communities to defend everything from hospitals to fire services.'[178] Yet he also told the *Financial Times* that he was 'not planning to co-ordinate strikes with other unions ... [adding] If there are disputes in rail, shipping or bus industries and other transport industries at the same time over cutbacks, we would be fools not to co-ordinate the timing.'[179] Later that year, he told the TUC congress:

> If workers come under attack then it runs in the veins of the trade union movement's history to mobilise civil disobedience and resistance. We are back in that mode right now and we need to learn from the environmental and social justice campaigns like UK Uncut. From blocking motorways to disrupting Bono at Glastonbury, those are the kind of tactics we need to add to our campaigns.[180]

In his penultimate New Year message, he said: 'We ... pledge to make 2013 the year that we step up the class fightback.'[181] To these ends, he and the RMT supported the launch of the Coalition of Resistance in 2010 and its successor, the People's Assembly against Austerity, in 2013.[182]

Focusing upon strikes, he argued at the RMT's 2010 AGM that a 'sustained campaign of generalised strikes'[183] in both public and private sectors was required to defeat government austerity, and at the 2010 TUC congress he said:

176 Radio 4 *Today*, 21 October 2010: 'We will need community protests and combined and co-ordinated action to fend off these cuts and we should look across the Channel to the kind of resistance being mobilised by the French trade unions, which enjoys overwhelming public support, as an example of how to resist austerity cuts and attacks on standards of living.'

177 *Times* 28 December 2010.

178 *Evening Standard* 21 February 2011.

179 *Financial Times* 25 March 2011.

180 *Telegraph* 14 September 2011.

181 *Times* 2 January 2013.

182 The Coalition was initiated by Counterfire, a split from the SWP. It worked with unions and politicians from the Left. However, it failed to expand as desired, so a wider initiative, the People's Assembly, was launched by Counterfire working with an enlarged group of unions and politicians.

183 *Telegraph* 30 June 2010.

We are confronting the same enemy and we should bring our forces together. The TUC will not be calling for a general strike. What we will see, however, is groups of workers taking action at the same time. Workers will take to the streets as they did during the poll tax demonstrations. I am not advocating going round smashing shop windows, but I am saying there should be a campaign of civil disobedience.[184]

He made his last major call for this at the 2013 TUC congress, saying: 'The surge in planned industrial actions across sectors, including fire, post, transport and education gives us the ideal foundation [from] which to make good the trade union movement's commitment to co-ordinated and generalised strike action.'[185] The year before he argued, in supporting the POA motion looking at the practicalities of staging a general strike: 'Let's co-ordinate action, and if that means a general strike, let's do it and get on with it.'[186]

Crow's calls and desire for action were sincere and heartfelt, and personally he could not have done more to generate the momentum for them, speaking at countless meetings to urge workers and citizens to take action, and helping coordinate RMT strikes with other public sector strikes (before and after the single mass public sector strike of 30 November 2011). The RMT, led by Crow, could not have done more given its size and the fact that most of its members were not public sector workers. Yet Crow profoundly under-estimated the difficulties faced. His belief that there would be mass action indicated his over-estimation of the ripeness of the political situation for mass resistance and the growing appeal of socialism, with his subjective desire colouring his assessment of objective reality (as was the case with much of the far Left such as the Communist Party and his new fellow travellers, the Socialist Party). He made a number of bold predictions:

[T]here will undoubtedly be a fight back … this anger will mirror the growing resistance in Greece and elsewhere …[187]

Once people realise the full scale of the impact of the government's cuts for public services and the true costs for jobs and standards of living we can expect widespread resistance.[188]

184 *Times* 13 September 2010.
185 *Independent* 9 September 2013.
186 *Times* 13 September 2012.
187 *RMT News* May 2010.
188 *RMT News* June 2010.

This attack on the people who make this country tick will spark a furious backlash and will drive millions onto the streets in French-style protests to stop the great pensions robbery.[189]

We're going to see an explosion ... All of a sudden, they'll be disputing in one particular industry, and there'll be another dispute and another dispute, I can't say when it will happen or how it will happen, but there will be a spark, and it will take off.[190]

[There'll be] French-style protests to stop the [government's] great pensions robbery' [with Britain standing] on the edge of the biggest industrial confrontation in over 80 years.[191]

But there was to be no 'winter of discontent' and civil unrest was not 'inevitable'[192] as he believed. Crow over-estimated the development of popular anger and what might become of it, incredulously saying to the *Guardian*: 'you're telling me these people now are going to put up with 3.5 million to 4 million people on the dole with no prospects. These kids aren't going to have it.'[193] *The Times* also reported him as believing that the 'recession ... has made everyone more left-wing: "When people realised the magnitude of what was taking place, it made a huge difference."'[194]

Calling these flights of fancy is not inappropriate because they were wrong-headed.[195] Outside of the RMT, Crow's consistent exaggeration made him look more marginalised than was warranted. This was odd because occasionally he recognised the limitations. For example, friends of his neighbours 'who were in their mid-thirties, had not even heard of the TUC – the union movement's umbrella organisation. "Not one of them had a clue what the TUC was about. They had a bit of an idea about individual leaders, but that was it" Crow sa[id].'[196] He also showed that he understood that the 'problem is that about 33% of the

---

189 *Guardian* 8 October 2010.
190 *Financial Times* 25 March 2011.
191 *Sunday Times* 26 June 2011. Others could be found in the *Guardian* (13 December 2010) and the *Sunday Times* (16 January 2011).
192 *Telegraph* 14 September 2011.
193 *Guardian* 20 June 2009. See also his comments on the degree of change among the public and union members in Murray (2003: 100).
194 *Times* 12 September 2009.
195 See his gross miscalculations over how much a one penny tax on each text and email would generate (respectively £968m PA and £12m PA) to pay off the national debt (*Observer* 19 December 2010; *Financial Times* 25 March 2011).
196 *Times* 18 November 2003.

workforce are now in a union, down from 67% in 1977'.[197] Interviewed by *LookLeft* in 2011, he said:

> The TUC, at the end of the day, is not going to call a general strike. With the laws we have at the moment, it would be impossible to call a general strike … you would have to ballot every single worker or ignore the laws. So I don't think there will be a general strike. What will happen … is groups of workers [like teachers and civil servants] will start taking action … So I think you will see co-ordinated action over three to four years. People will say 'well you're taking action today, and we are in dispute, so we will take action the same day'. I think that's what's going to happen.[198]

The strikes of 2011–12 and July and October 2014 did not prove Crow right, since they represented the end and not the beginning of a fight back (and an unsuccessful one at that). They did not represent the frequency or extent of action he advocated or wished for. For example, he believed that the Hutton report reform of public sector pensions would be 'the spark that lights the blue touch paper of co-ordinated strike action',[199] but the 30 November 2011 strike was the only instance of major strike action against the 2010–15 coalition government. The fight against the reform of public sector pensions was given up and replaced by the fight against a cap on public sector pay rises, though with no more success. No such widespread opposition was mounted against job cuts. The deficiencies in Crow's diagnosis and prognosis are attributable to his flawed understanding of the dynamics of popular rebellion: 'People are only political when something happens to them. Once an idea is ready to happen, and it's ready to hatch, it happens, and that's just happened in Libya and Egypt. It's just happened.'[200] This is not a criticism that Crow faced alone, since it was true for other left-wing union leaders and the radical Left. For Crow, as with others on the radical Left, the subjectivity of hope trumped the objective test of reality. The events of late 2014 and early 2015 – in terms of the demobilisation of strikes and industrial action in higher education, local government and the NHS – indicated how much had changed since the heady days of calls for a general strike and mass civil disobedience in 2010 and 2011.

197 *Observer* 4 September 2011. However, he over- and under-estimated the decline. Union membership was at its highest of 55% in 1979–80, and was 26% in 2011. In the same *Observer* interview, he also commented: 'For the first time in 60 or 70 years, people are seeing their pay packets getting smaller, prices going up, and their job security completely disappearing. I think they might be starting to see what a trade union's for.' Again, there was no evidence of a membership upturn.

198 *LookLeft* 2/7, 23 September 2011.

199 *Independent* 10 March 2011.

200 *Financial Times* 25 March 2011.

The pressure to elect Labour on 7 May 2015 by not 'rocking the boat' was felt.

Conclusion

No matter what criticism can be levelled at the politics behind his practice, they crucially provided Crow with his motivation to act and lead and, alongside his personality, influenced how he did this. All the time, the potential power of his RMT members was the anchor for this. Without this foundation, his politics and personality would not have become greater than the sum of their parts. Yet the politics behind his practice outside of the RMT and outside of its industrial bargaining did not necessarily help secure effective outcomes. This gives a sense of Crow and the RMT being masters of their own small domain but not masters beyond this. The explanation for this highlights the variations in power resources available to RMT and non-RMT members and the more complex dynamics of the arenas of struggle outside the rail transport sector. The next chapter continues to examine Crow's leadership, using the way he was portrayed and perceived to further illuminate how he acted in practice.

8. Perception and practice

As the 'most recognised face of British trade unionism',[1] Crow was subject to more media coverage and scrutiny than any other union leader. This provides not only an opportunity to contrast the public portrayal with the more complex reality behind the headlines, but also to subject the media perceptions to thoroughgoing scrutiny in order to reveal the frameworks they used and how reality often suggested the opposite. Building upon earlier chapters, this chapter begins by looking at the totality of Crow's media portrayal after he became general secretary. It then moves to consider some of the myths constructed about him in order to deconstruct them and show a multi-faceted and dynamic social process at work. This is followed by a comparison with Jimmy Knapp and an examination of the interplay of the key components of leadership, democracy, effectiveness and identity with regard to Crow and the RMT.

Media portrayal

Crow told the *Independent*: 'There's an old adage that if you're going to tell a lie, tell a big one. Our enemies surpassed themselves this time around.'[2] The enemies were the combined forces of the media, especially the right-wing tabloids. Lies were told and credulity was stretched to breaking point.[3] As the *Guardian* observed: 'In the rightwing press, he is public enemy number one, a wrecker, a dinosaur, a Fred Kite character, a Marxist militant.'[4] Editorials were biased and, in reporting, comments by politicians (such as Boris Johnson calling Crow 'demented') were used approvingly or uncritically, or the 'facts' were presented in a certain way to give a certain slant. Hence, the frequent mentions of

1 *Guardian* 1 October 2014.
2 *Independent* 29 June 2009.
3 See also *The media and the RMT*, Platform Films (http://www.platformfilms.co.uk/), which was made for *RMTv*.
4 *Guardian* 2 July 2004.

Millwall or Crow's shaven head were attempts to give thuggish connotations.[5] Nonetheless, much basic, incontestable information was provided, which led to a surprising number of positive assessments from some unexpected quarters. Reinforced by Crow's willingness to be interviewed by most media outlets (bar the *Sun*, *Star*, *Mail* and *Express*) and by his willingness to write to correct their stories, Crow was not completely unlike his portrayal. That is not to say that he got a fair ride. Even the more liberally inclined *Guardian* and *Mirror* were not uncritical, and sometimes bordered on hostile.

While Crow was critical of the media – often blaming them for his denigration[6] – he understood that he needed to use them. As a counterweight, he directed the RMT to develop a well-resourced and active press office using social media (such as live streaming its AGMs from 2008, *RMTv* from February 2009, enhancing its website, using Twitter and Facebook from 2009, and establishing its own intranet for members called *RMT Junction* in January 2010), though Crow was slow to use social media himself.[7] Indeed, Oliver New recalled:

> Although Bob used a Blackberry a bit he didn't really do computers, didn't Google, surf the net and generally got staff to deal with his e-mails. He got a bit better in the last few years, but not much. Bob didn't have papers on his desk. His computer and his filing system were inside his head.[8]

This consideration provides the basis upon which to assess his portrayal and reception in the media.

Usual suspects

The *Evening Standard*, unsurprisingly given its ownership, editorial line and London focus, was Crow's most consistent and harshest critic, calling him 'a classic canteen demagogue', captioning a photograph of him as 'THIS is the man who brought London to a halt today with a Tube strike' and venturing that he was 'a creature from the Jurassic era of industrial relations'.[9] At other times, it blatantly and wrongly stated

---

5 An obvious example comes from the *Evening Standard* (1 October 2002): 'It is no coincidence that the bullnecked, bullhorn-voiced Mr Crow is an ardent supporter of Millwall Football Club, whose thuggish fans rejoice in their unpopularity. "No one likes us, we don't care" they sing from the terraces, a chant which these days might as well be the slogan of Mr Crow and the RMT.'

6 The *Guardian* (10 December 2010) reported: '[I]t's no good endlessly blaming the media for his unpopularity, as he does.'

7 *RMT News* November 2009.

8 Email correspondence.

9 *Evening Standard* 18 July 2002, 18 July 2002, 15 July 2002, respectively.

that Crow had 'awarded himself a 12 per cent pay increase'[10] when this was not his decision. But the *Evening Standard* was not the only newspaper to scurrilously attack Crow. *The Times* opined that 'The RMT dinosaur is overdue for extinction.'[11] The *Telegraph* stated that Crow was 'a left-wing agitator straight out of the *I'm All Right Jack* school of Neanderthal militancy [who] routinely holds the capital and its environs to ransom'.[12] The prehistoric and outdated theme played itself out right to the end. A sceptical Jeremy Paxman asked Crow just five weeks before he died if he was a dinosaur, since unions were basically 'finished'. Crow retorted that not only were the dinosaurs around for quite a long time but who else was going to put working conditions, pay, pensions and world peace on the agenda if not the unions.[13] Untruths were not corrected by the media, so in the battle against the RMT, ignorance was bliss. Thus, the Conservative Party chair, Grant Shapps, accused Ed Miliband of only ever standing up for 'the likes of Len McCluskey and Bob Crow who bankroll his party',[14] and Vince Cable said: 'I make no apology for attacking spivs and gamblers who did more harm to the British economy than Bob Crow could achieve in his wildest Trotskyite fantasies.' Not even the *Guardian* bothered to point out that it would be difficult for Crow to have Trotskyite fantasies given his Communist Party heritage.[15]

Christian Wolmar was another of Crow's critics, even though Wolmar detested privatisation, 'new' Labour and neoliberalism.[16] He accused Crow of being a dinosaur – 'Britain's last diehard militant trade union leader'[17] – with far-fetched political dreams of leading a popular rebellion (nay revolution) against capitalism (an enthusiasm that his members allegedly did not share),[18] of over-reaching himself by organising several strikes too many on inappropriate grounds,[19] and of being generally politically counterproductive.[20] Wolmar did admit more freely

---

10 *Evening Standard* 12 August 2010.
11 *Times* 5 September 2007.
12 *Telegraph* 11 June 2009.
13 BBC 2 *Newsnight*, 4 February 2014.
14 *Evening Standard* 1 March 2014.
15 *Guardian* 23 September 2010
16 *Rail Magazine* 18 April 2010.
17 *Times* 7 September 2010.
18 'Bob Crow blows it', *Christian Says*, 2 April 2010, http://www.christianwolmar.co.uk/2010/04/bob-crow-blows-it/; Rail Magazine 23 September 2007.
19 *Times* 7 September 2010; *Rail Magazine* 23 September 2007, 18 April 2010; *Evening Standard* 25 November 2003.
20 *Rail Magazine* 18 April 2010; 'Union and management should grow up', *Christian Says*, 10 June 2009, http://www.christianwolmar.co.uk/2009/06/union-and-management-should-grow-up/; *Evening Standard* 5 February 2008.

than other critics that the RMT's semi-permanent state of strike mobilisation paid dividends for its members.[21] Yet this was countered by his conviction that Crow would get his comeuppance through various Tube strikes being flops,[22] and that the baleful approach that Crow deployed was 'striking first and negotiating second'[23] or 'shoot first, ask questions later'.[24] Although Crow wrote on occasion for the left-leaning *Mirror* and the liberally inclined *Guardian*, he was attacked by both.[25] The *Mirror* columnist Carole Malone wrote that Crow was a 'bully boy'[26] (though she thought better of him just before and after his death),[27] while the social democratic commentator Polly Toynbee commented: 'How the opposition relished the thuggish primitivism of the RMT leader, Bob Crow, and his crude attempt at strong-arming John Prescott by withdrawing union funds.'[28] To the likes of Toynbee, Crow said:

> It is no use deploring the excesses of grotesque boardroom pay scandals at the top, and then condemning employees who are fighting against the scandal of low pay at the bottom. Nor is it good for the country to have spineless unions, so feeble that they are unable to right transparent wrongs in the workplace. Weak unions are bad not just for their members, but for society.[29]

Although the *Independent* began an article on him by calling him 'the pantomime villain of modern industrial relations in Britain, and the tubby poster boy for the campaign to make it even more difficult to take strike action in this country',[30] it ended by saying:

> All these charges [over his holiday and home], whether you consider them legitimate or not, do not distract, however, from the fact that by a long way Bob Crow is the most effective union leader in Britain today. And he does it by focusing on one thing – getting the best deal for his members. He's very good at doing it, and he's very popular with his members as a consequence ... He is, whatever way you look at it, extremely popular with those he represents.[31]

21 *Rail Magazine* 18 April 2010; *Times* 7 September 2010.
22 *Times* 7 September 2010; *Evening Standard* 5 February 2008.
23 *Times* 7 September 2010.
24 *Rail Magazine* 18 April 2010.
25 See, for example, *Mirror* 4 January 2002; *Guardian* 12 June 2002.
26 *Sunday Mirror* 29 September 2002.
27 *Sunday Mirror* 9 February 2014, 12 March 2014.
28 *Guardian* 10 July 2002.
29 *Guardian* 11 January 2002.
30 *Independent* 5 February 2014.
31 *Independent* 5 February 2014.

Similarly, the *Observer* commented that Crow 'was back on the public enemy list last week after his RMT trade union announced two 48-hour tube strikes', but then added:

> for those commuters bemoaning the looming disruption to their working day, it is worth noting that Crow helps the British economy in his own way. One consequence of the RMT's industrial muscle is that rail, bus and tube workers consistently achieve above-inflation pay settlements. Given the iniquitous consequences of wage stagnation since the 1990s ... it could be argued ... Crow is addressing the signature economic issue of our time with a success that has escaped multiple governments on both sides of the Atlantic. No one ... disagrees with the aspiration of better pay and a higher standard of living for all. And at the expense of the occasional difficult journey to work, Crow achieves it.[32]

Writing in the *Evening Standard*, even former *Times* editor Simon Jenkins was sometimes capable of grudging respect: 'Crow is not a figure from the past ... He knows his market and knows how to exploit it';[33] 'Crow is a latter-day Arthur Scargill, except that Scargill failed to get the measure of his industry, while Crow so far has the measure of his. Crow has become "the acceptable face of unacceptable trade unionism".'[34] At other times this was more normal *Evening Standard* fare: 'Today's Tube strike should be in the Natural History Museum. It is about little more than Bob Crow's machismo. Every year the boss of the Tube drivers' union feels an urge to remind Londoners that he is a big stud.'[35] The *Telegraph* ventured some respect and praise: 'The result is that Bob Crow is able, indirectly, to present himself as the voice of reason – and that's not something any of us should be happy about.'[36] *The Times* commented, in response to Crow saying 'Our job is to represent our members', that 'It is a job he does quite brilliantly ... In short, as a trade unionist, Bob Crow is in a class of his own.'[37] Ironically, it was Wolmar who most insightfully noted the media's failure to damage Crow: 'frequent media attacks upon him largely did not stick, because of Crow's skill at handling [the media] ... which meant he always came across as straightforward and honest ... Even when espousing ideas that most of the public would regard as outlandish, he managed to sound reasonable and matter of fact.'[38]

32 *Observer* 12 January 2014.
33 *Evening Standard* 4 February 2014.
34 *Evening Standard* 10 May 2011.
35 *Evening Standard* 7 September 2010.
36 *Telegraph* 8 February 2012.
37 *Times* 31 January 2012.
38 *Guardian* 12 March 2014. The standfirst to Seumas Milne's piece (*Guardian*

Media darling

Ironically, Crow was something of a 'media darling' since he nearly always agreed to be interviewed by any journalist or to write pieces when requested,[39] because of his desire to represent his members as widely as possible, and because he gave voluminous numbers of colourful quotes in the course of doing so.[40] He was also an inveterate letter writer, defending himself and the RMT in the *Guardian*, *Telegraph*, *Times*, *Evening Standard* and *Independent*. His press officer said of him: 'Bob's in demand cos he's got something interesting to say. You couldn't say that about all these union leaders who don't say anything interesting, could you?'[41] Journalists often said that they enjoyed interviewing him and ended up liking him despite their preconceptions.[42] He was a straight talker, operating without the supervision of a press officer. Thus, the *Independent* said, 'unlike some other union leaders, the general secretary of the RMT union has not been house-trained by public relations consultants. What you see is what you get';[43] according to the *Guardian*, he was 'never one to hide behind a "no comment" or his loyal union PR man'.[44] In recognition of his profile and importance, Crow appeared on *Question Time* four times (in 2002, 2007, 2010 and 2013; of union leaders, only Arthur Scargill made more appearances, with five),[45] on *Any Questions* six times between 2009 and 2013, and on *Have I Got News For You* on 27 November 2009. Of the latter he

13 March 2014) included the sentence: 'That's why demonising Bob Crow was a failure.'

39 One of the few occasions when he declined to be interviewed was after he was entered in Debrett's *People of Today* in 2004. The RMT's media representative told the *Telegraph* (9 January 2004) that he was 'too busy' to talk about this. In the period from 2002, he wrote for the *Guardian* on 17 May 2013 on the EU, 1 November 2011 on safety, 19 May 2011 on rail profits, 6 September 2010 on the Tube, 25 August 2010 on a Tube strike, 9 June 2009 on a Tube dispute, 3 April 2009 on shipping, 21 October 2005 on rail safety, 23 March 2005 on rail nationalisation, 5 November 2003 on rail safety, 12 May 2003 on rail profits, 1 May 2002 (with Rix) on Labour and 11 January 2002 on workers' rights.

40 Some detractors thought he became a 'rent a quote' on matters far beyond the railways. However, his being asked for comments and quotes reflected the paucity of critical voices in British politics, and the way Crow operated encouraged some other general secretaries to begin to comment a little more widely than on just their immediate industrial issues.

41 *Guardian* 13 December 2010.

42 For example, Carole Malone of the *Mirror* (9 February 2014) and Decca Aitkenhead of the *Guardian* (12 March 2014). Christine Buckley found him polite, charming and attentive at dinner (*Guardian* online 11 March 2014).

43 *Independent* 19 April 2004.

44 *Guardian* 2 July 2004.

45 He was denied a place on the programme immediately before the 2009

said: 'As a long-standing fan … I am well pleased to be the first union leader invited on to the show. I'm looking forward to sparring with the panel. I've sat across the table from some sharp operators, but this poses a different challenge.'[46] However, despite having a sense of humour, he did not sparkle as might have been expected, and came across as rather earnest by trying too hard to be straightforwardly political.

Popular myths

The tabloid press widely personalised the RMT on to Crow. The *Mirror* called him 'the commander-in-chief … the Big Daddy of all union bosses',[47] and proceeded to expand its 'great man' theory of the RMT:

> his greatest strength was that he was fearless … when Bob Crow sounded his war cry across the Capital … he would bring the city to its knees in a heartbeat if he thought it would get his members what he believed they deserved. And not only did they worship him for it. They believed he was unbeatable. Indestructible. A force no man could defeat. And no man did … Everyone wanted to be in Bob's gang because what he demanded – he got.[48]

So it was that Bob Crow called strikes and Bob Crow disrupted commuters' lives, rather than RMT members. Seldom was it recognised – even by the *Financial Times*[49] and the *Guardian*[50] – that only the CoE had the authority to order ballots and call industrial action. Although not of the same political significance, and intended as a compliment this time, it was also said that Crow increased RMT membership and gained pay rises for its members, ignoring the role of others. This error was again committed across the spectrum.[51] Sometimes, the way Crow

European elections because No2EU was too small a political party (*The Socialist* 28 May 2009).

46 *Independent* 24 November 2009.

47 *Mirror* 9 February 2014.

48 *Mirror* 12 March 2014. Earlier (*Mirror* 9 February 2014), it was reported: 'the fact is what Bob Crow wants for his members – he gets!'

49 For example: 'His actions led the Conservatives to consider new laws to protect essential services … His militant tactics … Crow was known for his frequent use of industrial action ballots as a weapon' (*Financial Times* 12 March 2014). Other examples included '[he] regularly brought London's transport system to a standstill through industrial action' (*Financial Times* 25 March 2011) and 'He is not afraid to go into battle for his members' (*Financial Times* 6 September 2007).

50 For example, 'he was unafraid to call a strike' (*Guardian* 12 March 2014), 'Last week Crow almost brought London to a stop. Again' (*Guardian* 20 June 2009), and 'no union leader calls more industrial action ballots than Crow' (*Guardian* 2 July 2004).

51 See, for example, the *Guardian* (13 December 2010): 'If Bob Crow were a

characterised himself did not help: 'Of course, commuters are angry with me. But if you join a trade union you expect it to fight for you. And that's what I'm doing ... I will fight anyone I have to fight to get what I think they deserve';[52] 'I don't shirk from taking industrial action';[53] 'I have not arranged to call a strike on the royal wedding.'[54] Interviewed by the *Guardian*, he was asked if he knew 'how many strikes he had called since taking over the RMT: "Nah." It's reported to be more than any other union leader in any other industry. "Probably, yeah," he agrees.'[55] Seldom was it possible to identify the more measured media tones of 'Under his leadership, the RMT has ...' or 'With Bob Crow's guidance, the RMT decided to ...' Even these formulations would not have done justice to the RMT as a collective body. The general sense given was that Crow ran the RMT, whether benignly or not. Thus, he was the RMT 'boss', and it was wilfully forgotten that he was elected and accountable, and that the RMT was a democratic organisation. Hence, there are a number of popular myths that are worth delving into, namely that Crow was 'strike happy' and that he ran the RMT as 'a personal fiefdom'.[56]

Strike-happy militant?

The usual charges were that 1) Crow compelled the RMT to adopt a 'strike first, negotiate later' approach[57] and 2) that he was so militant that he would not and could not make deals, and hence more strikes were precipitated or prolonged. Seldom did the media give much weight to the employers' role and influence in generating disputes (especially on the Underground where management became increasingly hard-nosed). Consequently, Crow was correct to blame management for causing strikes. At one level, this seemed counter-intuitive, since union

---

business leader, he would probably be celebrated as a great British success story. Since taking charge in 2002 he has increased the profits of his shareholders year on year [i.e. the pay of members], even through the most testing of economic times, while expanding his business by 50% [i.e. the RMT membership]'; and 'In any other profession, if he was on performance-related pay, he would have got a bonus every year' (*Guardian* 13 March 2014). The *Evening Standard* (4 February 2014) reported that 'At a basic £44,000 salary plus perks, he has made [Tube drivers] among the highest-paid workers in the public sector'.

52 *Mirror* 12 March 2014. These quotes are from notes of the interview with him that was published on 9 February 2014.
53 *Guardian* 14 February 2002.
54 *Financial Times* 25 March 2011.
55 *Guardian* 13 December 2010.
56 *Telegraph* 11 June 2009.
57 See, for example, *Guardian* 2 July 2004.

members decide whether or not to strike – and clearly most do not, with levels of strike activity in Britain at historically low levels. But on another level, Crow was right that management cause strikes because, notwithstanding workers' agency, management provide the causes of strikes since unions *react* to management. Equally importantly, in most cases successful strike ballots were used without striking to gain settlements. Other forms of industrial action short of striking (work-to-rules, go-slows and overtime bans) were also deployed. Moreover, the process by which ballots and strikes were called saw the CoE play the sovereign role, whereby Crow said: 'We believe it's a demand of the membership. We don't automatically say there will be a ballot if our members want one, but if our shop stewards say they want to ballot, the Executive Committee normally grants it.'[58] Crow 'always made clear he would lend support to strikes … if he felt they "had legs"'.[59]

So before calling a strike, the RMT under Crow skilfully and frequently used ballot results in favour of strikes and notifications of action to get most of what it wanted. As Crow explained: 'A lot of these companies don't take you seriously until you have a ballot and it concentrates their minds. We only ballot for two reasons – if a company imposes worse conditions on our members or if they refuse to negotiate … We have won a lot more deals through balloting than not balloting … We settle two-thirds of them before going to strike.'[60] This was recognised by a few commentators: 'for the most part agreements were reached before workers walked out';[61] 'Crow makes more threats than he carries out … his tactic of balloting first and negotiating later has often extracted concessions.'[62] This indicated that Crow understood that the perception of power was important, and that exaggeration had a useful role to play in industrial bargaining where members could deliver upon the threat of action if need be. The bête noire of the Left, journalist Andrew Gilligan, noted that under Crow the RMT's 'real weapon is not the strike, but the strike ballot'[63] on the London Underground.[64] This was also the view of Crow's successor, Mick Cash:

58 BBC Radio 4 *The Report*, 8 October 2009.
59 Unjum Mirza, email correspondence.
60 BBC Radio 4 *The Report*, 8 October 2009.
61 *Guardian* 12 March 2014.
62 *Financial Times* 30 March 2010.
63 *Evening Standard* 27 February 2006.
64 However, the *Guardian* (12 May 2011) commented: 'For now, then, the capital has been spared its 22nd withdrawal of RMT labour in the past three years'; and the *Evening Standard* (27 March 2012) reported: 'Leaked RMT figures show that during Tory Mr Johnson's four years in office there have been 15 strikes by the union led by Bob Crow, compared with eight during the two terms of his

I got taught early doors – pick your fights, and the thing I've seen in the last 12 years is that's what we do: we negotiate first, we seek to get deals, but if we can't we give our members the opportunity to have their say. There is a danger people say we've got one trick in our box. But it wasn't like that under Bob and it certainly isn't going to be under me.[65]

Crow was not an advocate of unofficial or unballoted action, making his statement 'Why bother with ballots – where does it get us?'[66] a case of grandstanding to a rally.[67] Recognising the force of the aforementioned points, Crow said: 'It's a myth that there are lots of strikes going on. Our members are losing more time through being assaulted and injured at work than they are by taking strike action.'[68] Of course, crucial to the ability to use ballots as a tool of leverage was winning a mandate. Crow stated in 2009: 'Up until the recession, we'd won every single ballot. This year we've won 92 to 93 of them out of 100 we've had, not a bad record.'[69] This was a slight over-statement as there were some ballots lost prior to 2009 (and some lost after as well).[70]

Before looking at figures for balloting, it is important to reiterate that for Crow, striking was a means to an end, even if it was one that had to be used more than he wished (given the loss of wages). Asked in a *Guardian* interview 'Does he consider [striking] a mark of his success or of his failure?', he responded: 'I couldn't care less if we had no strikes in 10 years, or we had a million strikes.' The journalist's reaction was disbelief: 'I'm not sure his indifference can be entirely authentic, because Crow's whole argument is that his union is successful because it is will-

predecessor and current Labour rival for the mayoralty, Ken Livingstone. But while the number who walked out when Mr Livingstone was Mayor totalled 19,052, under Tory Mr Johnson that number fell more than 8,000 to 10,865.'

65 *Guardian* 1 October 2014. Arrowsmith (2003: 160) also found evidence of tactical use of ballots with regard to Virgin.

66 *Socialist Review* December 2003.

67 See also Berlin (2006: 154) and Pendleton (1991b: 217). The 1989 pay revolt was the last major instance of unofficial action on the railways. After that, in 1998 there were much smaller unofficial strikes against the victimisation of Steve Hedley and Bill Ashcroft. These actions were repudiated by the RMT.

68 *Telegraph* 16 February 2002.

69 BBC Radio 4 *The Report*, 8 October 2009.

70 Some examples were South West Trains (March 2003, July 2012), c2c (March 2003) and Network Rail signalling staff (May 2008). In the case of South West Trains in 2003, this was influenced by the company training 150 managers to do the guards' job (*Times* 7 March 2003). The latter was lost by a margin of 1,203 for striking to 2,015 against. *The Times* (23 May 2008) quoted an RMT source as saying: 'It is very unusual for us to lose a strike ballot by such a large margin'. See also Darlington (2014b: 71) for the period 2002–09.

ing to strike.'[71] However, this did not undermine Crow's stance – with some employers it took a strike to get satisfactory outcomes while with others it did not, so the means were subservient to the ends. Just occasionally, a strike was needed to compel management to meet the RMT to allow it to put its case and negotiate. The last Tube strike under Crow was a case in point. He considered it

> a resounding success 'because now they're going to sit down and hear what we have to say' over making sure redundancies are voluntary with the option for redeployment. 'If we'd had an opportunity to speak to the mayor, at least we could have briefed him on exactly what we are in dispute about'. So why didn't Crow accept Johnson's invitation on Monday to call off the strike and sit down with him to talk? 'Because if we hadn't gone on strike, we wouldn't be sitting down at Acas on Friday. And because, don't forget, the last time we had a strike he said: "Call it off and we'll meet you," and he never met me. He's never met me. He won't let us meet.'[72]

Turning to the balloting figures, it would be more accurate to characterise the RMT under Crow as being in a semi-permanent state of mobilisation than as being 'strike prone'. Thus, Darlington reported:

> on London Underground between January 2002 and December 2012 the union balloted in favour of industrial action on at least 87 different occasions, with ballots leading to strikes … on 41 different occasions, resulting in a total of 72 full days of strike action overall. On the national railway network during the same period, the union balloted in favour of industrial action on at least 131 different occasions, with ballots leading to strikes on 54 different occasions, resulting in a total of 176 full days of strike action overall. In the two industries combined this represented a total of at least 218 ballots, 95 of which led to strikes, resulting in a total of 248 full days of strike action overall.[73]

Thereafter, the balance between the number of ballots and the number of strikes stayed roughly the same, but the numbers of each grew; between May 2010 and March 2014 250 ballots were organised, with 75 ballots between January and June 2009.[74] Thus, the RMT has a very strong claim to be – on a proportionate basis – the union that holds more ballots than any other, that secures more 'yes' votes than any other

---

71 *Guardian* 13 December 2010.

72 *Guardian* 7 February 2014.

73 Darlington (2014b: 72). Darlington (2012: 521) and Connolly and Darlington (2012: 239) reported the earlier figures for January 2002 to December 2009.

74 The figures are May–31 December 2010, 30; 2011, 84; 2012, 90; 2013, 34; and January–11 March 2014, 12 (from http://www.rmt.org.uk/about/ballot-results/). The 2009 figures come from *RMT News* (July 2009).

and that takes strike action more often than any other. When asked by the *Financial Times* 'Does [the RMT] strike more than the other unions?', Crow replied: 'I bloody well hope so.'[75] He was equally proud of the balloting statistics in 2009: 'We've had 100 so far. It's a record and it's only September.'[76]

Of his supposed personal fiefdom, Crow repeatedly pointed out: 'What people misunderstand in all that is that the members get a vote. They are not fools and they won't be used. They've got mortgages and they don't want to lose money';[77] 'Every time we've taken action we've had a ballot and respected our members' wishes'; 'Our members vote in a secret ballot, and I respect their wishes';[78] 'I expect members to vote yes to strike action but, yes or no, I will respect their wishes';[79] 'Some of the media are particularly ignorant about how industrial relations come about and seem to believe that strikes get called at my whim and not as a result of a vote by angry members.'[80] He also made clear that the ballots 'are authorised by the union's executive committee, not me'.[81] Former CoE member Janine Booth reminded observers that 'Once he became the General Secretary, Bob was not even in the meetings which called ballots or strikes on the Tube or on other companies: that was not part of his role.'[82] The media expectation that upon his election in 2002, ASLEF and the RMT would constantly strike together in order to exert maximum leverage (certainly while Rix was ASLEF general secretary) was not borne out to any great extent, even although Crow told the *Telegraph*: 'Where there's a common interest, we try to meet and decide tactics.'[83]

In sum, the RMT under Crow's leadership never took any industrial action without going through the process of declaring a dispute and engaging in negotiations. There were countless examples where action was called off, so that mandates were not implemented. That said, there were clearly many cases where they were, reflecting clashes between management positions and union demands. Management was often intransigent and demands often seemed ambitious by comparison to those of other unions inside and outside sectors that the RMT organ-

75 *Financial Times* 25 March 2011.
76 BBC Radio 4 *The Report*, 8 October 2009.
77 *Times* 9 May 2009.
78 *Guardian* 13 December 2010.
79 *Independent* 19 April 2004.
80 *RMT News* June 2009.
81 *Evening Standard* 22 September 1999.
82 *Solidarity* 19 March 2014.
83 *Telegraph* 16 February 2002.

ised. Thus, a not uncommon headline in, for example, the *Guardian* was 'Tube strike starts *after* talks break down' (emphasis added).[84] Yet a consideration of the agreements signed by the RMT to end disputes whether involving industrial action or not shows that it was very often prepared to compromise when certain red lines were not crossed (such as no compulsory redundancies, or pay rises matching inflation). This was because the RMT, as Crow put it, knew 'when to turn the gas on and when to turn it off',[85] meaning that its CoE and negotiating officers made judgements about how far and fast to pressurise management in terms of what could be gained and what action members could and would sustain. Crow expanded on this, saying: 'In negotiations, you have to know how far you can go. You can't be 100 miles in front of the members or 100 miles behind them. If they want to fight, you have to fight for them. And you can't ask for the moon if your members don't think that's achievable.'[86]

Darlington commented: 'Per thousand members, the RMT has probably organised more ballots for industrial action, secured "yes" votes in such ballots, and then taken more strike action than any other union in Britain over recent years.'[87] What this does not take into account is that the RMT on its transport side had far more bargaining units and employers to deal with per 1,000 members than most other unions. The significance of this is twofold. First, all other things being equal, there is a greater propensity for mobilising and taking action where there is a plethora of smaller bargaining units than where there is a handful of large bargaining units, because the threat of action is more potent in larger bargaining units while organising in smaller bargaining units is relatively easier. For example, the threat of a national rail strike is more potent in terms of the potential disruption caused than the threat of a regional rail strike. This difference is likely to compel more caution in using the former than the latter. Second, the absolute number of ballots and strikes per 1,000 members will always look bigger where a greater number of smaller bargaining units exists. However, the number of workers involved and the number of days not worked per 1,000 workers would not. So the impact of more bargaining units because of the decentralisation and fragmentation of previously unified and centralised structures should be recognised, otherwise the strike propensity

---

84 *Guardian* 9 June 2009.
85 *Times* 9 May 2009.
86 *Financial Times* 10 September 2004.
87 Darlington (2014b: 72). This point was also made earlier (Darlington 2008: 26, 2009a: 5, 2010: 22, 2012: 521). See also Connolly and Darlington (2012: 239).

of the RMT is over-estimated, and that of other unions like the PCS is under-estimated.

When it comes to allegations that Crow was so militant that he could not strike a deal, it was seldom recognised that he did less negotiating than was generally assumed. While he did more as an AGS, once he became general secretary, as the *Guardian* reported: 'he himself doesn't even play any part in the negotiations; post-privatisation, the RMT now has to deal with more than 500 different companies, so the role of negotiating has been devolved down to local level'.[88] But Phil McGarry stressed that the large number of companies operating on the railways and the Underground meant that there were insufficient RMT officers for the general secretary not to play some role in negotiations. The number of companies was possibly much higher, since Crow had previously written that 'We have over 3,000 different companies working on the railways.'[89] Negotiations were carried out by other national officers, CoE members and regional organisers.[90] To the extent that Crow did take part in negotiations, these either concerned the public politics of negotiating or the most important disputes such as those on London Underground. The *Independent* quoted one industry source as saying that 'It is tempting to write him off as some sort of baseball cap-wearing yob with an O-Level in Marxism. The reality is that he is someone who is paid to get the best for his members and will eventually do a deal.'[91] Christian Wolmar reported that 'rail industry managers who had to sit on the opposite side of the negotiation table from Crow were virtually unanimous in their assessment that "you could always cut a deal

88 *Guardian* 7 February 2014. Darlington (2009a: 12) put the figure at over 100 bargaining units in the late 2000s.

89 *Morning Star* 14 January 2002. In 2003, Crow wrote: 'Privatisation fragmented our railways beyond recognition. Today there are 25 train operating companies, six freight operators, three rolling-stock companies, two infrastructure controllers in Network Rail and Eurotunnel, and seven main infrastructure maintenance contractors. Dig a little deeper, and you find a complex network of contractors and subcontractors: nearly 120,000 certified workers employed by almost 1,500 employers, two-thirds of which employ fewer than 25 workers' (*Guardian* 12 May 2003). Previously, the *Mirror* (15 May 2002) reported: 'The number of companies maintaining the railways has risen 11-fold in less than a decade. After privatisation in 1994, only 120 firms worked in the railway industry, a figure which is now approaching 1,400. And it could be as high as 2,000, according to *Keeping Track* magazine which compiles a list of contractors and suppliers.'

90 Companies and organisations that operated across regions like Network Rail, East Coast and Virgin were dealt with by national officers. For example, Mick Cash was the lead officer for Network Rail members while he was an AGS.

91 *Independent* 6 September 2007.

with Bob"'.[92] An ACAS official observed in 2008 that 'when he turns up in person to negotiations you know he wants to do a deal'.[93] The *Independent* reported Crow as being similar to his successor: '"[Cash] was always the type of bloke who would engineer the deal when he could", a friend said. "Actually, Bob was like that too, but he pretended that he wasn't."'[94]

> *Internal democracy and processes: captive or captain?*

Whether through wilful ignorance or deliberate deception, Crow was frequently portrayed in the tabloids as a general in charge of his own private army. What was scarcely ever mentioned was that he was elected and accountable. Common descriptions were 'boss', 'chief' and 'baron', so there was seldom much recognition of the RMT's internal democratic processes. Between AGMs, the CoE was charged with 'administer[ing] the business and affairs of the Union ... oversee[ing] the work of the General Secretary and the work of other officials and employees'.[95] The RMT constitution stipulates that 'The General Secretary shall obey the instructions of the Council of Executives',[96] where the president and general secretary have the right to speak at its meetings but not vote. Members are elected every three years.[97] The CoE (or sometimes the general grades committee) has the sole authority to call industrial action ballots and industrial action. This meant formally that the agenda Crow worked to was set by the CoE. He was then charged with prosecuting and articulating it – sometimes known as 'fronting' it. For example, in a diary for the *Independent*, Crow wrote:

> Spent the day talking mostly to journalists from various newspapers and getting my photo taken at the office. I tried once more to underline the union's point of view and to get them to see us in a fairer and more positive light. I am hopeful that we could soon start to win the PR battle.[98]

That is not to say Crow had no influence over the CoE:

> If the Mayor of London, Transport Commissioner or the Government do not take action to suspend these contracts, then I shall be recommending

92 *Guardian* 12 March 2014.
93 Personal recollection.
94 *Independent* 2 May 2014.
95 RMT rule book, http://www.rmt.org.uk/about/rmt-rule-book/.
96 RMT rule book, http://www.rmt.org.uk/about/rmt-rule-book/.
97 It is also worth noting the rotation of CoE elections (roughly on a 33% basis per year over a three-year cycle), so not all members are elected at the same time. Semi-continuous membership of the CoE is only possible by a member becoming the president.
98 *Independent* 12 January 2002.

to my executive and to the other rail unions on London Underground that we ballot to take strike action to defend the safety of our members and the travelling public.[99]

Mr Crow revealed he would be recommending to his senior colleagues a campaign of action which could include walkouts lasting six hours to strikes aimed at causing chaos during three-day periods.[100]

Crow ... said late on Friday that he would recommend to his executive that the strike be called off.[101]

Indeed, as a powerful figure, especially when working with the president,[102] Crow could sway and lead the CoE (and AGMs). In addition to his personality and politics, he had the advantage of years of experience and of being in post full-time, which gave him knowledge, skill and authority. By comparison, CoE members were only elected for three years before going back to their 'tools' and they could not stand for another three years. CoE members could not be delegates to AGMs. Crow was also a clever operator and would influence AGM decisions – in order to set the CoE's agenda – by taking motions to his own branch, London Underground Engineering, and taking opportunities to speak to other branches. As with the senior elected officials, he did not have a vote at the AGM, merely the right to speak. On one occasion this right was used very effectively. In 2009, he 'broke the union's rule that the General Secretary should defend existing RMT policy, instead giving a tub-thumping speech for the boycott – earning himself a reprimand from the President, but only after it was too late to affect the outcome ... [namely] the AGM vot[ing] for a boycott of Israeli goods, overturning RMT's "solidarity not boycott" policy'.[103] He could also be a sharp operator at other times: responding to the suggestion that he might have struck his own share of underhand agreements in the past, he said: 'Don't tell my executive committee ... everything is done above board.'[104]

Crow's role in influencing the CoE was made easier by the absence of

99 *Independent* 20 October 2003.
100 *Independent* 19 April 2004.
101 *Times* 21 April 2008.
102 The position of president was filled by senior figures, so the president's support for the general secretary was of great use. For example, Tony Donaghey had been a local, regional and branch representative and served on the executive four times.
103 'Top table wins on all the issues', *Solidarity* 9 July 2009, http://www.workersliberty.org/story/2009/07/09/top-table-wins-all-issues.
104 Radio 4, 10 March 2014.

a Broad Left within the RMT, so that the Left operated largely through the officer corps. This allowed him to stamp his authority more easily on the national union, thereby facilitating political congruence around his agenda and person. Such a Broad Left organisation would have provided some counterbalance to him (especially if CoE members were members). But the CFDU had long since ceased to exist and an attempt to relaunch it in 2007 was unsuccessful.[105] What did exist were groupings like the Alliance for Workers' Liberty (AWL), the SWP and the Socialist Party and their publications such as *Off the Rails*, *Tube Worker*, *Across the Tracks* and *The Red Line*. Even together they did not constitute a force that would increase levels of accountability. That said, it should not be assumed that Crow had ideas that were diametrically opposed to those of the CoE (and vice versa) so that he had a job of work to do in getting his way. Rather, there was already much common ground and differences were usually over relatively minor issues such as tactics and details, not strategy and bargaining objectives.

Sometimes there was a counter-narrative – that Crow was less militant than portrayed and was a prisoner of militants. For example, the *Guardian* reported: 'Crow is usually depicted as the diehard dinosaur in all this, but one TfL big cheese tells me "Bob is actually a reasonable bloke. But he can't agree to anything; it's the Executive Committee and the members who agree things"';[106] 'Sources say Crow is actually quite a moderate and flexible trade unionist, but must play the intransigent militant to pacify hardcore members of the RMT's executive committee, or else he'll be out of a job, [with Crow opining] "What, you're saying we've got a hard-left executive? Well, if so it's certainly got a soft centre."'[107] The *Independent* commented: 'Mr Crow ... was himself less hard-line than some of the other senior union officials ... It was often said that Bob Crow was more pragmatic than he appeared, but was pushed into militancy by others in the union, notably Pat Sikorski.'[108] The *Evening Standard* believed that 'The strike is being orchestrated, not just by Bob Crow, but by a militant clique within the RMT [comprising] ... Steve Hedley, Brian Munro and Pat Sikorski each [of whom] have a long history of battling Tube managers and leading militant

---

105 See McIlroy and Daniels (2009: 155). With the possible exception of the PCS, most Broad Left groupings ceased to exist in a meaningful way once the national unions in which they operated became dominated at senior officer level by individuals from those groupings.
106 *Guardian* 4 June 2009.
107 *Guardian* 7 February 2014.
108 *Independent* 2 May 2014.

campaigns.'[109] Christian Wolmar reported that 'Amazingly, Bob Crow claims he is actually a voice of moderation compared with some of the members of his executive committee who are far more extremist.'[110] And Christine Buckley wrote that Crow was 'an effective union leader, not just for the considerable work he did for his members but also for how he steered the RMT. I've been at RMT conferences where often Bob was the only voice of reason.'[111] Overall, the *Guardian* said,

> the word 'moderate' to describe Crow popped up surprisingly often in conversations with railway managers. This was partly because Crow was wont to warn negotiators that his executive was on the warpath and he would need concessions to keep them happy. However, it was also the case that there were executive members who were further left politically than Crow and far more eager to see disruptive industrial action.[112]

Elsewhere in the *Guardian*, with reference to a Tube dispute over redundancies and the closure of ticket offices, it was ventured that:

> The big, giggly in-joke shared by Tube unions, management and clued-in politicians alike is that Crow is actually considered a straightforward, if hard-nosed, operator with whom it is possible to do business. A companion view is that he is, at least to some extent, the prisoner of an executive and activists strongly influenced by, shall we say, the more specialised sectors of the Outer Left.[113]

In 2002, the *Observer* noted: 'Last summer while some members of the RMT executive advocated all-out strike action on the London Underground in the run-up to the general election, Crow took a more measured line.'[114] Further back in the 1980s and 1990s, Martin Eady recalled: 'If political principles get in the way of practical advances for the membership then they are bad principles. You should not counterpose principles and pragmatism and I don't think Bob did so. He was no different to most of us on this.'[115] Hence, there was some evidence of differences over strategy and tactics between Crow, CoE members and some officers, but no more so than could be found in other unions.

109 *Evening Standard* 5 May 2011. Sikorski was then an AGS, Munro Bakerloo branch secretary and Hedley a London regional officer.

110 *Rail Magazine* 23 September 2007. Wolmar reiterated this elsewhere (*New Statesman* 20 January 2006; *Evening Standard* 6 February 2008).

111 *Guardian* 12 March 2014.

112 *Guardian* 12 March 2014.

113 *Guardian* 5 February 2014. By 'specialised sectors of the Outer Left' was meant the AWL, SWP and Socialist Party. AWL members working on London Underground had produced the monthly bulletin *Tube Worker* since 1991.

114 *Observer* 17 February 2002.

115 Email correspondence.

Knapp and Crow

Some perspective on Crow can be gained by comparing him to his predecessor. Jimmy Knapp became an NUR national official at the age of 31 in 1971, and general secretary of the NUR in 1983 and of the RMT in 1990. He remained in post until late 2000 (whereupon Vernon Hince, senior AGS, became acting general secretary until the general secretaryship election in February 2002). Knapp died after a long battle with cancer in August 2001. Thus, like Crow, Knapp had shown promise of rising as far as he did by an early age.[116] There were other similarities, not least their deaths in office, their unwillingness to tone down their accents and ways of speaking for the media, and their ardent football support – for Knapp, Crystal Palace and Kilmarnock. The right wing had also tried to stop Knapp becoming an official through the examination system.[117] Knapp faced considerable opposition upon being elected: 'Unity House ... NUR's head office ... was still run by the old Weighellite bureaucracy, and there were still people undermining Jimmy Knapp, and undermining any left wing member of the Executive. They were reputed to be taking orders from Sidney Weighell.'[118] As recounted earlier, Crow successfully neutered the right-wing opposition in the union.

The view of much of the Left of the RMT (especially CFDU) and of Crow supporters was that although Knapp was of the Left when compared to Weighell, he was not particularly left-wing and was insufficiently vociferous in prosecuting union policy to government.[119] These criticisms came together in the belief that Knapp was not robust enough in challenging rail privatisation and part-privatisation of the Underground, and 'new' Labour's move to endorse neoliberalism.[120] In particular, Knapp was said to be too reliant upon John Prescott's promise that Labour would renationalise the railways in 1997. Knapp was dismayed when this did not happen and felt betrayed, but this did not alter the reality of continued privatisation. Certainly, Knapp was more modest and humble than Crow – though that is not to suggest that Crow

116 By the age of 18, Knapp had become a branch collector and by 21 he was a branch secretary. He moved to London in 1972 to work as a divisional officer, and worked in the NUR headquarters from 1981.

117 Berlin (2006: 45)

118 Martin Eady, interviewed by Dave Welsh and Roraima Joebear on 20 May 2010 for the *Britain at Work* Oral History Project. See also Berlin (2006: 45).

119 See also Berlin (2006: 46, 143–144).

120 See the sometimes implicit and sometimes explicit subtext of Berlin (2006: 135–136, 143–144).

was arrogant and conceited. Crow was a far more energetic character who could seldom be accused of foot dragging, as Knapp often was.

It is widely perceived that there were more strikes under Crow's leadership than Knapp's (either on an absolute or relative basis).[121] This is assumed to speak to Crow's militancy and Knapp's moderation. But the reality is more complex. As explained before, the bargaining structure is an important variable in explaining strike propensity. Giving a flavour of this, Crow commented: 'The reason why it's perceived as so many ballots now is that before we just had the RMT negotiation with the railway board – now we have 200 companies in the railways.'[122] Essentially, a greater number of bargaining units is likely to lead to a greater number of strikes, all other things being equal. But all was not equal, as the existence of the Railway Staff National Tribunal until its abolition in 1992[123] and the declining use of ACAS thereafter indicated the availability of conciliation, mediation and, critically, arbitration provided something of a safety valve, so that strikes during much of Knapp's leadership would also have been less likely. The prevailing mood of rail workers was another critical differentiating factor between the periods of Knapp's and Crow's tenure. The 1990s were difficult for the RMT. British Rail's abolition of check-off in 1993, privatisation, redundancies and the removal of bargaining structures and attendant facility time for senior reps all hit the RMT hard.[124] The RMT was weakened by membership loss and reduced organising and bargaining capacity. By contrast, from the late 1990s the return of Labour governments, expanding passenger numbers and staff shortages helped change the mood. Crow inherited these factors, which facilitated the increased potency of strike threats and strikes themselves to gain better pay and conditions. He was prepared to take advantage of them whereas Knapp might not have been. But strikes against privatisation *per se* and the breaking of the anti-union laws, in spite of Crow's advocacy, were absent under his tenure as they had been under Knapp. And the RMT under Crow did not win all its industrial battles. It won most on favourable terms through a series of limited strikes characterised as 'smash and grab',[125] but there were also some long drawn-out battles during which

121 This is likely but cannot be definitely established because the categories of official strike statistics do not isolate transport from communication. And from the 2000s, transport, storage and communication were lumped together.

122 BBC Radio 4 *The Report*, 8 October 2009.

123 See Gourvish (2002).

124 See Berlin (2006: 77–78) and Darlington (2009a: 16).

125 Unjum Mirza, email correspondence. The term was also used by the *Daily Mail* (12 March 2014), as in Crow 'saw class war as an ongoing smash-and-grab raid'.

RMT members lost considerable wages (for example, Arriva Northern, SWT,[126] Virgin Cross Country,[127] Tyne and Wear Metro,[128] Scotrail[129] and Network Rail).[130] In this regard, it is worth recalling that under Knapp, signal workers held 17 one-day strikes in 1994, suggesting that even for such a strategically placed group of workers, strikes were not especially effective. Under Crow, cognisance of this led to innovation. The RMT did not suffer any major strike defeats under Crow's leadership.[131] Crow was never turned over by the CoE or AGMs as were Knapp in 1985 and Weighell in 1983.

Union democracy

Many Left-led unions claimed to be 'member led'. The RMT under Crow was no different.[132] However, at the World Federation of Trade Unions in 2012, Crow more candidly commented: 'We are trying to have a union that respects its members, where the leadership represents the members' wishes. We are trying to be as open and democratic as possible. We are trying to build a union where the members feel that they can actually change the directions of the union.'[133] President Peter Pinkney added his voice, saying:

> I stood on a platform of wanting to minimise the distance between the leadership of the union and the members at a workplace and branch level. So my priority will be getting out to workplaces and talking to people. I

126 SWT was arguably the most aggressive of the TOCs.

127 There were 14 24-hour Sunday strikes by guards in 2006. Prior to this, Arrowsmith (2003: 151) found that Virgin had engaged with rather than confronted the RMT and ASLEF.

128 Over eighteen months between 2012 and 2013, RMT cleaners employed by Churchill took 33 days of strike action.

129 RMT members took six days of strike action against the use of driver-only trains on the Airdrie–Bathgate line, but the action ended after internal divisions over its effectiveness (*Sunday Herald* 8 August 2010).

130 There were long-running disputes about the pay and conditions of maintenance workers in Network Rail after it was taken back in house (see *Observer* 26 October 2003; *Times* 9 August 2008).

131 Christian Wolmar believed that the RMT had come unstuck by over-reaching itself during a New Year Tube strike because the strike flopped (*New Statesman* 20 January 2006). This was not borne out by subsequent events.

132 See Gall (*Morning Star* 17 May 2005). RMT president Peter Pinkney made the same claim: 'I'm proud to be in a trade union that is rank and file, membership led' (*Morning Star* 11 September 2014). Crow (2012a: 155) said the RMT was 'a fighting and democratic industrial union'.

133 'An Interview with Bob Crow', *Marxism-Leninism Today* 9 May 2012, http://mltoday.com/an-interview-with-bob-crow.

want to base the initiatives I take as President on what members at a rank-and-file level want ... I don't believe the Executive and the national officers should be having the final say about industrial strategy and disputes ... My fundamental aim as president is to help make the union more rank-and-file led ... The union should be led from the workplace level up.[134]

Meanwhile, the RMT said of itself: 'RMT is a progressive, democratic and highly professional trade union ... RMT members can rely on their union to protect and promote their interests in the workplace.'[135] None of this is to question the RMT's democratic processes, especially as they were more democratic than most.[136] Indeed, it is worth recalling Darlington's summation:

the reform of union government that occurred in the wake of Crow's election was highly significant. As a consequence, there is now election (rather than appointment) of all national and regional employed union officers (who are subject to re-election after five years) and a directly elected lay-member CoE (whose members must relinquish their post after a three-year term of office). In addition, central decision-making powers lie in the hands of the lay national grade conferences and the Annual General Meeting (with delegates excluded from attending for more than a three-year successive period).[137]

Thus, all the key positions – general secretary, national president, junior and senior AGS, national secretary and regional organisers – were elected (being more than is required by law), although it is worth recalling that in 2009 Crow opposed reducing the length of membership required to be able to attend AGMs on the basis that having five years' continuous membership displayed loyalty to the union and allowed experience to be built up.[138] Moreover, branches can submit motions not just to AGMs but also the CoE.

But being member-led involves much more than simply democratic process, for the quantity and quality of membership participation are critical; it is more than merely leaders gaining positive support for their policies and actions among activists and members. Rather, being member-led involves union members themselves proposing policies and

134 'The union should be led from the workplace', *Solidarity* 16 January 2013, http://www.workersliberty.org/story/2013/01/15/union-should-be-led-workplace.

135 'About us', https://www.rmt.org.uk/about/.

136 See Darlington (2009a: 17). The RMT elects its officers far more extensively than the PCS.

137 Darlington (2009b: 97).

138 'Rail union: a step forward for democracy', *Solidarity* 19 November 2009, http://www.workersliberty.org/story/2009/11/19/rail-union-step-forward-democracy.

actions, and ensuring that leaders carry them out. So it is instructive to examine Crow's praxis of directed democracy, which approximated to *primus inter pares*. Paul Jackson recounted that 'Bob was authoritarian on one level. He was a man of action and got things done.'[139] Martin Eady recalled that:

> As General Secretary ... Bob often involved lay reps in negotiations. As an example, in the talks which ended the 2007 strike on the privatised Metronet, for whom I worked, he chose a team of Functional Reps, including me, to accompany the full-time officer. But there was never any doubt that Bob was the one in charge. This was the dispute which led to us being re-nationalised. Bob would always consult lay reps before considering industrial action, and he would say 'tell me the truth, not what you think I might want to hear'.[140]

In the Metronet dispute, Les Harvey revealed that, while Crow commanded an audience, he 'could adapt to the dynamics of that audience quickly'; with workers facing a 5% pension loss, 'Bob spoke of a deal but the strength of feeling of the reps was for no deal, just to strike and get the 5% back. Bob saw and felt that passion so on his feet he went from deal maker to firebrand, and then led the most successful strike in LU's history!'[141] Meanwhile a former CoE member commented:

> Bob was certainly not one of those General Secretaries you sometimes see who just routinely ignored any [CoE] decision he doesn't agree with. On the few occasions the [CoE] voted differently from the way he wanted us to, he just got on with carrying it out. Proposals got to the [CoE] via various routes. But members and branches found their routes rather more tortuous than the leadership did! An initiative that Bob was enthusiastic about would find a ready passage onto the agenda ... He fought hard for the Executive to make the decisions that he wanted them to make. But Executive members could have asserted themselves a lot more to disagree or put different points of view. With Bob having a big personality, forthright views and a popular leadership style, some Executive members found it tough to go against his recommendations – and some did so rarely or maybe never![142]

Another CoE member recalled:

> The thing about Bob was his confidence ... He knew where he was going and got on with it ... He was in control, knew what he was doing and wasn't afraid of making a mistake. Industrially, Bob was very democratic,

---

139 Email correspondence.
140 Email correspondence
141 Email correspondence.
142 Email correspondence.

although there were rare times in critical disputes when he would lean on executive council members if he thought things were going wrong. Generally, he didn't involve himself in executive council decisions on industrial matters ... The non-seafaring industrial discussion and decisions are taken by the General Grades Committee [GGC]. Bob very rarely attended [these] meetings as he was too busy. Decisions were taken by the GGC, led by the relevant GGC member. [But] matters of politics, union policy, finance and legal issues are taken by the full CoE, which Bob almost always attended and led. His views almost certainly carried the day. Occasionally, they didn't but this wouldn't be on issues that he regarded as important. If he thought there might be a problem, he would talk to people beforehand to get things sorted.[143]

In addition to opportunities afforded by frequent branch visits and grade conference speeches, Unjum Mirza reported that Crow had another way of introducing issues on to the union's agenda: 'Each year, he would always address his branch with motions that he'd like addressed at the AGM. He read out and addressed each motion, opened a debate and accepted the branch vote after a show of hands as to whether it was acceptable for the AGM.' To many in the RMT, this made the union seem a 'bottom-up' democracy, but scratching below the surface it revealed shrewd leadership skills.

As the RMT did not (unlike the PCS)[144] publish annual data on numbers of workplace representatives, it is impossible to know whether the RMT activist base rose under Crow.[145] There is also no data to compare the Crow and Knapp eras. Moreover, no study has been conducted – as it has been on the PCS[146] – to determine the relationship between membership levels and striking. Available evidence is of a more passive form of member activity, mainly concerning ballots. Thus, it would be hard to say that the 88% vote for retaining the political fund in 2004 was a 'ringing endorsement'[147] as Crow did, since the turnout was only 37% (even though this was higher than in previous RMT and NUR ballots).[148] The same could be said of the 2014 political fund ballot

---

143 Oliver New, email correspondence.
144 In the form of its *National Organising Strategy* annual documents.
145 The nearest estimate came in early 2011 (*RMT News* March 2011), when Alan Pottage reported a database of 5,000 activists and reps which was a doubling of numbers (though not from a specified date). Pottage also reported an increase in young member conference delegates in the same issue from nine in 2008 to 50 registered for the 2011 conference.
146 See McCarthy (2009); Hodder *et al.* (2016).
147 *Labour Research* January 2005.
148 See also McIlroy (2012: 255).

result – 96% in favour on a 31% turnout.[149] Between 2002 and 2009, Darlington found that votes for industrial action had a mean of 83% support but turnouts were again much lower – a mean of 39% on the Underground and 66% on the railways.[150] In terms of participation in the RMT political fund – by deciding not to opt out – the percentage of paying members dropped from the high nineties to the low eighties between 2003/04 and 2013/14 (see Table 1). Although McIlroy believed that this did 'not suggest politicisation',[151] the lack of data does not allow a firm conclusion to be reached because the numbers tell us little – around 9,000 members opting out may suggest an objection to supporting the radical Left and not Labour. In Darlington's study of strikes, there was no clear evidence of rising, falling or stagnating member participation.[152] In terms of TUSC and No2EU, participation as candidates and activists was limited, even if some participants were high-profile. In the absence of data, the most likely scenario is that Crow's appeal was confined to those who were already activists.

This is to question, therefore, whether the RMT (or any union) can be said to be 'member-led', because unions overall are in such a poor state of health – as is working-class consciousness and working-class struggle – and this gravely affects membership participation and, thus, control. Indeed, electing 'awkward squad' leaders indicated that many members wanted leaders to fight for them when they were not fighting for themselves (as judged by falling strike levels). There is also little sense in which unions like the RMT are member-led if comparators of past shop steward movements are used, since they represented self-organised members who were able to significantly direct their unions' actions. Indeed, believing that the RMT was member-led is to unwittingly denigrate Crow's leadership skills. The critical issue, then, is whether 'awkward squad' leaders like Crow had the capacity to ensure that their unions started becoming more membership-led. What Crow did was necessary but not sufficient because of the ideological and political hegemony of neoliberalism. Another critical issue concerns whether, in an era of denuded membership involvement, the RMT (or any other union) is even activist-led. Even with the CoE, there was little sense that it – as the activist *crème de la crème* – was directed by activists from below. Crow's significance here was in giving voice to those without

---

149 RMT circular, NP222/14, 3 November 2014. In November 2015, the PCS's political fund was renewed in a ballot of 91% on a 23% turnout.
  150 Darlington (2010: 22).
  151 McIlroy (2012: 255).
  152 Darlington (2014b: 71–74).

much of a voice and encouraging lay activism, but within the parameters of directed democracy.

It is also pertinent to recall that formal organisational processes do not necessarily determine outcomes, because of internal cultures. Thus, a leading activist ventured, in the context of the 2009 RMT AGM, that:

> While the structures do not prevent delegates criticising the leadership, I feel that aspects of the AGM's culture suppressed criticism. We have a dominant General Secretary with a big personality, impressive speaking style and a decent (though flawed) record of standing up for members. This – together with a powerful desire for unity, for huddling together against the storm of the employers' attacks – can quieten dissent even if the structures do not.[153]

Indeed, one consequence of directed democracy was a culture of deference:

> Bob was held in incredibly high esteem ... common remarks in conversations ... with colleagues at work (not activists on the whole, just 'ordinary members') in the days after his death were along the lines of: 'It was great knowing we had someone like that fighting our corner' [and] 'We've lost our general in the middle of a war' ... The downside ... was ... something of a cult of personality developed around him ... I don't think [he] particularly cultivated that himself [especially as] he was perfectly prepared to engage with criticism of his role, his politics, [his] pay ... the cult of personality/ culture of deference ... was more cultivated by others around him ... For example, in the [2014] general secretary election, some people responded to the workers' wage issue by saying 'Are you saying Bob was overpaid?' as if it was a personal attack on him.[154]

In the World Federation of Trade Unions interview, Crow commented that 'The union is there to make sure that its members' pay and conditions are preserved and constantly improved ... Our role at the work places is to protect our members from employers' negligence.'[155] He told the *Mirror*: 'If you join one you expect it to fight for your rights and your job – and that's what I'm doing.'[156] A decade earlier, a further indication that the RMT was not as member-led as it was often said to be – or wanted to be – came again from Crow himself: 'we are a trade union and our members pay their money for us to get them the best possible pay

153 'Top table wins on all the issues', *Solidarity* 9 July 2009, http://www.workersliberty.org/story/2009/07/09/top-table-wins-all-issues.
154 Anonymised young RMT activist, email correspondence.
155 *Marxism-Leninism Today* 9 May 2012.
156 *Mirror* 9 February 2014.

and conditions and that's what we intend doing'.[157] These statements indicate that the servicing notion of buying representation was rather more prevalent than was assumed. Indeed, the RMT promotional video to recruit members strongly emphasised what the union could do for members and not what members could do for themselves.[158] In a further telling comment, Crow said: 'I will be the captain, steering the ship, but the members will make all the decisions.'[159] He meant that he would be their humble and loyal servant, carrying out their wishes. Yet from the terms used, and in view of his way of operating, it is more accurate to recall that the captain is the senior figure, giving – rather than receiving – the orders.

As noted earlier, Crow's ability, as an individual, to dominate the RMT was aided by the absence of an organised broad Left and the relatively small and homogeneous nature of the RMT's membership, suggesting the creation of political congruence. What did exist was an influential network of senior radical Left activists who shared common industrial and political perspectives.[160] As Oliver New recalled:

> I don't think Bob had a group around him – he tried to support and work with everyone. But, of course, he shared views with some more than others … he would particularly discuss politics with a handful of CPB people. Then there was a group within the union from the old left wing of the union, prior to Bob's election, some of who he appointed into organising positions on the staff.[161]

As with the way Crow related to other left-wing union general secretaries, it suited his style of personality and leadership not to have to participate in – and be bound by – any formal Left grouping.[162] This

---

157 *BBC Forum* interview, 9 September 2002, http://news.bbc.co.uk/2/hi/talking_point/forum/2234265.stm; see also *RMT – Your Union*, Platform Films, 2005, London.

158 *RMT – Your Union*, Platform Films, 2005, London.

159 *Mirror* 11 March 2014. The (original) source of this quote, which was widely used at the time of Crow's death, could not be found in any national newspaper prior to this period. It is presumed to have come from the Press Association (given its widespread usage), and to refer to Crow's perspective in his election campaign for the general secretaryship in 2002.

160 Notwithstanding that the Right organised around Cash, Knapp presided over a much more politically divided union.

161 Oliver New, email correspondence.

162 Most of the 'awkward squad' union leaders (with the exception of Serwotka) were elected without there being formal Left organisations in existence. This contrasts with left-wing leaders elected in previous decades, such as Scargill and Ken Gill. Much of this can be attributed to the declining influence of the Communist Party.

allowed the launching of initiatives and responses to events in a way that maximised his personal stamp. In so doing, he provided a centralised form of leadership, evidenced by, *inter alia*, operating uniformly across an enlarged number of employers and the absence of unofficial strikes.

Union effectiveness

Democracy and participation should not be made synonymous with effectiveness, because majority will is not about means or ends *per se*. So it is interesting to note two developments. In 2009, Crow launched a drive across the union's 12 regions to bolster branch organisation by carrying out 'health checks' (concerning the frequency of meetings, workplace visits by branch officials, membership communication, and visits from regional organisers), because some branches did not meet or have quorate meetings, some workplaces did not have reps and there was over £500,000 in branch funds unused.[163] Stemming from a motion passed at the 2011 AGM but put on hold due the repercussions of the proposed TSSA merger, a review of internal structures and processes was begun. In late 2013, submissions were taken from branches. While suggesting a relatively clean bill of health, the submissions showed concerns over issues of control and accountability due to overlapping complexity of structures (region, sector), some structures that reflected redundant historical influences resulting in over- and under-representation of particular groups, and an imbalance between the GGC members being full-time CoE officials and the remainder being part-time.[164] The latter was a longstanding issue for some, given that the GGC (essentially the rail section of the CoE) could make decisions about disputes (such as accepting deals or calling off strikes) where representatives of provincial rail members dominated.[165] Although not raised in the review, there was also longstanding concern that the small number of AGM delegates prevented wider participation.[166]

While disputes involving industrial action in the RMT's road (buses,

---

163 General Secretary's Report, 2009 AGM.

164 This reflected the fact that the facility of release for both groups was different, and that the shipping and offshore grade members had more difficulty attending meetings. Gordon and Upchurch (2012: 264) suggested that participation by different sections of the RMT membership was not all it could be.

165 This was an issue in 2001.

166 See, for example, 'Top table wins on all the issues', *Solidarity* 9 July 2009, http://www.workersliberty.org/story/2009/07/09/top-table-wins-all-issues; and 'RMT AGM: Bigger, More Democratic', *Off The Rails*, Autumn 2007, http://www.workersliberty.org/node/9507.

freight, taxis) and seafaring sections were not uncommon,[167] they never neared the levels found in the rail section. Terms and conditions in the former were poorer than in the latter. In seafaring, redundancies were more common. Despite Crow trying to instil confidence and encourage resistance, the power differential between RMT members in the former and latter sectors remained because of differences in labour markets (such as crewing under flags of convenience), the availability of alternatives, workers' strategic positioning, immediacy of impact of action and so on. Although the RMT never forgot these members, as evidenced by the organisation of sector conferences and campaigns reported in *RMT News*, there was no breakthrough in resolving these weaknesses.

Union identity

Although Crow stressed that the RMT – and its members – did not want to run the transport industry and that the union's priority was to improve terms and conditions, this was a partial truth. Under his leadership, with rail in particular, there was an industry mentality that claimed that the workers themselves were best placed through their experience, skills and material interests to exert control over 'their' industry, especially on safety and service provision. This mentality considerably increased under privatisation as a result of falling safety and service standards and continued public subsidy. It became the cornerstone of a close affinity of the members with their union, forming an industrial identity in which worker, union and sector came together.[168] Another cornerstone was the aspiration to – and progress made in pursuing – industrial unionism whereby the RMT organised industrially and across grades with transport and maritime industries. For Crow, industrial unionism was

> a legacy that continues to inform the principles and practice [of the RMT] … The core of that legacy is the significance of industrial unionism as a means of building the strongest possible unity across grades, rejecting narrow sectionalism in favour of solidarity [with the] cleaners' campaigns … a clear example of how RMT as an industrial union has been able to deploy solidarity, even within current legal constraints, to organise and win among a group of low-paid, vulnerable workers employed by hard-nosed contract companies.[169]

167 See, for example, First Devon and Cornwall buses in 2005 (*Times* 1 July 2005) and P&O in 2004 (*Independent* 29 September 2004).
168 This in spite of the historical decline in traditional work identity found by Strangleman (2004) in the rail industry. One such instance was the decline of the aristocracy of labour of highly skilled and highly remunerated workers.
169 Crow (2012a: 149, 155).

Crow recognised that, while driver members had more leverage, leverage could be generated by and for other RMT members such as unskilled cleaners, and he played a major role in transferring the union's identity and culture to cleaners (and maintaining it with caterers). Overall, and although the RMT organises a multitude of different workers, there was less sense of internal sectionalism than was found in other unions with different trade and industry sections.[170] Some obvious manifestations of higher than normal levels of union identity were the wearing of union badges and ties at work and union T-shirts and baseball caps outside work; viewing the criticism of outsiders as invalid because they were non-members; fierce defence of their general secretary as something approaching untouchable; and a sense of a union family through socialising with fellow members. In other words, there was a loyalty to, and pride in, the RMT displayed by members which crystallised around Crow, comprising a combination of market, class and societal orientations: the market orientation involved using labour market advantage for sectional gain, the class orientation involved the espousal of common interests for workers in the political arena, and the societal orientation involved the advocacy of citizens' interest.[171] Although there were tensions between these different orientations, they remained true to the RMT's aims of protecting and advancing members' interests and seeking socialism. In each Crow sought to align and wield RMT members' power, material interests and ideology into a holistic transformational project.

Conclusion

Unsurprisingly, the media portrayal that informed the public perception obscured a considerably more complex social reality about how Crow operated as a leader within the RMT. Based on the manufacture of his own power resources and *modus operandi*, Crow's practice of directed democracy saw him play the leading role, notwithstanding other influential actors within the union that helped construct and moderate his leadership. Added to the members' potential power, levels of union effectiveness were high. In other words, he provided the leadership to deploy their potential power effectively, turning it into usable leverage. In this, his members followed him, and did so largely uncritically, because his forceful personality and politics were critical to facilitating

170 This is not just because of the dominance of over- and underground rail members within the union.
171 See Hyman (2001) on the three categories.

this outcome. But, in turn, it should be recognised that his personality and politics rested upon the foundations of phenomena such as group cohesion and union identity. The next and final chapter examines the legend that Crow became as well as his legacy.

9. Legacy and legend

In its end of year review of 2014, the *Independent* commented that Crow was 'one of those public figures who seemed to loom larger than his organisation. With his dominant personality, his left-wing politics and his belief in using industrial muscle to obtain a better deal for his members, he was the nearest the ... union movement had to a celebrity, even if the [RMT] ... he led ... was barely a 20th the size of the biggest unions'.[1] In other words, he was a leader, fighter and socialist. The former FBU general secretary and then RMT national education officer, Andy Gilchrist, believed that: 'It's not too much to say it's unlikely I or indeed any of us will see his like again',[2] while former CoE member Janine Booth said: 'Bob was one of the best union leaders in the country, if not the best.'[3] This concluding chapter brings together the different themes and threads of previous ones to provide an overall assessment of Crow, his strengths, weaknesses and contribution. With the exception of Serwotka, Crow was the most 'awkward' of the 'awkward squad'[4] in both economic and political terms.[5] Serwotka's accusation in September 2014 that 'When history is written, up to this point the unions will be seen to have failed. They haven't been up to the task'[6] could not be levelled at Crow's leadership of the RMT.[7] This was because, as a RMT spokesperson told *The Times*: 'Bob Crow doesn't just talk the talk

1 *Independent* 30 December 2014.

2 Email correspondence.

3 *Telegraph* 12 March 2014.

4 The term was coined in 2001 by Kevin Maguire (*Guardian* 12 September 2001). See also Murray (2003: 133).

5 Indeed, this was view of the *Guardian* (2 July 2003) as early as 2003. Matt Wrack was not elected as FBU general secretary until 2005.

6 *Guardian* 6 September 2014.

7 An interview with Serwotka confirmed this view of Crow. He added that Crow was not affected by a 'deep seated fatalism' or 'defeatism', as Serwotka believed other union leaders were (*Guardian* 11 May 2012; *Morning Star* 3 January 2012, respectively). Subsequently, he said: 'As general secretary I think that, along with Bob Crow, I've been the most high profile critic of Labour in the trade union movement' (*Socialist Worker* 27 February 2016).

– he walks the walk';[8] he was, according to the *Morning Star*, a 'titan of socialism'.[9] Crow's contribution was anchored upon his persona, politics and the potential power of his members. Towards the end of his life, respect for him was growing, with the *Guardian* and *Mirror* commenting respectively: 'most of us might secretly like to have someone like Crow fighting our corner'[10] and he was 'a man you would want to fight your corner'.[11]

Before examining his leadership and its legacy, it is worth remembering that within days of his death, RMT members had applied the epithet 'RIP legend' to him. Along with 'loved by the workers, feared by the bosses', those words adorned banners and placards at his funeral and at the 2014 London May Day march. An RMT online book of condolence received nearly 2,500 messages from supporters and well-wishers between the day following his death and the end of April 2014.[12] Although his funeral on 24 March was a small private affair, thousands of supporters and sympathisers lined the cortege's route from Snakes Lane East, Woodford, to the City of London cemetery and crematorium in Manor Park. His coffin was clapped through the cemetery gates by hundreds, leading *Union News* to pointedly ask 'which other general secretary['s death] would provoke such an outpouring of grief?'[13] In a tribute to her step-father, Natasha Hoarau announced at the London May Day march that she would stand in the 2014 European elections for the organisation that he would have stood for in London had he not died.[14] Later she wrote: 'Bob was often told that he was in a minority, but that never bothered him as he would often say that minority views can become majority views very quickly. He also taught me to never give up.'[15] In a very unusual move,

8 *Times* 5 September 2007.

9 *Morning Star* 2 January 2015. Tony Benn was also accorded this characterisation.

10 *Guardian* 13 December 2010.

11 *Mirror* 9 February 2014.

12 See http://www.rmt.org.uk/bob-crow/. There was also a physical book of condolence at the RMT's headquarters and this remained open for some six months after his death (*Guardian* 1 October 2014).

13 *Union News* 24 March 2014. It helped that Crow was in office and in the midst of current struggles when he died, as the funeral for a union leader who had long since left the battlefield would inevitably have been smaller than that for one who had died in office. One person who did not attend his funeral was Boris Johnson, with the consequence that Crow's quip that he would meet Johnson at 'his funeral' (*Financial Times* 25 March 2011) turned out not to be realised. It was unclear whether Crow had meant his or Johnson's funeral. The context was Johnson's refusal ever to meet Crow in an official capacity.

14 *RMT News* April–May 2014.

15 *Morning Star* 10 May 2014.

TfL put up posters of Crow on the Underground to commemorate him.[16] This was matched by over fifty transport employers agreeing to a special dispensation of the regular uniform arrangements for RMT members, allowing them to wear a black tie or armband on the day of his funeral.[17] Posthumously, Crow was awarded the Silver Badge by trades union councils for his campaigning work for them.[18] The RMT's 2014 AGM decided to 'rename its education and training centre to commemorate him. Delegates supported a name change to the Bob Crow RMT National Education Centre as well as erecting a statue of him to be placed outside [it].'[19] A plaque was unveiled to his memory at the STUC headquarters on 13 September 2014. A week earlier, a video tribute was paid to him at the TUC congress with the soundtrack being a specially commissioned song.[20] When the RMT unveiled a plaque at its Aberdeen and Glasgow offices in honour of Crow in November 2014, Natasha Hoarau recalled: 'He was loved by so many for his strength of character when fighting for others. He never put himself first and valued the underdog and he didn't just talk the talk with empty words, he walked the walk and was a man of action.'[21] Another plaque was unveiled to him at Millwall FC at their last game of the season.[22] Finally, and echoing the traditions of the International Brigades during the Spanish Civil War, a group of British and Irish volunteers, as part of the International Freedom Battalion fighting the Islamic State of Iraq and Syria (ISIS) alongside Kurdish People's Protection Units, named their brigade the Bob Crow Brigade in 2016.[23]

The measure of the man

Crow was culturally and psychologically working class in his tastes and orientations, but he was not materially or politically working class, because of his role as a union general secretary, which gave him a different position in society along with superior financial resources to those of

16 Acquiring the rights to use the photograph cost £1,050, with the image being sent electronically, printed and displayed at stations at negligible cost (*Morning Star* 14 July 2014).

17 RMT press release, 21 March 2014.

18 *Morning Star* 16 July 2014. Crow was chair of the trades union council's joint consultative committee, and successfully moved the RMT's motion at the 2008 TUC to allow trades councils to submit motions to annual TUC congresses.

19 *RMT News* July–August 2014, p. 20.

20 Set to the tune of the Clash's 'London Calling'; see https://www.youtube.com/watch?v=7faxXtpC9Lk.

21 *RMT News* November–December 2014.

22 *RMT News* July–August 2014.

23 *Independent* 16 September 2016.

working-class people, and because of his radical socialist politics. Indeed, if Crow was working class in these aspects, he would not have stood out as much as he did, nor been as important as he was. Nonetheless, he presented himself, and crucially was seen by others (especially on the Left), as the 'real deal', a working-class boy with a manual background made good in the cause of fighting for workers and socialism. He led a militant union in a militant way, with his authenticity enhanced by his cultural, psychological and political dispositions.

Crow had a developed sense of righteous indignation concerning the plight of RMT members, workers and the working class, and was unfazed and undaunted in prosecuting their interests by the hostility and ridicule heaped upon him. Indeed, and up to a point, he wore this as a badge of honour, since it affirmed and validated that what he was doing was correct.[24] For example, he stated that 'I have been trained to believe that if the media attack you, you must be doing something right'[25] and 'I have always thought that if the right-wing press weren't attacking me I would probably not be doing my job properly.'[26] Indeed, the *Evening Standard*'s attack on him from 1996, entitled 'Last stand of the dinosaurs', was framed in his office.[27] Sometimes, he expressed this as 'I'm like Millwall – a dog with a bad name',[28] telling an interviewer: 'I always speak my mind. People either accept it or they don't.'[29] All these traits made him remarkable. But the clincher for members and activists was that he was not aloof. He enjoyed getting around branches to present awards or give talks, speaking at section conferences and visiting RMT picket lines.[30] He was not one to sit in an office and did not fear or dislike his members. To be in contact with members in this way was about taking the temperature as well as encouraging developments that he favoured. Crow was also authentic in other senses – he was a

---

24 *Guardian* 2 July 2004; *RMT News* October 2010; *Guardian* 12 March 2014. In the latter, Decca Aitkenhead wrote: 'There was never any doubt that he relished his reputation as the unacceptable face of trade unionism ... He saw himself as one of the Labour movement's last true Marxist class warriors ... he considered his unpopularity among the media and political classes a signifier of success, because he wore it like a badge of honour.'

25 In Murray (2003: 99).

26 *RMT News* November 2010.

27 *Evening Standard* 11 July 1996.

28 *Telegraph* 16 February 2002.

29 In Murray (2003: 103).

30 *RMT News* published photographic evidence of this on a monthly basis. There were few occasions when Crow did not visit his members' picket lines. One instance of him being prevented from visiting a picket line was when he had to attend the RMT AGM in Portsmouth in 2004.

workaholic and did not just call for a new party of labour but tried to develop the basis for one.

Unlike many other union leaders or politicians, Crow was not evasive or defensive when questioned by journalists or political foes about the RMT or his politics. He came across as sincere and passionate in his dogged, defiant defence of himself, the RMT, workers and socialism. As a result, when putting across his arguments, he was blunt and force-ful. He used a language and a vocabulary that some found off-putting but that chimed with many more, especially RMT members. To the minority, it lacked sophistication and erudition. To the majority, it was a no-nonsense style that was understandable and unashamed. In these ways, Crow became the living embodiment of the RMT's industrial and political agenda. His physique also spoke to these qualities of being strong and sturdy when he needed to be. Overall, he 'talked the talk' and 'walked the walk', contrasting with most other left-wing union leaders who did not make nearly such a powerful synergy of their person, per-sona and politics. Crow's synergy meant that the whole was greater than the sum of the parts. Doing this for RMT members, and with successful outcomes, meant that he was also able to be an advocate for workers in general – that they be treated with respect and be valued – and in so doing was a better advocate than nearly all other union leaders. But as this biography has stressed, none of this could have been done without the palpable bargaining power of RMT members. That said, Crow was not the only significant left-wing figure in the RMT, others being most obviously Greg Tucker, Bobby Law, John Leach, Peter Pinkney, Pat Sikorski, Steve Hedley and Alex Gordon. The point is that Crow became not only general secretary but also the undisputed leader of the Left in the RMT, which serves to emphasise that he had a persona and personal skills that were far superior to those of others. The following sections examine the most important aspects of this.

Being a leader

Crow developed leadership skills without the benefit of formal training, which indicates that personality, experience and political worldview were as critical as any mentoring system or theory-based classroom instruction. He did this from an early age and with dedication and industriousness, as Martin Eady recalled: 'His commitment and sheer hard work saw him gradually develop into the great leader that he was.' Crow developed skills to carry out the leadership functions, namely agenda setting, strategising, negotiating, communicating, cau-cusing and alliance formation, and managing people and resources. Communication often comprised 'fronting' CoE decisions to members and media, requiring the presentation of arguments and response to criticism, while agenda setting involved influencing AGM and CoE decisions. Strategising required agreeing and implementing ways and means of obtaining goals and objectives. Crow showed that he could work with the different strands of the radical Left (communist, syndicalist, Trotskyist) both inside and outside the RMT as a result of his skills of caucusing and alliance formation. Crow's presentation style gave the sense of leading from the front, embodying the RMT brand of militancy. This meant that he never publicly undermined his members' interests or resilience by indicating that he was less than fully supportive of them.[31]

The components of leadership encompass the dialectic of leading and reflecting, meaning influencing members' views while also taking on board and representing their views. In this sense, leadership requires being ahead of most members' industrial and political consciousness, but not too far ahead. Crow understood this vanguardism while providing transformational leadership to encourage and facilitate membership resistance. With no formal faction dominating the RMT, he provided this in a centralised manner. In only one function did he come up short, namely, legacy planning. Although his death was unexpected, he had considered not standing again, and it became evident with four radical Left candidates to potentially succeed him that no steps had been taken to establish a single successor. Moreover, because he had been so dominant, obvious successors did not emerge. By far and away the two most important aptitudes Crow displayed were to simultaneously 'front' and 'frame' disputes militantly, and then negotiate pragmatically ('fronting' and 'framing' being agenda-setting and mobilisation aspects). For example, Paul Jackson recounted: 'He was pragmatic. Get in, threaten and get out with something. He could do a deal for certain. Sometimes maybe too quick, maybe sometimes too slow, but the truth is, he knew what we would win and what we wouldn't.'[32] Affecting both militancy and pragmatism was a clever strategy, since the former facilitated the latter but on a basis where pragmatism allowed deals that comprised ambitious demands. To effectively carry out these functions requires that individuals have highly developed sets of the aforementioned skills, and to have those skills demands that individuals be self-confident and assertive, with well-developed emotional intelligence.

As union leader and leading left-winger, Crow carried off a difficult

---

31 On one occasion, Crow was a little too frank, saying in front of a manager at a disciplinary hearing for a white-collar RMT member that other (manual) RMT members would not come out on strike to stop the member's sacking.

32 Email correspondence.

balancing act, namely being the same as but also different from his members and his audiences. His mannerisms and tastes were often the same as theirs so there was a palpable sense in which he 'was one of us', as Paul Jackson put it,[33] or was at least still manifestly from the members' ilk. But he was also different from them because he was a leader who could instil courage and confidence to act collectively for radical, socialist ends. In this sense, he provided leadership for others and, in doing so, he was far more transformative than transactional because he cognitively helped people to do things that they wanted to do but did not necessarily feel capable of doing.[34] Being predominantly transformative means using more the inspiration of ideas and examples, whereas being transactional means relying upon instrumental and material motivations. Part of being transformative was raising people's expectations by defiantly spelling out things the way he saw them and by offering an alternative based upon a socialist critique of capitalism, the Conservative–Liberal Democrat coalition government and Labour. Indeed, as Peter Pinkney recalled, 'he instilled bravery, determination and confidence into all those who heard him and worked with him'.[35] Applied to RMT members, the essential aspects of inspiration and encouragement concerned strike mobilisation strategy, thus boosting their self-confidence and collective power.

Crow realised that carrying out such a role meant being a bit out of the ordinary:

> To be a general secretary of a union you've got to be larger than life ... You can't walk around with a grey suit on and eat a cheese sandwich every lunchtime. You want someone who's got a bit of spark about them [but without being] gobby, flash or arrogant ... I suppose [I like to be seen as] talkative, a man with an opinion. And perhaps sometimes where some people might keep their mouth shut I have expressed a point of view where sometimes you should listen a bit more.[36]

This suggests that he embellished certain characteristics in his personality in order to play the part of 'Bob Crow, the public figure', given that he was quite shy and humble in private. This was a trait common in

33 Email correspondence.
34 This was a characteristic of other union leaders such as Scargill. By contrast, and although on the Left, Clive Jenkins led the ASTMS in a more transactional manner (Melling 2004).
35 *RMT News* April 2014.
36 Radio 4 *PM*, 10 March 2014. See also 'RMT leader Bob Crow talks salary, strikes and Boris', http://www.bbc.com/news/uk-politics-26529361, 11 March 2014.

other leaders.[37] This is not to suggest that he was insincere, faked it or consciously courted celebrity.[38] Jeff Porter observed:

> In the later years, Bob became almost a caricature of his real self ... as a television performer he came across as louder than he was in real life. Perhaps, it was because knowing him before he became famous, he just seemed quieter and more reflective. He always held the opinions he espoused on TV so it was not his opinions which were the caricature but the loudness with which he expressed them.[39]

For the Crow the public figure, the big personality was required to give effective delivery to the content of industrial bargaining and socialist politics.[40] This persona helped him perform when under pressure in the sense of being able to go into character, this being a form of deep acting.

But despite Crow's influence, it was surprising just how introspective the RMT continued to be. Its internal organisational culture determined that its *modus operandi* was somewhat closed off to others in the union movement. For example, engagement with the Left and the wider movement on any terms other than its own was uncommon, and at local and regional levels the RMT was pretty much the start and finish of most activists' horizons. RMT involvement in the NSSN became minimal after its first few years.[41] This introspection and sectionalism – despite the RMT's being vocal in the TUC, central to TUSC and so on – can be partly accounted for by the impact of the distinctive culture of the rail sector and by the RMT being a small specialist transport union. But it can also be accounted for by the RMT being able to win many of its industrial battles on its own because of its strength, and its centralised nature whereby its general secretary is seen as almost the sole voice of authority. This tendency was reinforced and extended under Crow's leadership. Consequently, there was much very much the view among activists and active members that Crow would do 'the job' for them. For example, seldom did RMT activists go in large numbers to events outside the RMT at which Crow spoke in order to support him. For his followers within the RMT, he was seen as doing something that they could not,

37 See Gall (2012a: 244–248) on Tommy Sheridan 'getting into character'.
38 As did a number of individuals on the employer and management side of the rail industry (see Radio 4 *Profile*, 4 April 2010, http://www.bbc.co.uk/programmes/b00rq2kx).
39 Jeff Porter, email correspondence.
40 See also *Telegraph* 12 March 2014.
41 The NSSN became a *de facto* franchise of the Socialist Party from 2011 after a split over broadening its campaigning direction. This was despite an initial disagreement between the RMT, led by Crow and Gordon, and the Socialist Party over strategy (see *The Socialist* 12, 19 January 2012).

namely, realising their potential by articulating arguments forcefully. Outside the RMT, Crow was seen by followers as giving legitimacy to their causes and politics, so that he was feted by the radical Left in terms of speaking at their meetings, offering his support and so on.

Employing nuance

Crow was often portrayed as ham-fisted and bone-headed[42] but there was nuance and measure to what he argued.[43] For example, in an introduction to a pamphlet on health and safety, Crow couched his argument carefully, describing the need to 'eliminate *unnecessary* [emphasis added] risk', the 'tendency' rather than the iron law of employers' drive to minimise costs and maximise profits, a union-organised workforce being '*usually* [emphasis added] a safer workforce', and that 'the law *as it stands* [emphasis added] has important limitations'.[44] And, while favouring rail renationalisation, he also advocated taking contracted-out services such as infrastructure maintenance back in house, merging Network Rail with the Strategic Rail Authority to create a unified management structure and vertical reintegration of the rail industry as steps towards public ownership.[45] With the RMT being a major part of the 'Take Back the Track' campaign, he argued that the campaign involved 'getting Railtrack first of all back into public ownership, then bringing the rest of the train operating companies, and the whole lot eventually'.[46] His desire for renationalisation was not just for RMT members' benefit but also for citizens as passengers and as taxpayers, since he warned that increased rail subsidies were 'useless if [they] ended up in the pockets of shareholders'.[47] Indeed, he did not advocate a return to the 'state socialist' nationalisation of the past, but a model of far more democratic and participative common ownership:

42 There are many examples of this in the press, but those by Christian Wolmar are as good as any given that they come from a specialist commentator: 'Think before you strike, Bob', *Evening Standard* 6 February 2008; 'Bob Crow blows it', *Christian Says*, 2 April 2010, http://www.christianwolmar.co.uk/2010/04/bob-crow-blows-it/; and 'A strike too far?', *Times* 7 September 2010.

43 This indicates that the contrast with Serwotka (see earlier) should not be exaggerated.

44 Crow (2007: 3).

45 *Independent* 13 May 2002; *Guardian* 12 May 2003; and Crow (2008: 21). See also *The Times* (18 November 2003), where he stated: 'We are not against private contractors per se. In fact there are some areas, such as building the Channel Tunnel high-speed rail link, where we think they can't be replaced.'

46 *Socialist Review* May 2001.

47 *Morning Star* 22, 25 July 2002.

This need not simply be a return to Whitehall centralisation. The new body could include representatives from passenger groups, unions, business and other stakeholders. The Scottish parliament, the Welsh assembly and Transport for London could have prominent roles in planning and funding local services, and the possibility of regional assemblies in England also provides the opportunity for greater regional direction over the railways.[48]

On Labour, Crow told the *Guardian*: 'It is not that we are marching too slowly towards our goals, we are being led in the wrong direction',[49] but recognising the radical Left's weakness, he understood that carefully crafted appeals to reason were needed – even when he believed Labour was beyond the pale – in order to unmask it to those not yet converted to his perspective. Thus, for many years he lambasted Labour for courting political suicide if it did this or that when it was quite clear it would not change course. For example, he said: 'Unless Blair stops cosying up to big business and obeying every command from the warmonger across the Atlantic, he risks causing a meltdown in support from the very people who put Labour into power';[50] 'We welcome the review of the Employment Relations Act, but the Government would be committing political suicide if it caved in again to the demands of the employers';[51] 'By lining up with the Tory-led coalition on the assault on public sector pay, Ed Balls will today sign Labour's electoral suicide note as he alienates his core voters in their millions.'[52]

Public speaking

Crow's style as a public speaker was passionate, unflinching, instinctive and unapologetic. He used exaggerated modes of expression, deploying superlatives in figurative ways to express his strong feelings and to stir up strong feelings among his audiences. His linguistic extravagance led some to mock him, accusing him of a cartoon style. *The Times* believed that he was 'abrasive and confrontational ... a stereotypical militant and a brilliant orator – if you like the vein-bulging, finger-pointing, grammar mangling, lectern-thumping variety of demagoguery'[53] and that he spoke

48 *Guardian* 12 May 2003. The idea of a participative model of ownership and control was explored in a pamphlet written for the RMT by the then SSP head of policy, Alan McCombes, in 2005.
49 *Guardian* 25 June 2002.
50 *Times* 9 September 2002.
51 *Times* 10 September 2002.
52 *Guardian* 14 January 2012. See also the *New Statesman*'s 'Trade Union Guide', 14 September 2009.
53 *Times* 14 September 2010.

'as if he has been cast as a truculent union leader in a 1950s comedy'.[54] The RMT's official historian believed that Crow was 'outspoken to the point of bluntness'.[55] The usual convention of speaking in a personal capacity (designated by the letters 'pc' after the speaker's name on the leaflets advertising meetings) seldom applied to Crow because what he said prosecuted the RMT's three primary objectives and because he was such an authoritative figure within the union.

His bluntness and colour were critical to his ability to motivate, encourage and inspire others, especially as a transformational leader.[56] In the context of (internal) union affairs, his exaggerated style came across as less pronounced because RMT members on underground and overground rail, by and large, had the power to deliver effective action. This was not the case for those who were receptive to his message outside the RMT. Not only did he speak without notes – 'from the hip' as Paul Jackson put it[57] or as Ann Henderson recalled, '[his] contributions ... were to the point, impatient and urgent'[58] – but his accomplished performances involved more than mere tub-thumping invective, as diagnosis and prognosis were covered equally. He could, of course, do diatribe and vilification, with the *Evening Standard* noting that 'he retains his grassroots command of invective'.[59] The TSSA former general secretary, Gerry Doherty, recalled: 'Sure he was abrasive at times, loud-mouthed, maybe, but absolutely committed to the cause and more than able and willing to debate his corner with the very best of them'[60] and Christine Buckley wrote: 'Bob may have said this more than 1,000 times since his teens but he made the arguments with as much vigour and belief as if he'd first come across the ideas.'[61]

His style of public speaking was seemingly rudimentary because of its simplicity. The supposed attraction of sophistication should not, however, be confused with effectiveness. Without trying to bamboozle audiences into agreement or action through sophistry and highfalutin' words, Crow put over clear but basic arguments that addressed the big issues of the day. His style was simple without being overly simplistic. His maxims were well chosen: 'Fear is contagious, but not as contagious as courage'; 'If you fight you may lose, if you don't fight you certainly

54 *Times* 10 May 2011.
55 Berlin (2006: 147).
56 Another example of this was Joseph Mambuliya, chair of the RMT London Underground cleaners' grade committee (*The Socialist* 25 March 2015).
57 Email correspondence.
58 Email correspondence.
59 *Evening Standard* 16 May 2001.
60 *TSSA Journal* April 2014.
61 *Guardian* 12 March 2014.

will lose'; 'Don't fear them, fight them'; 'If you don't own it, you don't control it'; and 'The only people who don't make mistakes are people who don't do anything.' He made a small number of key points that reinforced each other and that left audiences in no uncertainty about the crucial message of his overall argument or its force.[62] There was never much grey in what he argued. His contrasts were always stark, being the dichotomies of capital and labour, workers and bosses, right and wrong, capitalism and socialism. Often his humour and his examples came from direct experiences. When they did not, contemporary or historical examples were used. He almost always spoke in the first person, never hiding behind the supposed neutrality and impartiality of the third person. The *Independent* gave a good insight into his public speaking abilities:

> On the rostrum, Crow is fiery – one of the few orators at the TUC who can be relied upon to pull a crowd. He jabs his finger at the ceiling as he demands re-nationalisation and the repeal of Thatcher's anti-union legislation … Did he have any training? 'No, I did it myself. I never have notes. And everything I say, is what I say. No-one else writes it.' Humour, he adds, is essential. 'They're sitting there all day, bored to tears. That's what they're looking for, a bit of humour. If you can get a bit of humour, you can win them over.'[63]

Alex Gordon summed up his style thus:

> He had no airs and graces. Not a trace of pomposity attached to him, yet his powers of communication were exceptional. I have not heard any … union or political leader since Arthur Scargill at the peak of his powers who could speak to an audience with the power of Bob Crow. On several occasions I have seen him reduce audiences to tears of anger and uproarious laughter at the same time.[64]

Serwotka's style contrasted with Crow's. Although not entirely dissimilar, Serwotka's *modus operandi* was a calmer, more patient, reasoned and cerebral one, especially when setting out his strategies for resistance. This difference primarily reflected the fact that while RMT members, in general, could exercise simple, immediate economic power, PCS members, in general, sought to exercise a less immediate political power. According to Serwotka, it was a case of 'horses for

---

62 For example, Christian Wolmar (*Guardian* 12 March 2014) noted: 'One fellow trade unionist remembers travelling to Washington with him as part of the International Transport Workers' Federation for discussions with the World Bank: "there would be jokes and routine denunciations of the Conservatives, but these were only padding for the two or three key messages Crow wanted to get across".'
63 *Independent* 13 September 2007.
64 *National Shop Stewards Network Bulletin* 13 March 2014.

courses'[65] rather than 'each to their own'. In this sense, both were shaped by – but also shaped – their respective unions.

Crow's grammar and syntax were imperfect, leading to Crow-isms' or 'Bob-isms'.[66] Mangling the English language in his combined cockney and Essex estuary English,[67] he told Radio 4: 'if the employers had unfettered regulation, they would basically take all our rights off us completely'.[68] Clearly, he meant if the employers had unfettered power through not being subject to regulation. Earlier, he said having Railtrack in charge of safety was like 'having a butcher responsible for the safety of meat in his shop'.[69] Again, what he meant was clear, but trying to update putting the 'fox in charge of the henhouse' did not come off. The day before he died he told the BBC: 'We are all civil servants – we are serving civilisation. That is what a civil servant does.'[70] The *Independent* observed that 'he often gets his words magnificently tangled. During a dispute about tea-breaks he appeared on London regional news to say: "It has got to the point where some of my members are no longer allowed out for a urination."'[71] When asked on BBC 2's *Newsnight* why workers still joined unions, Crow replied for 'one thing and one thing only', then proceeded to give six different reasons.[72] The *Independent* reported that he got 'so steamed up about pensions this week that he referred repeatedly to "final-year salaries" when he seemed to be talking about final-salary schemes'.[73] Celebrating his life, the socialist comedian Mark Steel tweeted on 11 March 2014 that he was 'a man full of passion and organisation and gloriously mispronounced words ... The last speech I saw Bob make, he almost exploded ... ending [with] "our world MUST HAVE more equalness"'. This was a much kinder assessment than that offered by *The Times* of a speech at the 2003 TUC congress, when it claimed that he gave 'one of the most passionate, and least com-

---

65 Interview.

66 This does not include common patterns of speech, such as being 'a man who rarely gets out a sentence which does not begin: "At the end of the day ..."' (*Evening Standard* 30 January 2002; *Guardian* 13 December 2010; BBC 2 *Newsnight*, 4 February 2014). Another common idiom used by Crow was 'The reality is ...' Former CoE member Oliver New coined the term 'Bob-isms' ('Bob Crow: Only the good die young', *Left Unity* website, 11 March 2014).

67 The *Weekly Worker* (13 March 2014) put this more tactfully, noting that he had a style of 'simple (if sometimes disjointed) phrasing'.

68 Radio 4 *Profile*, 4 April 2010, http://www.bbc.co.uk/programmes/b00rq2kx.

69 *Evening News* (Edinburgh) 22 February 2000.

70 Radio 4 *PM*, 10 March 2014.

71 *Independent* 30 July 2008.

72 BBC 2 *Newsnight*, 4 February 2014.

73 *Independent* 9 March 2002.

prehensible speeches I have ever heard, dispensing with both grammar and, even more impressively, with the need to breathe'.[74]

However, the Crowisms and mangling were strengths, for they added to his authenticity and sincerity. He was never ashamed of this because it helped him 'talk the talk' on a level that RMT members and other workers could understand and relate to. Unjum Mirza recalled:

> Essentially, a 'Crow-ism' was when Bob in the midst of a blistering speech would jumble up his words making us all laugh while [still] driving home the political message ... my favourite had to be ... after we'd been kicked out of Labour. On the platform with Bob was John McDonnell MP. Bob wanted to stress that while 'Labour does not stand up for working people', he was proud to stand shoulder to shoulder with McDonnell and others like Benn and Corbyn ... then came the 'Crowism': 'And I say brothers and sisters, I stand shoulder to shoulder with John and anyone from Labour that stands up and fights for working people. I say don't throw the baby out the bathroom window' – we all arose from our seats applauding a great speech while a few of us looked over to each other as if to confirm: 'He really did say that didn't he?'[75]

Paul Jackson recounted:

> He often made the odd slip in his speeches that made them more human and more 'one of us'. For example he had a famous quote 'if you fight, you won't always win, if you don't fight, you will always lose' and occasionally he'd get it round the wrong way: 'if you don't fight, you will always win'. At our branch the week before he died, he was talking about Cuba and said guacamole instead of Guantanamo [Bay].[76]

The same sense of strength could also be found in Crow's use of exaggeration through clichés because of the forcefulness and sharpness they created.[77]

Flights of fancy

Crow was so keen and energetic to confront employers and the Right, and to stop their attacks on unions and the Left, that he often strayed

74 *Times* 10 September 2002.
75 Email correspondence.
76 Email correspondence.
77 Some further examples were his statement that 'The railways' safety culture was sacrificed on the altar of the market when the Tories smashed the railway system to pieces in 1996' (*Guardian* 14 January 2003), and his characterisation of the situation of the railways as 'A desperate rearrangement of deckchairs won't stop rail privatisation sinking in a sea of chaos and ever-deepening debt' (*Guardian* 20 April 2004).

into territory where he lacked credibility.[78] Notwithstanding his capacity for measure and nuance, there was also a tendency to exaggerate the prospects for fighting back and for success in doing so.[79] The tendency was most pronounced in political matters. In industrial relations, it was far lessened pronounced. This situation came about because in the former, unlike the latter, the existence of the requisite social forces to repel attacks and make advances was open to doubt. For example, advocating a one-day general strike to stop the Conservative–Liberal Democrat austerity programme was fine on one level as the next step in resistance (even though it would take more than a one-day strike to achieve this). But it was not on another, because the union movement was not in a position to mount an effective general strike given low private-sector density (15%), limited loyalty of members and the atrophy of union organisation (even if the RMT was a partial if powerful exception to this). So the call for a general strike lacked credibility because it could not be effectively delivered.

The transition from making propaganda against – and agitating against – the government and capitalism to mass mobilisation against them was fraught, highlighting the challenge for socialists of finding the means of bridging the chasm between how society is and how society should be. Unfortunately, the dominant socialist perspective has comprised a form of voluntarism, whereby exhortation and exaggeration are used to tell activists that workers can and will revolt in order to motivate activists to go out and persuade workers to revolt. It did not suit Crow's politics or style to openly or fully acknowledge such difficulties and to act accordingly (though he did not 'talk up' the prospects for action and advance to the point of disbelief as many on the Left did). The exaggeration that Crow deployed – and represented – was a double-edged sword. It was necessary to motivate and support activists but it did not find wholesale endorsement among union (RMT and non-RMT) members, since they often found it somewhat far-fetched. Yet by accommodating the message to such members, the resource represented by activists would have been denuded. Arguably, Serwotka managed the tension

78 This was sometimes also a fault of Serwotka who – like Crow – told the same Coalition of Resistance audience outside Downing Street in 2010 it could emulate the French in holding general strikes with accompanying mass marches (*Financial Times* 22 October 2010). The RMT's own commissioned history by Berlin was indicative of this tendency. The title was a statement of aspiration and the history began eleven years before the RMT existed.

79 Sometimes this also operated retrospectively. For example, Crow (2013a: xiii) argued that the public exposure of the financial madness of PPP on the Underground was a victory – despite the continuation of the scheme.

between propaganda and agitation and moving between the current present and the desired future better than Crow, because he came across as a more patient, methodical and reasoned. But even for Serwotka, the tension still manifestly existed and was not easily resolved, and he was not above making the same exhortations for mass action as Crow did.[80]

Crow's Achilles' heel was that his enthusiasm and determination to see the fulfilment of his long-held ideal of workers fighting back obscured the clarity of his strategic vision. What he achieved within the RMT on industrial relations matters could not be replicated within the wider union movement, especially as the RMT was so small and idiosyncratic, and few union members had the power of RMT members. There was a sense that subjective will could trump objective reality within the RMT because most of its members had significant industrial leverage – it was merely a case of convincing them to use it. Crow's predictions that workers in general would fight back and that there would be an upturn in militancy[81] were well-meant and sincere but, nevertheless, wrong-headed because, like much of the far Left, he allowed his optimism and desire to trump any objective assessment of the state of the struggle as it was. It was almost as if his enthusiasm – and maybe a little impatience – got the better of him. But it may also have been because, while the RMT membership could deliver effective industrial action, he did not quite appreciate that it was easier for them than for others to do so. However, at least Crow offered a strategy for resistance and social change, rather than simply pronouncing pious words about how bad things were and asserting that 'something' needed to be done about it. This habit of diagnosis without prognosis was a weakness that Tony Benn – who died in the same week as Crow and was something of a hero to him – was prone to.

Political achievements

In noting that 'Crow's problem seems to be that the very qualities that make him a formidable union leader don't translate into broader public appeal ... the political agitator's [role] is not the same as [that of] trade union leader',[82] the *Guardian* misjudged him. His appeal was wide and deep (as the reaction to his death showed) but this could not be tested in terms of standing for domestic political office (since the RMT constitution barred this). Along with Serwotka, his appeal was much

---

80 See p 00, note 78 above.
81 See, for example, *Newcastle Journal* 4 September 2002
82 *Guardian* 13 December 2010.

wider than his own union, since it extended into the labour movement and beyond.[83] Some indication of this was given by him being ranked as one of the most influential figures on the Left, regularly making the list of the top 100 Left figures. The year before he died he was number 72, the previous year he had been number 99, and his ranking was 55 in 2011.[84] In the year of his death he was ranked 80th in a list of 100 most trustworthy figures in public life.[85] His appeal was an indictment of Labour, since traditionally unions spoke to industrial, and not political, concerns. Facilitated by both personality and politics prior to 2004, and then by party disaffiliation after 2004, Crow's appeal was based on his being a voice for the voiceless and an advocate for activists and activism. This particularly applied to union members outside the RMT as they were less powerful than most RMT members.[86] Nonetheless, voice and effectiveness should not be conflated, even though Crow took steps to attain more than just voice. As a result of his self-belief expressed in the force of his personality and political thinking, Crow made some arguments convincing that other leaders could not. This was very much the case within the RMT but less so outside it, the difference again relating to RMT members' greater ability to take effective industrial action.

Yet Crow was unable to create a substantial new socialist political force, unite existing socialist parties, return rail or bus transport to public ownership, stop further privatisation (of London Underground under PPP),[87] move Labour to the Left or persuade union affiliates of Labour to disaffiliate. This is why the *Independent* noted: 'As a political leader, he achieved less.'[88] Of course, these were Herculean tasks, no matter how energetic and strong the individual was in combination with others. Yet they were all interlinked, indicating how shrunken

83 For instance, Alan Pottage wrote: 'RMT members knew that Bob had come to appeal to a wider constituency, he spoke for his social class, stood up for them, understood us in a way only another working class man can. He was respected for his fighting spirit both in and outside his union' (*Scottish Left Review* May–June 2014). But it is also worth recalling that, in addition to Crow's attested communication abilities, the public face of the RMT was pretty much always the general secretary. Thus, it was primarily the general secretary who conducted media interviews and all press releases were sent out in the name of the general secretary, with no other officials being quoted.

84 *Telegraph* 27 September 2013, 3 October 2012, 27 September 2011, respectively.

85 *Independent* 6 February 2014.

86 The same was true of Tommy Sheridan in his heyday – he was a voice for the voiceless (see Gall 2012a: 120).

87 Although there were successes with Merseyrail track maintenance and the Royal Fleet Auxiliary.

88 *Independent* 12 March 2014.

and divided the radical Left had become and how dominant neoliberalism remained. Indeed, the Left inside and outside Labour was weaker
when Crow died than when he had become a major figure twenty years
earlier. Despite both Crow and the RMT punching well above their
weight, their influence was too little to achieve these political goals.[89]
The RMT was too small and specialist a union to exert the kind of
political influence that a large, general union could have had (assuming
that its members also possessed strategic leverage). And, as with other
left-wing unions like the FBU and the PCS, the RMT found that the biggest three unions were combined immovable objects. For Crow (and the
RMT) this represented something of a 'Catch 22' situation. Despite their
individually and organisationally supporting TUSC, a new and sizeable
socialist force could not emerge because a host of other unions would
not support it and, until other unions supported a new and sizeable
socialist force, one would not emerge.[90] All this meant that the 'radical
political unionism' vaunted by some and best epitomised by the RMT
lacked the necessary wider traction.[91]

Therefore, it is tempting to view Crow more as a heroic talisman
for others on the political Left. He gave them hope when hopelessness
abounded, with neoliberalism maintaining its hegemony despite its
crisis. He instilled in many activists a particular radical oppositional
perspective where fighting back was seen as a good in itself. He was able
to do this not only because he led a pugnacious union but also because
of his politics and personality. This takes nothing away from his being
a 'hero' to his members[92] or to workers more widely.[93] But it is salutary
to recall that, despite repeated severe problems, rail privatisation stayed
on track regardless of his repeated predictions that the end was nigh
(after Railtrack went into administration (2001), and Connex (2003)
and National Express (2011) returned their franchises). For example, in
2003 he said of Network Rail taking maintenance back in-house: 'This
is a major step towards the complete renationalisation of the railways.
It is clear that privatisation is in its coffin and waiting for the hole to be
dug';[94] and in 2009 the East Coast debacle marked 'the beginning of

89 See also McIlroy (2012: 255) and Gordon and Upchurch (2012: 262).
90 The individual support of leading officers from the FBU, PCS and POA unions
did not alter this, especially as many were Socialist Party members.
91 See Darlington (2014b) and Upchurch and Mathers (2011).
92 *Financial Times* 12 March 2014; *Herald* 14 May 2014.
93 George Galloway, *Guardian* 12 March 2014; *Mirror* 9 February 2014; and
TUC general secretary, Frances O'Grady, at the London May Day rally in 2014 (*The
Socialist* 7 May 2014).
94 *Telegraph* 24 October 2003.

the end' for privatisation.[95] It was not wrong to seek advantage in these political opportunities, but it was somewhat foolhardy to predict with such certainty what would then happen. As suggested elsewhere, his subjective desire trumped objective reality.

Industrial achievements

Previous chapters set out Crow's considerable contribution to achieving RMT's industrial goals on members' pay and working conditions. Despite their falling out, Ken Livingstone was able to state upon Crow's death: 'His members are one of the few groups of working-class people who have still got well-paid jobs and a lot of that is down to him.'[96] In understanding this achievement, it has to be borne in mind that it was not just that the majority of RMT members had potential power as a result of their strategic location, since it was vital that they also had a high level of group cohesion in order to be able to transform this potential into actual power in pursuit of their industrial interests. Crow helped sharpen the sense of group cohesion, encouraging this transformation as well as skilfully using the consequent leverage. This was because Crow understood through praxis that in the capital–labour struggle, labour power resources can in the main be socially constructed through the efforts of activists, officers and leaders. Moreover, the frequent use of threats and chest-beating indicated that he also understood that one's opponent's perception of one's power was a crucial component of actual power (in terms of it being a bargaining tool). So within the RMT's industrial remit what seemed like exaggeration served a useful purpose.

Where industrial and political goals overlapped, in the case of stopping and reversing privatisation and contracting out, there was less success, given that industrial advance was predicated upon (leftwards) political advance. And while there were no strikes against privatisation and in favour of renationalisation *per se*, the effect of London Underground strikes was to deter further privatisation because the strikes indicated a restless workforce that would cause investors problems. Organising strikes against privatisation and in favour of renationalisation faced some obvious obstacles – such as being declared unlawful for being political – but these were not insuperable, as strikes against contracting out by other unions had shown. Here, as on a few other occasions, Crow's rhetoric was not matched by reality. Yet under him, the RMT in words and deeds spearheaded the attempt to revitalise widespread union

95 *Times* 14 November 2009.
96 *Financial Times* 12 March 2014.

militancy, thereby challenging the practice of 'social partnership' with employers and the 'new realism' strategy of relying upon Labour governments to reform employment laws because unions were too enfeebled to do so themselves. Even the limited availability of arbitration was used in a militant manner and for militant ends. Crow and the RMT had many advantages in doing this compared with others.[97]

The different levels of success recorded in the industrial and political arenas, as alluded to before, could also in part be attributed to Crow applying the same perspective that he applied to RMT members to non-RMT members, thereby underplaying the relative power of his members and the relative powerlessness of most other union members. Thus, Crow could convincingly threaten TOCs but far less so governments, since to do so would have required non-RMT members to act more like RMT members and on the basis of RMT members' leverage.

Militancy, mobilisation, power and political congruence

Reprising these theoretical and conceptual issues, this study of Crow has been set within two central relationships under capitalism – namely, capital–labour and leader–follower – where a dialectical materialist approach has been used to understand their intra- and interactions. In other words, within the framework of the interplay of agency–environment, the elements of intention, process and outcome of Crow's leadership were examined, especially through the triad of person, politics and power in which RMT members' interests were held to be uppermost. It has become clear that Crow was an intelligent and responsible militant leader for the RMT because of his ability to play a major role in helping direct its resources (principally members' power) using the force of his personality and politics. Under Crow, the RMT had ambitious industrial and political goals, engaged in extensive membership mobilisation in pursuit of these, and held to a socialist worldview where the industrial was not separated from the political. Thus, while embedding and advanced industrial militancy, Crow also provided an ideological critique of capitalism in its neoliberal stage while simultaneously emphasising that capitalism *per se* is characterised by exploitation, oppression and alienation. However, as noted above, he recorded greater success

97 The FBU suffered from central government removing its responsibility for service provision during industrial disputes, while the PCS was often unable to stop or delay the work of government departments. Both unions also experienced governmental hostility to public sector striking, with Labour's unwillingness to support such action meaning that it no longer generated the political heat that it once would have done.

in the industrial than the political arenas – because outside the RMT, he did not have the same power base to work from and so his political message and the power of his personality had less traction and currency.

In terms of mobilisation theory, he was not just a significant framer of issues and significant facilitator of developing grievances, for he also played a large part in assisting members to generate the confidence needed to undertake collective actions to resolve their grievances. However, some caution is needed so as not to overstate Crow's contribution. There were clearly cases where he was directly involved in RMT members' disputes, in terms of framing grievances, and leading and fronting action. But he was not involved in all disputes directly or to any great degree (especially when general secretary). Neither was he involved in developing discontent into grievances (and then into disputes) in all cases. Rather, his influence was often more indirect in terms of providing activists with an organisatinonal culture that bestowed legitimacy on developing militant interests, goals and means. Even though the relationship between mobilisation and political congruence was not a simple one of cause and effect, this process of mobilisation was predicated upon political congruence, whereby Crow was the pivotal element in an informal network that (democratically) captured control of the RMT,[98] establishing a hegemony for militancy (by creating common norms and expectations as a form of consciousness across the different sections of the union) and instituting a united, non-factionalised national leadership. This was a considerable achievement given that, unlike Weighell, Knapp or Cash, Crow came from the relatively small London Underground section of membership[99] and not the much bigger (overground) railways section. Along with the differences in size of this base came cultural differences.

Out of the achievement of political congruence came union renewal and revitalisation in terms of membership growth, bargaining leverage and outcomes and militant political stances. While there were limits to the extent that members actively supported the RMT's industrial and political agenda under Crow, commitment and participation were sufficiently high to ensure that industrial militancy was effective. Politically, less was achieved in terms of membership subscription and participation. So although the RMT had 'over 3,000 industrial members' of

98 This was like the situation in the CWU but unlike the PCS or Unite, as no formal Broad Left organisation was used as the vehicle to gain control.

99 In 2005, Crow stated that the RMT had 8,000 members on London Underground (*RMT – Your Union*, Platform Films, 2005, London), amounting to some 11% of RMT membership.

Labour in the mid-1990s but only 300 Labour members by 2004,[100] the hold of labourism – a form of top-down social democracy defined as 'an ideology of social reform, within the framework of capitalism, with no serious ambition of transcending that framework'[101] – was still strong, judged by the limited extent of RMT members' involvement in activities and organisations of the radical Left. Finally, and recalling Batstone's three sources of union power, the experience of Crow and the RMT indicates that the category of 'political influence' requires some refinement so that it is less based upon affiliation to Labour and more upon direct influence over government and political parties as a result of the political leverage of strikes and the formation of producer–user alliances.

Aftermath

Not long after Crow was elected, the *Financial Times* commented: 'He's young enough to keep the job for a generation.'[102] This was not to be, and with Crow's unexpected death there was no legacy planning. In early April 2014, a timetable for electing a new general secretary was announced. Nominations opened a week later, closing in early July with the ballot running from July to September. All the candidates from the radical Left (Alex Gordon, Steve Hedley, John Leach and Alan Pottage) pledged to continue Crow's legacy, as did Mick Cash.[103] Pottage told the *Herald*:

> You are there to put the boot on the throat of the employer and make sure you win. Ninety nine per cent of our problems are negotiated, but we know the main victories we have achieved for our members ... have come from our members being strong enough to take industrial action ... I feel there is no-one better placed to continue [Crow's] legacy than myself. It means being unpopular, but as long as you are popular with your membership and your class that is what counts.[104]

100 Berlin (2006: 133, 159).
101 Miliband (1972: 376).
102 *Financial Times* 10 September 2004.
103 Cash showed warmth and respect towards Crow when he was interviewed after his death (*Guardian* 1 October 2014). Here, there may have been a similarity with the relationship between Crow and Knapp, in as much as the degree of conflict between the two did not play out as some might have expected.
104 *Herald* 14 May 2014. He also told the *Evening News* (22 August 2014): 'My views are the same as Bob's, that we need to have a strong union, one that will stand up and make a case against things like rail fares going up, and cutting staff to add to the profits of private operators.'

Meanwhile, Cash said: 'I will use all my leadership experience to make sure the RMT remains a militant, member-led union.'[105] On 22 September 2014, Cash was elected, receiving 8,938 votes (with Pottage gaining 4,006, Hedley 1,885, Leach 1,428 and Gordon 1,176). Absolute turnout was lower than in 2002 (with 17,433 against 18,560) and the relative turnout was lower too (23% against 32%).[106] Post-Crow, the election demonstrated that the radical Left was divided in a way it had not been for many years, with the four unsuccessful candidates together not gaining Cash's vote (8,495 to his 8,938).[107] However, Cash's victory reflected more than a divided Left. He was the most senior and longstanding officer to contest the election, had bargaining responsibility for the largest single group within the RMT (namely, Network Rail) and was not the clear antithesis of Crow.[108] Cash's election saw Hedley move up to senior AGS and the election for the subsequent vacancy for AGS was won on 31 March 2015 by Mick Lynch (beating Pottage and John Tilley).[109]

Cash greeted his victory by saying:

> I am proud and honoured to have been given the enormous responsibility of now taking our fighting and militant union forwards, six months after the bitter loss to the labour movement of Bob Crow. Let me make this clear. There will be no deviation from the industrial, political and organising strategy mapped out by RMT under Bob's leadership. Our fight on pay,

105 *Morning Star* 5 April 2014.

106 The turnout was still better than that of nearly all the other unions in general secretary elections (Unite's 16% in 2010 and 15% in 2013, and the PCS's 21% in 2009, though ASLEF had 46% in 2011).

107 Although an imperfect measure, the time to decide upon a single Left candidate would have been after the branch nominations. The candidate with the greatest number of nominations would then go forward. To facilitate this, some kind of inclusive Left organisation (formal or informal) would have been needed. Traditionally, broad Left or reform movements have played this role. The United Left in Unite and Left Unity in the PCS currently play this role, while the National Seamen's Reform Movement played this role in the NUS in the 1960s (leading to the election of Jim Slater), and the 'Not on the Agenda' group had this role in the CWU in the 1990s (leading to the election of Billy Hayes) (see Gall 2001). However, the unwillingness of the rivals to agree on a single candidate may have been increased by the view that in the event of Cash winning, the post of senior AGS would become vacant. Hence standing for the position of general secretary would be good preparation for standing in the subsequent AGS election.

108 Upon Cash's election, the *Guardian* (1 October 2014) commented that he and Crow 'were said to be more similar in their outlook than early public rhetoric appeared'.

109 Lynch was RMT secretary at Eurostar and CoE member for London and Anglia.

jobs, working conditions, pensions and safety continues on every front and in every industry where we organise members.[110]

The 'no deviation' message was repeated twice in the October 2014 edition of *RMT News*[111] and then at the 2015 AGM.[112] Under Cash, the RMT was in a broadly similar state of semi-permanent strike mobilisation as before when judged by frequency of industrial action ballots: from 11 March 2014 to 22 September 2014, 37 were organised.[113] In Cash's first year as general secretary there were 76, with 53 in his second year.[114] The *Independent* speculated that 'It is also possible – though not certain – that strikes would be rarer if Mr Cash were to become general secretary.'[115] This was not detectable to any degree (although cleaners figured less significantly than before). Cash's handling of the London Underground dispute in 2015 on night working and the dispute with Southern trains over driver-only operations[116] were very much in line with Crow's hard bargaining and selective striking tactics. Given his comments in 1999 about the RMT being too 'strike happy', Cash's statements and actions attested to Crow's impact in playing a leading role in normalising industrial and political militancy within the RMT and critically among its lay activists and employed union officers (as per a process of political congruence). So, after his election, Cash stated: 'The reason [the RMT has] had the profile was that we were out there fighting. That's what we'll continue to do.'[117] Almost two years after this, he proudly recalled the 'militancy' of RMT members when

110 RMT press release, 22 September 2014.

111 In his editorial, Cash stated: 'It is important to understand that there will be no deviation from the industrial and political strategy mapped out under Bob's leadership', and in the news section he said: 'There will be no deviation from the industrial, political and organising strategy mapped out by RMT under Bob's leadership.'

112 *RMT News* May 2015.

113 See http://www.rmt.org.uk/about/ballot-results/.

114 See http://www.rmt.org.uk/about/ballot-results/.

115 *Independent* 2 May 2014.

116 The return of disputes over driver-only operations in 2015–16 at First Great Western, Merseyrail and Northern Rail, with prolonged strike action taken on Scotrail and Southern trains, indicated that the battle to preserve the guards' safety-critical role was not one that had been won forever under Crow's leadership. This indicated that although the McNulty report had been published in 2011, it was still on the agenda for implementation under the Conservative government of 2015 onwards. The Southern trains dispute took on the nature of a 'reforming conflict', given the comments of the senior Department of Transport civil servant, Peter Wilkinson, about the need to break the hold of the rail unions at a public meeting in Crawley in February 2016.

117 *Guardian* 1 October 2014.

resisting moves towards driver-only operations.[118] Such were the battles that the RMT fought under Cash's early leadership that the *Guardian* asked: 'Has the RMT union's moderate Mick Cash turned militant?'[119] Interviewed earlier by the *Independent*, Cash stated that he was 'thinking about giving up on Labour altogether and starting afresh',[120] and he told the ASLEF 2015 AGM: 'I can't see in my time as general secretary that we will get back into the Labour Party. Because we have a huge problem with the party that was born out of our movement endorsing policies that work against this movement.'[121] To this end, the RMT donated £10,000 to TUSC in late 2014, but no RMT national officers or officials attended the TUSC conference of early 2015 save John Reid, CoE and Socialist Party member.[122] Cash did not speak at TUSC rallies and campaign launches as Crow had[123] and the RMT donated £25,000 to Jeremy Corbyn's campaign for the Labour leadership after its AGM voted to back Corbyn.[124] Although he welcomed Corbyn's victory and first speeches, Cash made clear the issue of re-affiliation could not be discussed until the 2016 AGM at the earliest.[125] In the event, the AGM decided to continue to participate in TUSC because it was believed to be essential to maintain an electoral alternative to Labour that was fully anti-austerity while also backing Corbyn,[126] and to this end, the union again donated £25,000 to Corbyn for his re-election campaign in 2016.[127] Meanwhile, Pinkney told the 2015 TUSC conference: 'TUSC is not dead and we're not reaffiliating to the Labour Party. What if Jeremy's ousted in six months and the right wingers are back in charge?

118 *Morning Star* 14 September 2016.

119 *Guardian* 13 August 2016.

120 *Independent* 6 October 2014.

121 *Morning Star* 14 May 2015.

122 *Weekly Worker* 29 January 2015. It is worth noting that support for TUSC within the RMT was far from universal. Peter Pinkney (*RMT News* November–December 2014) advocated support for the Greens. The RMT donated £7,000 to the campaign to re-elect Caroline Lucas in Brighton Pavilion (*Sunday Sun* 8 February 2015). There was considerable debate about supporting the Greens in *RMT News* (January, February, March 2015).

123 The most he did, along with other senior RMT figures (both lay and employed) and other senior officers from other unions, was to protest at the media boycott of anti-austerity candidates in the 2014 local council elections by signing an open letter on 21 May 2014. However, it should also be noted that Crow 'studiously avoided all mention of the [TUSC] coalition … on his Question Time appearances' (*A Very Public Sociologist* blog 13 April 2015).

124 *Daily Mirror* 14 August 2015.

125 RMT press releases, 14, 15 September 2015.

126 *The Socialist* 6 July 2016.

127 *Morning Star* 21 September 2016.

We'll continue to support TUSC – and wait and see on the Labour Party.'[128] On Labour's planned rail renationalisation under Corbyn, the RMT was not critical of the phased-in process of return to public ownership as the TSSA was.[129]

Yet the question remained, for the longer term, about whether Cash had the personal and political wherewithal and skills to carry on Crow's legacy in the commanding way in which it had been established and executed. Cash was no challenger to Crow as a powerful speaker or media performer, since he lacked the self-assurance and swagger that Crow had. With this came a far lower profile for the RMT and its general secretary. Certainly, Cash was aware of this, saying: 'Bob was unique. The way he presented himself and the RMT was how he operated ... I have to find my way'[130] and 'Of course, I'm different to Bob in many respects.'[131] Subsequent media interviews picked upon the difference too.[132] Could it be the case that if the person is removed, then so too is much of the influence, profile and strength? It was Pinkney, not Cash, who moved the RMT's contested but ultimately successful motion at the 2015 TUC congress calling for a generalised strike if any union or activist was criminalised for defying the Trade Union Bill. On other significant occasions, the current president Sean Hoyle has also moved crucial motions and made key speeches, while other RMT officers have given media interviews (such as Paul Cox, the RMT south-east regional organiser, on the Southern Trains dispute).

128 *Socialist Worker* 3 October 2015. See also *The Socialist* 30 September 2015. The effective putting of TUSC into abeyance by the Socialist Party (*Socialism Today* November 2016) and the application by leading members of the Socialist Party to rejoin Labour (*The Socialist* 16 November 2016) brought into serious doubt whether TUSC had much of a future.

129 See RMT press release, 21 September 2015. For the TSSA's position, see *Morning Star* 30 September 2015. However, Pinkney did raise criticism of Corbyn, demanding an immediate renationalisation of all franchises (*The Socialist* 30 September 2015).

130 *Guardian* 1 October 2014.

131 *Evening Standard* 26 September 2014.

132 See, for example, 'Mick Cash: "passengers pay a premium for privatisation"', *Guardian* website 8 April 2015. The difference was not complete, however: 'Until he starts defending his transport workers against what he perceives as damaging political short-termism, Mick Cash seems utterly different from his controversial predecessor Bob Crow ... In contrast, my first impression of Cash ... is that of a mild mannered historian, enthusiastic rather than forceful and certainly not a weight-lifter. However, it seems Cash's moderate reputation may be down to little more than how personable he is. His level of determination to fight on behalf of the RMT's [members] soon shows itself to be indistinguishable from Crow's.'

Final remarks

Crow inhabited a certain period with historically peculiar conditions. While most union leaders were unwilling and unable to be trenchant critics of 'new' Labour, Crow was, giving him a cutting edge few others had (even though his voice was a little more crowded out when the Tories returned to office). Similarly, the RMT under Crow seemed to be fighting and winning more than other unions as strike activity in general declined. Crow's premature death robbed him of being able to cast his influence over a plethora of key events in subsequent years. The Scottish independence referendum of 2014, the Trade Union Bill (which became law in May 2016) and continued government austerity measures, the rise and fall of Syriza, the EU referendum (and attendant campaign)[133] and the terms of Brexit were among the most important of these. Above all, Jeremy Corbyn's election to the leadership of Labour would have presented Crow with a particular challenge given that Corbyn,[134] along with John McDonnell as shadow chancellor, were from the socialist Left and returned Labour to the policy of rail renationalisation. Crow had told the RMT grades conference delegates in 2002: 'I have never been and never will be a member of the Labour Party';[135] he had said to *Socialist Worker* in 2005: '[Labour's radicalism is] gone. It's finished. And they have adopted a scorched earth policy behind them so there is no democracy left inside';[136] and he had told gatherings of unions and the Left in 2006 and 2009 that Labour 'can't be changed' and was 'dead'.[137] In a testament to the sea change represented by Corbyn winning the leadership, the FBU re-affiliated and both Matt Wrack and Mark Serwotka rejoined Labour.[138]

133 The RMT maintained its Leave position, being only one of three unions to take such a position, the others being ASLEF and the bakers' union, BFAWU.

134 Under Crow's leadership, the RMT had supported both Corbyn and McDonnell as candidates in the 2005 general election, gifting their campaigns, along with those of nine other Labour candidates, £1,500 each and the assistance of union officials and CoE members (RMT circular NP166/05, 5 April 2005).

135 *Socialist Review* July 2002.

136 *Socialist Worker* 17 September 2005. Intriguingly, he did suggest that Labour could be swung back to the Left if the party conference was 'changed back to being a resolution-based conference', and commented that 'I suppose it is possible to turn it around. But it would be a hell of a job' (in Murray 2003: 101).

137 *The Socialist* 26 January 2006, 25 November 2009.

138 *Morning Star* 3 March 2016. It would have been interesting to see whether Crow would have concurred with the analysis of his political collaborators, the Socialist Party, which not only described Labour under Corbyn as a battle between two parties (*The Socialist* 28 September, 2 December 2015, 10 February 2016) but would also like to affiliate as a party to Labour (BBC 2 *Daily Politics*, 8 December 2015).

Crow was fondly remembered in *RMT News* after his death, being referred to as a 'great' man and 'great' general secretary,[139] because while he had weaknesses, his strengths vastly outnumbered them. In recognition of this, the most fitting way to end this biography is to recall what Peter Pinkney said in his address to the 2014 RMT AGM: 'They say you don't know what you've got until it's gone but in this case that is not true',[140] and to remember that it was common to hear non-RMT union members say: 'I wish we had Bob Crow as our leader', 'If only our union had someone like him leading us we'd be a damn sight better off' or 'I wish I could join the RMT.' These are surely the best eulogies any union leader could hope for.

---

139 *RMT News* September 2015. Other examples were in the July–August 2015 edition. With regard to Crow stimulating a fellow US union to reorganise and revitalise itself, it was reported that Crow was often on American TV, as his portrait was in the office of the New York Transport Workers' Union where the union president is usually interviewed. Money is still being raised for the Bob Crow cancer fund through sponsored cycling and hiking events undertaken by RMT members. In mid-2016, Nicola Hoarau completed the Inca Trail in Peru to raise money for the fund (*RMT News* July–August 2016).

140 *RMT News* April 2014; *Morning Star* 24 June 2014, respectively. In his last *RMT News* column as president (November–December 2015), Pinkney wrote: 'I miss him very much both as a friend and as an inspiration. We have been able to carry on because of the great legacy that he has left us.'

Appendix 1: Testimonies

Within the RMT: anonymised CoE member 2011–14, anonymised young RMT activist, Martin Eady (CoE member 1988–89, president, London Transport District Council), Les Harvey (executive member, London Underground Engineering branch), Ann Henderson (Glasgow No. 6 branch secretary 1988–92, RMT Broad Left secretary, and RMT Scottish Parliament liaison officer 2004–07), Paul Jackson (branch secretary, London Underground Engineering 2006–), Phil McGarry (Scottish Regional Organiser), Unjum Mirza (Political Officer for London Transport Region 2003–12), Oliver New (CoE member 2007–10), Jeff Porter (assistant branch secretary, Stratford 1987–90, secretary Hammersmith and City branch 1996–2002), Pam Singer (Neasden 3 branch secretary, 1990–96 and co-founder and regional secretary of RMT Women's Advisory Committee) and Martin Wicks (former RMT Network Rail staff side representative). Outside the RMT: Billy Hayes (former CWU general secretary), Mick Rix (former ASLEF general secretary), Andy Gilchrist (former FBU general secretary), Mark Serwotka (PCS general secretary), John McDonnell MP and Mick Whelan (ASLEF general secretary). Testimonies were gathered between August 2014 and April 2016.

Appendix 2: Tributes to Crow

The TSSA general secretary, Manuel Cortes, said that Crow 'was admired by his members and feared by employers which is exactly how he liked it. It was a privilege to campaign and fight alongside him because he never gave an inch. He was often under-estimated by politicians, employers and the media because he stayed true to his working class roots. He was more than happy to be under-estimated as long as he got the right results for his members'.[1] Similar tributes came from the general secretaries of Nautilus International, the International Transport Workers' Federation, the Prison Officers' Association, NUJ, TUC, Unite, UNISON, GMB and UCU. Even unions that had little industrial or political connection with Crow or the RMT (like USDAW and Community) felt compelled to offer words of praise and condolence. Former *Times* industrial editor Christine Buckley believed: 'In these days of declining membership, union leaders are not household names. But he was. Everyone knew Bob Crow'.[2]

---

1 In a similar statement, he said: 'The thing with Bob was that he was respected by employers and loved by his members because he did the best he could to ensure they got the best possible deal on offer. I am proud and privileged to have stood alongside Bob. He was tenacious, and he carried the overwhelming support of his members. While many bosses might not have said it in public, he carried their respect. He understood that his job was to get the best possible deal for his members. That is what he always did' (*Guardian* 12 March 2014).
2 Personal email correspondence, 19 November 2015.

Bibliography

Arrowsmith, J. (2003), 'Post-privatisation industrial relations in the UK rail and electricity industries', *Industrial Relations Journal*, 34/2: 150–163.

Batstone, E. (1988), 'The frontier of control', in D. Gallie (ed.), *Employment in Britain*, Blackwell, Oxford, pp. 218–247.

Benn, T. (2013), *A Blaze of Autumn Sunshine*, Random House, London.

Berlin, M. (2006), *Never on our Knees: A History of the RMT, 1979–2006*, Pluto Press, London.

Carrier, D. (2012), 'From heroes to zeros – how the press report the work of public sector employees', in J. Manson (ed.), *Public Service on the Brink*, Imprint Academic, Exeter, pp. 242–269.

Connolly, H., and Darlington, R. (2012), 'Radical political unionism in France and Britain: a comparative study of SUD-Rail and the RMT', *European Journal of Industrial Relations*, 18/3: 235–250.

Croucher, R., and Upchurch, M. (2012), 'Political congruence: a conceptual framework and historical case study', *Labor History*, 53/2: 205–223.

Crow, B. (2007), 'Introduction', in U. Mirza, *I Do Mind Dying: The politics of health and safety*, RMT London Transport Regional Council, London, pp. 3–4.

Crow, B. (2008), 'Rail privatisation – a failed experiment', in A. Fisher (ed.), *Building the New Common Sense: Social ownership for the 21st century*, Left Economics Advisory Project, London, pp. 19–22.

Crow, B. (2009), 'Foreword', in J. Nicolson, *A Turbulent Life*, Praxis Press, Glasgow, p. 5.

Crow, B. (2012a), 'The enduring legacy of industrial unionism', *Historical Studies in Industrial Relations*, 33: 149–155.

Crow, B. (2012b), 'Introduction', in J. Boyd (ed.), *Social Europe is a Con: Selected essays and articles*, Democrat Press, London, p. 4.

Crow, B. (2013a), 'Foreword', in J. Booth, *Plundering London Underground: New Labour, private capital and public service 1997–2010*, Merlin Press, Brecon, p. 4.

Crow, B. (2013b), 'Labour and the trade unions', *Scottish Left Review*, 79: 16–17.

Cumbers, A., MacKinnon, D., and Shaw, J. (2010), 'Labour, organisational rescaling and the politics of production: union renewal in the privatised rail industry', *Work, Employment and Society*, 24/1: 127–144.

Darlington, R. (2001), 'Union militancy and left-wing leadership on London Underground', *Industrial Relations Journal*, 32/1: 2–21.

Darlington, R. (2008), 'Strike mobilisation and union revitalisation', *RMT News*, 9/9: 26–27.

Darlington, R. (2009a), 'Leadership and union militancy: the case of the RMT', *Capital and Class*, 33/3: 3–32.

Darlington, R. (2009b), 'Organising, militancy and revitalisation: the case of the RMT', in G. Gall (ed.), *Union Revitalisation in Advanced Economies: Assessing the contribution of 'union organising'*, Palgrave Macmillan, Basingstoke, 2009, pp. 83–106.

Darlington, R. (2010), 'A striking union: the case of the RMT', *RMT News*, 12/3: 22–23.

Darlington, R. (2012), 'The interplay of structure and agency dynamics in strike activity', *Employee Relations*, 34/5: 518–533.

Darlington, R. (2014a), 'The rank and file and the trade union bureaucracy', *International Socialism*, 142: 57–82.

Darlington, R. (2014b), 'Britain: striking unionism with a political cutting-edge', in H. Connolly, L. Kretsos and C. Phelan (eds), *Radical Unions in Europe and the Future of Collective Interest Representation*, volume 20, Peter Lang, Oxford, pp. 69–88.

Darlington, R., and Upchurch, M. (2012), 'A reappraisal of the rank-and-file/bureaucracy debate', *Capital and Class*, 36/1: 73–91.

Eady, M. (2010), '1989 – the summer of discontent: an account of the unofficial strikes on the London Underground', *Labour Heritage Bulletin*, Autumn.

Eady, M. (2016), *Hold on Tight: London Transport and the trade unions*, Capital Transport Publishing, London.

Fairbrother, P. (2000), *Trade Unions at the Crossroads*, Mansell, London.

Ferner, A. (1985), 'Political constraints and management strategies: the case of working practices in British Rail', *British Journal of Industrial Relations*, 23/1: 47–70.

Gall, G. (2001), 'The organisation of organised discontent: the case of the postal workers in Britain', *British Journal of Industrial Relations*, 39/3: 393–409.

Gall, G. (2003), *The Meaning of Militancy? Postal workers and industrial relations*, Ashgate, Farnham.

Gall, G. (2006), 'Injunctions as a legal weapon in industrial disputes in Britain, 1995–2005', *British Journal of Industrial Relations*, 44/2: 327–349.

Gall, G. (2012a), *Tommy Sheridan: From hero to zero? A political biography*, Welsh Academic Press, Cardiff.

Gall, G. (2012b), 'The flexible rostering dispute', *ASLEF Journal*, April, pp. 12–13.

Gall, G. (2016), 'Injunctions as a legal weapon in collective industrial disputes in Britain, 2005–2014', *British Journal of Industrial Relations*, pp. 1–28, 8 June, doi: 10.1111/bjir.12187.

Gall, G., and Fiorito, J. (2011), 'The backward march of labour halted? Or, what is to be done with "union organising"? The cases of Britain and the USA', *Capital and Class*, 35/2: 233–251.

Gordon, A., and Upchurch, M. (2012), 'Railing against neoliberalism: radical political unionism in SUD-Rail and RMT', *European Journal of Industrial Relations*, 18/3: 259–265.

Gourvish, T. (2002), *British Rail 1974–1997: From integration to privatisation*, Oxford University Press, Oxford.

Halpin, K. (2012), *Memoirs of a Militant: Sharply and to the point*, Praxis Press, Glasgow.

Hodder, A., Williams, M., Kelly, J. and McCarthy, N. (2016) 'Does Strike Action Stimulate Trade Union Membership Growth?' *British Journal of Industrial Relations*, 1–22, 8 June, doi: 10.1111/bjir.12188

Hyman, R. (2001), *Understanding European Trade Unionism: Between market, class and society*, Sage, London.

Kelly, J. (1988), *Trade Unions and Socialist Politics*, Verso, London.

Kelly, J. (1996), 'Union militancy and social partnership', in P. Ackers, C. Smith and P. Smith (eds), *The New Workplace and Trade Unionism: Critical perspectives on work and organisation*, Routledge, London, pp. 77–109.

Kelly, J. (1998), *Rethinking Industrial Relations: Mobilisation, collectivism and long waves*, Routledge, London.

Lyddon, D. (2009), 'Strikes: industrial conflict under New Labour', in G. Daniels and J. McIlroy (eds), *Trade Unions in a Neoliberal World: British trade unions under New Labour*, Routledge, Abingdon, pp. 316–341.

MacUaid, L. (2011), 'Bob Crow's death "a huge blow to militant class-struggle unionism"', 11 March, http://links.org.au/node/3760.

Maksymiw, W., Eaton, J., and Gill, C. (1990), *The British Trade Union Directory*, Longman, Harlow.

McCarthy, N. (2009), 'Union mobilisation in a recognised environment – a case study of mobilisation', in G. Gall (ed.), *Union Revitalisation in Advanced Economies: Assessing the contribution of 'union organising'*, Palgrave Macmillan, Basingstoke, pp. 107–130.

McIlroy, J. (2011), 'Britain: how neo-liberalism cut unions down to size', in G. Gall, A. Wilkinson and R. Hurd (eds), *The International Handbook of Labour Unions: Responses to neo-liberalism*, Edward Elgar, Cheltenham, pp. 82–104.

McIlroy, J. (2012), 'Radical political unionism reassessed', *European Journal of Industrial Relations*, 18/3: 251–258.

McIlroy, J., and Daniels, G. (2009), 'An anatomy of British trade unionism since 1997: organisation, structure and factionalism', in G. Daniels and J. McIlroy (eds), *Trade Unions in a Neoliberal World: British trade unions under New Labour*, Routledge, Abingdon, pp. 127–164.

Melling, J. (2004), 'Leading the white-collar union: Clive Jenkins, the management of trade-union officers, and the politics of the British labour movement, c.1968–1979', *International Review of Social History*, 49/1: 71–102.

Bibliography

Miliband, R. (1972), *Parliamentary Socialism: A study of the politics of Labour*, Merlin, London.

Mullins, B. (1999), 'State of the unions', *Socialism Today*, June.

Murray, A. (2003), *A New Labour Nightmare: The return of the awkward squad*, Verso, London.

Pendleton, A. (1991a), 'Integration and dealignment in public enterprise industrial relations: a study of British Rail', *British Journal of Industrial Relations*, 29/3: 411–426.

Pendleton, A. (1991b), 'Workplace industrial relations in British Rail: change and continuity in the 1980s', *Industrial Relations Journal*, 22/3: 210–222.

Pendleton, A. (1993), 'Railways', in A. Pendleton and J. Winterton (eds), *Public Enterprise in Transition: Industrial relations in state and privatised corporations*, Routledge, London, pp. 100–133.

Pendleton, A. (1997), 'The evolution of industrial relations in UK nationalised industries', *British Journal of Industrial Relations*, 35/2: 145–172.

Routledge, P. (2003), *The Bumper Book of British Lefties*, Politicos, London.

Russell, D. (2014), 'What Bob Crow meant to me', *Spiked*, 12 March, http://www.spiked-online.com/newsite/article/what-bob-crow-meant-to-me/14780#.VFzs9fmsVu4.

Seifert, R., and Sibley, T. (2005), *United They Stood*, Lawrence and Wishart, London.

Spencer, D., and Khamis, H. (1998), 'Why we have left the Socialist Labour Party: the dead hand of Stalinism without the lure of Moscow gold', *New Interventions*, 8/3.

Strangleman, T. (2004), *Work Identity at the End of the Line? Privatisation and culture change in the UK rail industry*, Palgrave, Basingstoke.

Tattersall, A. (2010), *Power in Coalition: Strategies for strong unions and social change*, Cornell University Press, Ithaca, NY.

Upchurch, M., Croucher, R., and Flynn, M. (2012a), 'Political congruence and trade union renewal', *Work, Employment and Society*, 26/5: 857–868.

Upchurch, M., Croucher, R., and Flynn, M. (2012b), 'Does political congruence help us understand trade union renewal?', in M. Hauptmeier and M. Vidal (eds), *Comparative Political Economy of Work: Critical perspectives on work and employment*, Palgrave, Basingstoke, pp. 272–289.

Upchurch, M., and Mathers, A. (2011), 'Neo-liberal globalisation and trade unionism: towards radical political unionism', *Critical Sociology*, 38/2: 265–280.

Index

Index

Index